# THE HUMAN ADVANTAGE

ALSO BY JAY RICHARDS

*The Hobbit Party*

*Infiltrated*

*Indivisible*

*Money, Greed, and God*

# THE HUMAN ADVANTAGE

## The Future of American Work
## in an Age of Smart Machines

### JAY W. RICHARDS

CROWN
FORUM
NEW YORK

All rights reserved.
Published in the United States by Crown Forum, an imprint of the Crown
Publishing Group, a division of Penguin Random House LLC, New York.
crownpublishing.com

CROWN FORUM with colophon is a registered trademark
of Penguin Random House LLC.

Library of Congress Cataloging-in-Publication Data available upon request.

ISBN 978-0-451-49616-4
Ebook ISBN 978-0-451-49618-8

PRINTED IN THE UNITED STATES OF AMERICA

Jacket design: Tal Goretsky
Jacket photographs: (hand and wrench) natasaadzic/Getty Images; (robot arm)
PhonlamaiPhoto/Getty Images

10 9 8 7 6 5 4 3 2 1

First Edition

*In memory of Michael Novak*

# CONTENTS

## PART III: HOW TO PURSUE HAPPINESS

# INTRODUCTION

When the disaster struck, Daniel and Kelli Segars could have been a statistic.

Daniel studied food and nutrition in college. In 2000 he started work as a personal trainer and nutrition counselor at a fitness club. Kelli earned degrees from Central Washington University in psychology and sociology—undergrad favorites that don't exactly chart a career path. In 2006 she found herself at the same club as Daniel, selling memberships. They fell in love, got married, and after a while mustered enough savings to do what everyone else in the greater Seattle area was trying to do at the time: They bought a house. The sale closed on a weekend. It was August 2008, the dawn of the Great Recession.

The following Monday, Kelli had her hours slashed and Daniel lost most of his clients. The Segars, like millions of other Americans, were slammed by what few experts had seen coming: the greatest financial crisis since the Great Depression. And the tsunami struck the very market in which the Segars had just invested their life savings: housing.

The Segars had no control over the crisis that soon swept over the globe, stripping away their livelihoods and threatening them with joblessness. They had control over one thing: their response to it. They could have blamed NAFTA or the WTO or the rise of the robots. They could have joined Occupy Wall Street and denounced a heartless global capitalism that allocated all the wealth for the "one percent" and left personal trainers to fend for themselves. They could have gotten depressed or climbed onto the government dole. Instead, the young couple found several part-time jobs to stay afloat. "Kelli wrote 'how-to' articles on the Internet at night," explains the *Seattle Times* in one of the couple's only published profiles, "while ironically working with an organization that helped unemployed people get back on their feet. Daniel apprenticed as a plumber."[1] These jobs paid the bills while Daniel and Kelli worked on a side hustle.

Given their fitness background, the Segars noticed that gimmicky workout videos had started to populate the Web. Most of these followed a simple formula: a grab bag of lessons led by a cut, steroid-swelled guy or a bleached-blond, spray-tanned gal who tries to motivate you with unrealistic promises, corny comments, and drill sergeant antics, all the while coaxing you to upgrade to the deluxe package.

Daniel and Kelli knew far more about fitness and nutrition than most of these characters. Granted, they knew nothing about video production, but no matter. The house they had bought was a financial albatross, but it did have a nearly finished garage. So they added some drywall and white paint, bought a few hundred dollars' worth of video equipment, and started to shoot their own videos. "We taught ourselves how to use editing software and though we have a cameraman (who has become a good friend over the last few years), we often still film and edit our own videos," Kelli told me in an email interview.

Their first pieces were just thirty-second snippets of single exercises: agility dots (level one), crunch with toe touch (level two), mountain climbers (level one), deep glute stretch (level one). Nothing groundbreaking or all that popular. But before long they discovered what people wanted: individual workouts and workout plans. Their website, FitnessBlender.com, went live in 2010 and became their full-time job two years later. As of this writing, their YouTube channel has over four million subscribers.

I'm one of them. I had used other gimmicky video programs. They were better than nothing, but I kept looking for something better. One day I found Fitness Blender. Its success is its simplicity: no corn, no music, no pitch to upgrade. Just a simple white background, a user-friendly search function, variety, and routines that don't call for fancy equipment.

Indeed, much of Fitness Blender's success is due to the Segars themselves. Daniel is cut and seems to always have the right amount of facial stubble. Kelli is statuesque with long, dark-blond hair. (As my annoyed wife says, "She doesn't need Spanx, but you can't help but like her.") At the same time, they're the "couple next door," the kind of people you could picture meeting at a block party. They even fluctuate a bit in their body-fat ratio. If you ever work out, you know how it goes. You throw out your back or get the flu or get depressed, and next thing you know you've added a useless layer of winter blubber that takes five times as long to work off. At Fitness Blender, you won't see anything as dramatic (and unsustainable) as the feats achieved on *The Biggest Loser*. But you can see Daniel and Kelli get fitter over time in multi-week routines. They're like personal trainers who are there for you. They feel your pain.

The strategy wouldn't have worked twenty years ago, since the Segars would have had to charge every user for their services. But YouTube, which is owned by Google, shares the profits from its ads with "partners"—the people who produce the video content. People like Daniel and Kelli Segars. Through ad revenue, royalties on their e-book meal plans and exercise guides, and donations, the couple makes a living without charging anyone by the hour. They won't become billionaires, but in the face of financial disaster they found a new way to live the American Dream.

The lesson here isn't that everyone is cut out to launch a You-Tube fitness channel with millions of subscribers if only they would show a little pluck and resolve. Indeed, the Segars' success was not assured. They could have gone broke before they got things turned around. But while millions of Americans doubt that those who work hard and act responsibly can prosper in this country, the Segars found a way. Their troubles are a microcosm of what's happening everywhere in our economy.

And they offer a model of what to do in a crisis. Their jobs were disrupted by events beyond their control. Rather than get angry or depressed or blame their bad luck on someone else, they got busy—using technology to deliver the value of their expertise in a new way. Producing YouTube videos is an obvious way to do this, albeit one that may not work for everyone. But our emerging economy holds promise far beyond the most obvious, for those who are willing to adapt.

## THE AMERICAN DREAM IN CRISIS

For over three hundred years, men, women, and children have left their native countries and come to America in search of *something*.

When Thomas Jefferson wrote the Declaration of Independence in 1776, he spoke of a God-given right to pursue happiness. French thinker Alexis de Tocqueville toured the fruited plains in the 1830s and talked to common Americans in cities, hamlets, and even prisons. He later described what he saw among Americans as "the charm of anticipated success." Americans were poor by highborn European standards, but seemed to lack the despair he often encountered in his native France. These Americans had hope for the future.

It was historian James Truslow Adams who coined the term "American Dream" in his 1931 book *The Epic of America* to refer to "that dream of a land in which life should be better and richer and fuller for everyone." This hope of future success is bipartisan and always championed. It's the promise at the heart of America's Experiment. For at least the last decade, though, Americans have worried that the Dream is in danger. The 2008 financial crisis, which was triggered by a bevy of bad policies, bad home loans, and bad securities built upon them, is an apt symbol for the fear over our country's future. But the lingering trauma isn't limited to housing. Recent college grads find themselves underemployed and waterlogged with student loan debt. Automation, offshoring, and outsourcing have displaced entire manufacturing sectors and consumed a number of white-collar jobs. Many millennials work several part-time jobs, with a side hustle that is a diversion rather than a sustainable career. Experts tell us that soon enough smart robots will take *all* the jobs.

Even when the unemployment rate drops, that has as much to do with people dropping out of the workforce as it does with finding new and worthwhile jobs. Nearly one in six men of working age do no meaningful work at all.[2] And far too many of these idle males between the ages of twenty-five and fifty-four are hooked on painkilling drugs.[3] We hear that the middle class has been hollowed out and its wages have stagnated.[4] Government debt is out of control. Social Security and Medicare careen toward insolvency.

All of this has led to bipartisan doubts about the sources of our past success. In the 2016 presidential election, for instance, Hillary Clinton went soft on trade agreements once championed by her husband. Donald Trump, the victor for the officially free-market party, often sounded like Bernie Sanders when he talked about the economy. Sanders, for his part, electrified the Democratic Party base by celebrating rather than hiding his socialism.

In a national downturn, we tend to contrast our present woes with an idealized past. Liberals invoke a post–World War II workingman's paradise guarded by strong unions and a generous, government-run safety net. Conservatives imagine a golden age when GIs and college grads could easily afford to buy a house in their twenties, nab a middle-class job, keep it for forty years, and retire to Florida.

Majorities in the United States and other developed nations now expect their children to be worse off than they are.[5] That fits a 2016 study that claims only half of US kids born in 1980 make more money than their parents did, in contrast to 92 percent of kids born in 1940. The half that do better come mostly from the upper-middle class.[6] French economist Thomas Piketty delivered a more academic take on the same theme. He decried a growing gap between rich and poor where the rich get richer and the poor get poorer. The message has long since trickled down. In another 2016 study, almost half of millennials thought the American Dream was dead.[7] Others *wish* it were dead, because they identify it not with hope, happiness, and fecundity but with inequality, greed, and environmental ruin.

Is this right? Was the last century a unique, unjust, and unsustainable moment of prosperity brought on by new industry and abundant fossil fuel? Have we already picked all the low-hanging fruit?[8] Should we now prepare for a future of mediocrity and decline?

There are reasons to worry, but they're not the reasons offered by those, like Piketty, who fixate on small pies and income gaps. No, often what ails us are the very "cures" prescribed by such thinkers. Our economy languishes under foolish policies that squelch growth and innovation, encourage bad habits, and discourage good ones. In some sectors, our economy is more cronyist than capitalist. We have an outdated and blinkered educational system that delivers far less value for everyday Americans but costs them far more money. And we suffer from the breakdown of the family, which prevents lower-income Americans from grabbing even the bottom rungs of the economic ladder.

These are grave challenges. In response, dozens of would-be

guides call for a whole new economy, some "third way" between capitalism and socialism where no one should have to work to pay the bills. This is not new. In every financial crisis and economic inflection point, false prophets offer up old myths, insist that the truths of economics no longer hold, and issue calls to upend the system. Most of the popular media miss the fact that the self-styled reformers call for a power-up of the policies that gave rise to the problems in the first place.

If millions of Americans are to achieve the American Dream, however, we must scatter the fog, debunk the myths, and shun the bad advice. In 2016 we avoided the pleas for Bernie Sanders–style socialism. But there are plenty of misguided schemes that fall short of a continent-wide revolt against the free market. We now hear appeals to "protect" domestic workers and industries from foreign competition, and calls to guarantee jobs or incomes with ever more government "aid." These ideas make for tasty sound bites. But do we really want a repeat of the 1930s, when a recession was followed by bad policies, policies that plunged the country into a decade-long depression?

We need to get a grip. For many Americans, the current doldrums are as much about an imagined past or future as present pain. Even now, on most real measures, Americans are healthier and wealthier, our water and air are vastly cleaner, and our use of energy is far leaner than was the case even four decades ago. Americans work, on average, eight fewer hours per week than they did in the 1960s.[9] Our grandparents in 1960 spent almost 18 percent of their income on food. On average, each of us spends less than 10 percent today.[10] (The rates in the decades and centuries before that were much higher.) Even in gloomy 2016, the absolute and average net worth of US households reached an all-time high. The bounty isn't just enjoyed by the one percent.[11] If you make at least $32,400 a year, you're in the top half of American incomes but in the top *1 percent* of income earners worldwide.[12]

Even more, we live in an age of historic innovation that has just gotten started. Income charts miss the high-tech treasures that we now enjoy, in part because so many are practically free. Technology has bettered the lives of people even in parts of the world that still lack most of the fruits of economic freedom and rule of law. The numbers are astonishing, as we'll see later. And as we'll also see, the information economy holds promises that our ancestors could not have grasped.

Alas, this good news is hidden under a bushel. A recent Legatum Institute poll of ten nations revealed that large majorities from the United States to Thailand to Brazil think the poor get poorer in countries with market economies.[13] Socialism and capitalism now have similar favorability ratings for Americans under thirty.[14] Why do so many notice only the costs and so few appreciate the blessings and promises of freedom?

For one thing, we like harmful myths more than helpful truths. How often have you heard or read one of these old chestnuts?

- Americans were better off in the past.
- Capitalism is all about greed.
- The American Dream is out of reach for the poor.
- The American Dream is about rugged individualism.
- The wealth of some causes poverty for others.
- Our economy is better off when protected from outside competition.
- The economy is a finite pie.
- All the economic growth is behind us.
- Freedom means doing whatever you want to do.
- Government-run safety nets are the best solution to American poverty.
- The best way to succeed is to follow your passion.
- Machines will take all the jobs.

L. P. Hartley said the past is a foreign country. For many of us, it's a foreign country that doesn't speak a lick of English. Ignorance of history makes us dupes of demagogues. The myth that people lived better lives in the past, for instance, doesn't survive even a passing glance at history. In the past, poverty and disease were the norm. The era of widespread wealth we now enjoy is the one shining exception. Our lives may fare poorly compared to a utopian ideal but not compared to every other period. To understand our moment, we must see it in historical context.

Or take the myth about greed. Ayn Rand, the twentieth century liberal's bête noire, argued that capitalism and altruism are incompatible and that selfishness is a *virtue*. She was not a critic of capitalism but its fierce champion. With friends like these, who needs enemies?

Then there are the defenses that, unlike Rand, aren't daft but are halfhearted. The system that has done more than any other to lift entire cultures out of poverty gets at best faint praise, as if it's a necessary evil that we would abandon if anything more wholesome came along that actually worked. It's no wonder that for many the "American Dream" conjures up images of a greedy individualist who obsesses over riches.

As a college professor and a person who writes and speaks about the economy, I've spent the last decade trying to do my part to debunk many such myths. At times it has come to feel like an endless game of Whac-A-Mole.[15] Why bother? Because these myths threaten our future. They keep us from seeking the very skills and virtues we need to succeed in tomorrow's economy and lead us to opt, instead, for bad government fixes. *What we believe about ourselves, our past, and our economy shapes what we do.* Harmful myths cripple millions of Americans. That's why we'll have to debunk fistfuls of them in the pages that follow.

Even more, a new, insidious myth is about to reach the status of conventional wisdom in our schools, in our economic literature, and in the press. It's the overarching myth I target in this book: *Machines will soon replace us.* If you've paid attention to the news and the commentary of "experts" in the last few years, chances are you've heard rumblings of this. Within a decade or two, we're told, automation will destroy the career paths that created our country's middle class. The rich will get richer, but most Americans will find themselves without jobs or prospects. This myth, if it catches on, could steal hope from a generation who have not yet achieved the American Dream, and inspire policies that will ensure that they don't.

This makes even more acute the real challenge of our time: the rapid disruption of jobs, firms, ways of life, and whole industries.[16] This is the most glaring cost of our information economy. A flux in income can make us feel worse off, even when we are better off than at earlier, more stable times.[17] Our great-grandparents might have treated this as a test or a fact of life. Many young Americans now treat it as an affront to their dignity.

Nevertheless, the challenge of disruption is the one we most need to meet, since it will get worse in the years to come. What economist Joseph Schumpeter called "creative destruction" is as old as capitalism itself. But these days both the creation *and* the destruction happen so fast that whole professions can appear and disappear within the span of a single generation. The process speeds up as the economy moves from the physical to the informational, from "atoms to bits." If anything like current trends continues, the near future will be quite different from the present, with even more fast-paced change.

The destruction Schumpeter referred to is the fruit of innovation. Any new service or technology will dispatch something to the compost bin even as it creates newer, better prospects across the economy.[18] Alas, stories about new industries emerging next year are cold comfort if you can't pay your mortgage this year. And aside from such mundane matters, behavioral economists have shown that human beings are loss-averse: We feel a loss far more than a gain, even if the gain is greater than the loss.

So how do we prepare for an even more volatile future? Good policies and ideas are necessary but not sufficient. We will need to learn new twists on old-fashioned virtues. Virtue—always the un-sung hero of the American Dream—will be more vital than ever in our higher-tech future. Unfortunately, the sources of virtue are all under assault, especially among poor Americans. Healthy families, churches, and schools are in far shorter supply than they were half a century ago. Yet we need them now more than ever.

We need not fear the rise of the robots, but we do need to pre-pare for it. Some of our habits and institutions from earlier stages are creaky and unfit for the new. Routine factory and office work is passing away. So is the hope of a single stable job with one em-ployer, and an education completed at age twenty-two that will sus-tain a career for the next forty-five years.

The first American Dream was owning a farm, and the second was owning a home. The third[19] is more universal but also less con-crete: *the collaborative creating and sharing of value itself.*[20] Produc-ing workout videos and math tutorials, selling handmade goods directly to a global market, crowdsourcing a tough engineering problem, fabricating jewelry in your basement, creating an auto-mated name-changing service for young brides, designing a logo, editing a manuscript for an author you've never met, managing a team distributed around the globe—these are just a few of the countless new ways to create value with and for others.

As machines aid and replace more and more of our work, we will need to focus on *what is uniquely human.* We will need to nur-ture virtues such as the willingness to bear risk, to trade security for opportunity, to learn from inevitable failures, to work with and for others, to create value, and to help others create value. The good news is that our hyper-connected information economy provides endless new ways to do that, with ever lower barriers to entry.

There is a new and exciting tomorrow for the American Dream, and for America itself. But, to achieve it, we must first understand how our current crisis came about.

# PART I

## HOW WE GOT HERE

# I

# FROM HUNTER-GATHERERS
# TO HOMEOWNERS

## The Evolution of the American Dream

Tanzania's Kalahari Bushmen are persistence hunters who track antelope until they wear them out. This might seem inefficient, but Bushmen are well designed for extreme long-distance running in the desert heat. They can also carry water. A large-horned kudu antelope can run fast for many miles. After eight hours of being tracked through the desert, though, the animal can reach such a point of thirst and fatigue that one small man can kill it with a simple wooden spear.[1]

Halfway across the world, the Dani people of the Indonesian province of Papua, Western New Guinea, are subject to the heavy rains of a large tropical island, so they get by on Stone Age farming methods. The Dani plant tubers such as sweet potatoes and cassava, grow banana trees, and cook pork in earthen ovens. Bedecked with ornate feathered headdresses but little more than waist straps to cover their nakedness, the Dani were first discovered by the outside world in the early twentieth century.

The Kalahari Bushmen and Dani give us two glimpses of what the long prehistory of humanity must have looked like: hunter-gatherers and primitive farmers who subsisted on whatever the land provided and accumulated no wealth over the course of their lives.

Civilization began with the domestication of animals and the advent of larger-scale farming. Still, for thousands of years, most people were desperately poor by modern standards. They lived at or just above subsistence, always at risk from disease, climate, and predation.

Only in the last few hundred years have large numbers of people created more wealth than they consumed, and lived much longer and healthier lives. Graphs that chart economic growth from about 8000 BC to the present show a nearly horizontal line for most of that history, which quickly curves upward in hockey-stick fashion in the last three centuries, with most of the spike coming in the last century.[2]

Before the sharp "elbow" of this line, life for most people was brutally hard by today's standards. Thomas Hobbes surely missed some of the joys and beauties of life in primitive societies. But his famous description of the imagined state of nature might just as well have applied to the past. "No arts; no letters; no society; and which is worst of all, continual fear, and danger of violent death; and the life of man, solitary, poor, nasty, brutish and short," Hobbes observed.[3]

Hobbes wrote from his ascendant perch in England—in 1651. In other words, he wrote just *before* the elbow of the curve had turned sharply upward. How much harsher and harder must the lives of our distant ancestors appear to us now, on the other side of Scottish inventor James Watt. Watt's work tripled the power of steam engines in the decade before 1776.[4] His miracle gave rise to massive factories, cities, railways, and everything else we associate with the Industrial Revolution.[5]

People moved from using wood to coal, oil, and natural gas. They learned to harness electricity, purify water, refrigerate food,

## The "Hockey Stick" Curve of Human History

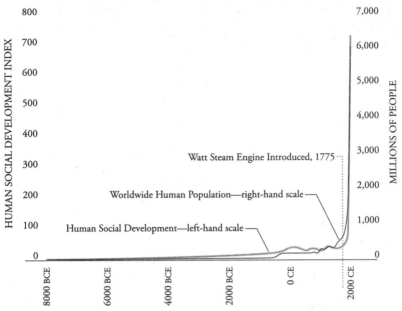

Shannon Henderson, after Brynjolfsson and McAfee, *The Second Machine Age*, p. 7

and build indoor plumbing.[6] With such advances came new forms of industry, transportation, and cities, as well as prosperity that previous generations could not have imagined. On average, the global population today is "about twenty times richer than it was during the long Agrarian age" before 1500 AD.[7]

There are now far more people living better, longer lives than ever before. This is especially true in the developed world, but even much of the developing world is catching up. Since 1990—as more countries have embraced trade and economic freedom—extreme poverty has been cut in half worldwide and continues to plummet.[8] The Brookings Institution projects that such poverty could disappear by 2030.[9]

Also, "life expectancy in the past 150 years has more than doubled," notes Danish economist Bjorn Lomborg. "One and a half centuries ago, more than 75% of the world's population lived in extreme poverty, consuming less than $1 a day, in 1985 money. This year [2015] the World Bank expects extreme poverty to fall below 10% for the first time in history."[10] There's more. Globally, infant mortality, malnutrition, and illiteracy are on the decline.[11] In 1962, people in fifty-one countries consumed, on average, under 2,000 calories. By 2013, only one country was still below that grim threshold.[12]

Any such major change comes with costs, of course—sometimes severe ones. Today we fear that all the growth is behind us, with little but stasis or decline ahead. We worry about jobs and living standards for our children in a world where machines do so much of the work.

No one can prove just what jobs the future will bring. What we do have is the proof of the past. Throughout history, every large economic shift has meant disruption, when one form of life gave way to another. A nomadic tribe of hunter-gatherers meets a kind of crisis when it settles down and starts to plow fields and plant seeds. So does a culture that moves from farms in the country to cities and factories. What's new about our time is not change itself but the pace of change. For most of human history, such major shifts were few and far between, and took place over thousands of years. For instance, the feudal era that followed the collapse of the Roman Empire lasted about a millennium. That was long enough for the trades to settle into guilds, and for jobs to pass from father to son. Many surnames in England and elsewhere—Miller, Miner, Baker, Chandler, Taylor, Carpenter, Tanner, and Smith—hint at how slowly things changed in that era.

The reason we speak of what came next as an Industrial *Revolution* is not because it came out of nowhere or swept aside all that took place before but because of the *time scale*.[13] Compared to the leisurely stroll along the foothills of human history—starting a flint fire here, chiseling a wheel there, domesticating cows over yonder—industrialization was a catapult into the stratosphere. Now the changes come fast and hard—over the course of a decade or even a year—though human nature has not changed at all. Taxi driver and insurance adjuster, webmaster and social media manager: These will never be surnames.

## THE FIRST AMERICAN DREAM

Even in the short history of the American Experiment, there have been disruptive shifts between three versions of the American Dream, each one lasting for a shorter period than the one that came before. The heart of the first American Dream was the farm. Having left an aristocratic, agrarian culture in Europe, where they worked as tenant farmers, America's early colonists dreamed of a place where they could not just work the land but *own* a piece of it. They believed that in the New World their family tree need not keep them rooted to the same patch of someone else's ground. For millions, the desire to own a farm meant freedom, independence— what today we call "self-employment"—and a morsel of wealth beyond mere survival.[14] Personal success was not guaranteed, but neither was it unthinkable.

As late as 1776, more than 90 percent of the colonial inhabitants of what would soon be the United States of America still lived on farms. This included American Founding Fathers such as John Adams, a Massachusetts lawyer, and Virginians Thomas Jefferson and George Washington, both of whom owned large plantations and slaves.

With the Homestead Act of 1862, enacted by Abraham Lincoln, and the promise of free or cheap land, the same agrarian spirit pushed western expansion. Hundreds of thousands of families packed up all their worldly assets on little more than a hope of fertile earth over the western horizon. Even as late as 1920 and well into the Industrial Revolution, more than half the US population still lived and worked on farms.[15] And more than half the compensated workforce was self-employed.

My grandfather on my mom's side of the family, V. B. Hubbard, was born in 1899 on a small family farm in Hill County, Texas. His family had hoped to buy a larger plot someday, so they scrimped and saved until they could purchase land in West Texas, near Odessa. My grandfather's earliest memory was of the 350-mile journey west with his parents and sisters in a covered wagon. Unfortunately, their new property was smack dab in the middle of the Dust Bowl. It was sandy and useless for growing crops. It still is.

This drama had played out for decades. Many of the common soldiers who fought in the Revolutionary War were paid with farmland. The best land had been nabbed by the time of the Civil War. By the early 1900s, it was slim pickings. So the Hubbards soon sold their barren patch of dirt—where, according to family lore, oil was later discovered. They then moved to the tiny town of Wheeler in the Texas Panhandle, population 904. They bought a house with cash. To be more precise, they bought a converted post office with three small rooms, a cold-water well, gas lights, and an outhouse connected to the town sewer.

The Hubbards had moved into town, but my grandfather's work remained tied to the land. He quit school in the seventh grade to pick cotton. As an adult, though, he ditched King Cotton and invested in a cutting-edge technology: a truck for hauling cedar posts, which at the time were used to build barbed-wire fences. At twenty-seven, "Posty," as he was called, married Etta Kate Crowder, who had grown up on a proper farm, and they started a family. His nickname and job soon became obsolete, since metal posts replaced cedar. He spent the rest of his life baling and hauling hay for cattle.

My mom and her five siblings also knew the pleasures of picking cotton at their uncle Clarence Crowder's farm. I grew up hearing stories of dust, mosquitoes, bleeding fingers, and sore backs. And the heat. Oh, the incessant heat. But by the 1950s my grandfather realized the old way of life was giving way to something new. Railroads, refrigeration, and labor-saving farm techniques meant far more and cheaper food for everyone. The downside was that small family farms and related jobs were no longer the dream they once were, especially in the dry Texas Panhandle. So V.B. and Etta Kate Hubbard, whom I knew as Papaw and Mamaw, pulled up their roots in Wheeler and moved with their six kids to Canyon, Texas, the closest town with a state university. They didn't know it at the time, but the Hubbards were embarking on the second American Dream—the one centered on owning a home.

Their third son, my uncle Gene, had just returned from the Korean War. He got a Veterans Administration loan to buy a house, where the whole family could live, less than a mile from West Texas State College. The move to Canyon meant that the kids could get college educations and clerical or teaching jobs. None of them ever returned to farm life. Picking cotton is fine, unless you can do almost anything else.

There are millions of such stories. In *The Grapes of Wrath*, poor Oklahoma farmers had it worse than my mom's family. Steinbeck's characters had to flee the Oklahoma Dust Bowl for faraway California in search of jobs. Progressive politicians such as William Jennings Bryan built careers on the loss of family farms, unable to see the big picture or imagine the better days ahead.

By the mid-twentieth century, a new social order had emerged. It was dominated by industry, cities, suburbs, financial markets, the Federal Reserve, private banks, and stock markets—all of this because we learned to produce vastly more food on less land than we used just a few decades earlier.[16]

In contrast to the previous two centuries, only 10 percent of workers were self-employed.[17] But contra the gloomy guesses of Thomas Malthus and Karl Marx, the teeming masses enjoyed longer and richer lives because of ingenuity, industry, and Henry Ford–like mass production. In this environment, most Americans dreamed not of owning a farm but of owning a home. That dream, like the one before, was not preordained. It happened for millions of common Americans only because of the right mix of laws and policies as well as personal and civic virtues. And as we'll see, with the right virtues and policies it can happen again in the twenty-first century.

## The Second American Dream

For decades now, the largest single asset and the center of family life for most Americans has been a home. While my maternal grandfather's career was mostly bound to the first American Dream, my paternal grandfather's career was bound to the second. Floyd Richards Sr. was born on a farm near Dallas in 1905 but spent his life in my hometown of Amarillo. He worked in construction and in due course started his own business, Floyd Richards Construction Co. The company built houses and churches, doing a little bit to make the second American Dream a reality.

Frank Capra captured that Dream in his 1946 classic, *It's a Wonderful Life*, starring Jimmy Stewart as George Bailey. Even as a child, George wants to leave his small-town home of Bedford Falls. He longs to travel to exotic places, go to college, move to the big city, and then build great skyscrapers and bridges. George's father, Peter Bailey, has a family business with his brother, Bailey Bros. Building & Loan, which provides the only mortgage loans in the small town.

When Peter Bailey reaches retirement age, he tells George that he hopes he will take over the family business. George rebuffs him, complaining that he can't imagine "this business of nickels and dimes, spending all your life trying to figure out how to save three cents on a length of pipe. . . . I'd go crazy. I want to do something big and something important."

"You know, George," Peter says calmly, "I feel that in a small way we are doing something important. Satisfying a fundamental urge. It's deep in the race for a man to want his own roof and walls and fireplace . . ." He is speaking of his humble neighbors who would otherwise have to rent a room at Potter's Field, a slum run by the miserly Mr. Potter.

George Bailey and Bedford Falls are a composite of Everytown, USA, in the middle of the twentieth century. By then, owning a house had become a realistic hope for many Americans—at least for those who could, and would, commit to the hard work and discipline required to save enough money to secure a mortgage. At the turn of the twentieth century, fewer than half of Americans owned their homes (46.5 percent). By 1960, almost 62 percent were homeowners.[18]

*It's a Wonderful Life* may be the only great movie to cast a banker qua banker as a hero. But historically it was spot-on. Few regular folks could have achieved either the first or second American Dreams without the right mix of laws and financial innovations to reward and reinforce fiscal virtue. That is, they could never have owned farms or houses without lenders who poured themselves into "this business of nickels and dimes," to quote George Bailey one last time. This part of the American story gets short shrift, so let's take a moment to give the George and Peter Baileys their due.

Though the *Mayflower* never would have crossed the Atlantic without financial credit, early American colonists had a dim view of debt. Two generations later, Benjamin Franklin depicted debt as a despotic master. "Maintain your Independency," he warned. "Be frugal and free."[19] A few generations on, Victorian-era Americans had made their peace with productive credit, such as for land. In the eyes of most Americans, borrowing money was okay as long as it was "used to purchase things that increased in value or had productive uses."[20] But the meaning of "productive use" expanded over time, as did the types of loans available to ordinary people.

Installment loans, which were first introduced by the US government rather than by retailers, played a major role. The finance historian Lendol Calder explains that after the Land Act of 1800, the federal government sold 19.4 million acres of public land using a loan program for individuals. Later, installment credit allowed humble farmers to buy mechanical farm equipment. Not technology alone but new technology *combined* with creative credit allowed farmers to reduce "the man-hours required to harvest an acre of grain from twenty hours to one."[21]

This much greater bounty meant fewer people needed to farm and more people could move to the city, sparking the second American Dream and the home-ownership boom of the twentieth century. One of the watershed inventions along the way was the sewing machine, which empowered millions of Americans—mostly women—to become income earners. I. M. Singer & Co. is remembered because its machines found their way into so many American homes. That only happened because Singer and other sewing machine companies made installment credit popular nationwide.[22]

Credit was bound to be applied to home purchases as well. Buying a house is not the same as investing in farmland or even a tractor. Owning a house doesn't, in itself, make your work more productive. Yet, even in a flat housing market—where prices don't change—buying a house with a mortgage loan can be a sort of investment. After all, if you live in a house and slowly pay off a thirty-year mortgage, you end up with a house. If you had rented it instead, at the end of that period you'd still have to pay rent and wouldn't own so much as a single two-by-four in the house where you'd spent half your life.

Just when technology and mass production were lowering the price of necessities, credit lifted the reach of lower-income Americans. Goods that had been a luxury for the wealthy in an earlier age were now within reach of the growing middle class. But besides these perks there were predictable costs of credit and prosperity, not just financial but cultural and moral costs. With home ownership, more disposable income, a postwar bounty, and ever-present credit came a much larger consumer culture.

That was surely a good thing, since a consumer culture is only possible when lots of people emerge from destitution. But such bounty had its downside—consumer*ism*. The "conspicuous consumption" that Thorstein Veblen detected in the "leisure class" in 1899[23] found its way even to the lower classes who could least

afford it a century later. Now Americans are burdened with almost $1 trillion in consumer debt at any given moment, more than $1 trillion in student loan debt, $8 trillion in mortgage debt, and a giant $20 trillion in government debt. That doesn't include the massive unfunded promises from Social Security and other entitlements.

How things have changed. My grandfather V. B. Hubbard never signed up for Social Security, never owned a credit card, and always kept his money safe from banks. He chose to deal in greenbacks, carrying giant folded wads of hundred-dollar bills in his shirt pocket. He also saved everything—and I mean *everything*. He recycled and reused long before it was fashionable to do so. Every doorknob in his house held dozens of spare rubber bands. His pants always had patches that he had sewn himself with a Singer treadle-powered (that is, foot-powered) sewing machine. A visitor from Dallas might have mistaken his backyard for a junkyard, with hazardous stacks of old tires, a ramshackle chicken coop, broken truck transmissions and engine blocks, sundry wooden trusses and two-by-fours, scrap metal, tools, and odd trinkets he imagined might someday be useful.

This extreme frugality was adaptive for most of human history and for most Americans until after World War II. In earlier times, the profligate poor were quickly evicted from the gene pool. We now treat this behavior as a psychological disorder. In 2013 "hoarding" found its way into the American Psychiatric Association's *Diagnostic and Statistical Manual*.[24] It's even the subject of a reality TV show, *Hoarders*.

These days, we don't work, earn, scrimp, and save like our grandparents did. We work, earn . . . and spend, usually on credit and often more than we've earned. And we pass the habit down with our genes. A recent study found that fewer than half of millennials have even $1,000 in the bank.[25]

We hate to admit it, but even our use of mortgages has become part of this pattern of spending rather than saving. For decades,

easy credit and rising home prices gave Americans the sense that a house was an investment—full stop. But it's mostly a consumer good that may retain its value. Then again, it may not, as many learned the hard way when the housing bubble burst in 2007 and 2008.

We also tend to go large. Our grandparents bought much smaller and humbler houses than we do, and were more diligent about paying off their mortgages. Many Americans now refinance their mortgages every few years to get cash out of equity. At the start of the crisis in early 2008, the amount of equity Americans had in their homes dipped below 50 percent for the first time since 1945.[26] I have heard young denizens of Dallas complain about having to live in a "used house." Seriously. How did families ever survive with only one bathroom?

Still, for the pursuit of happiness, the mortgage loan was a godsend. Rather than rely on the whims of feudal lords in the Old World and landlords in the New, it gave millions of families a place to call their own, a little castle set off from the state, the collective, and the miserly Mr. Potter. A house is a real asset that anchors a family to a fixed place, to a plot of soil, a proxy for the farmer's more direct tie to the land. The family home becomes the basic unit of the neighborhood, town, and parish.

The properly structured mortgage requires that the buyer have the discipline to scrimp and save for a down payment. Home ownership correlates with all sorts of other "positive social indicators," too, as a social scientist might say. If you own rather than rent a home, you're more likely to vote, plan for the future, obey the law, take care of your lawn, take an interest in local schools, and keep your job and your spouse. It literally keeps a family together, and spurs the breadwinner to do the same. It can provide the solid ground that allows for a peaceful life. It can even be used for collateral to get a productive loan. There is a reason home ownership was the second American Dream rather than the first. It could become a realistic hope for the masses only once society became productive

enough that most folks could leave the farm, and once the right financial tools could help them to do so.

## CRACKS IN THE FOUNDATION

Regrettably, politicians dreamed they could make the American Dream a reality for everyone by legislative fiat. The perks of home ownership led activists and politicians to push "affordable housing policies" designed to help poor Americans get home loans.

The efforts were modest at first. As far back as 1922, Herbert Hoover led a campaign to increase home ownership, and Franklin Roosevelt's New Deal brought most of the apparatus into place throughout the rest of the 1930s. At this stage, government-backed mortgages enforced strict lending standards. They directed loans to people with a track record of sound money management and away from people who might dig themselves into a hole they couldn't escape. But as with so many such programs, the plant that started small grew and grew and grew. Yes, go ahead and cue up the *Little Shop of Horrors* title song, because this plant did bloom into a man-eating monster.

Affordable housing policies picked up steam at the end of the century. By 2000, the steam had turned to smoke—dark, fetid, disorienting smoke. There were about twenty-four separate programs spread around federal office buildings in Washington, DC, meant to make the second American Dream a reality for all. Americans began to hear tales of "NINJA" loans. Their recipients, despite having "no income, no job or assets," somehow qualified for a mortgage.

NINJA loans were a portent of doom. By trying to control the price and supply of money, the Fed kept loan prices artificially low. Affordable housing policies degraded underwriting standards on mortgages and scrambled market signals and incentives. This turned a virtuous circle of work and saving into a vicious circle of bad lending and borrowing.

I mentioned above that while our grandparents' generation tended to be content with far more modest homes, we tend to go big. Part of that is due to rising prosperity. Part is due to cultural shifts unrelated to government policy. But part of the change is also due to easy credit engineered by the federal government.

There's no problem riding a bubble into the clear blue sky, as long as it doesn't burst. Alas, bubbles have a bad habit of doing just that. At the peak of the hot housing market in 2007, fully half of all mortgages were risky loans that would have been unthinkable even thirty years earlier. Two-thirds of these loans were held by federal agencies or entities that operated under government control. And many of the worst loans were issued in the few short years just before the collapse.

The housing crisis was a perfect storm, created when the consumer culture collided with government social engineering. If policies had not encouraged foolish risk and dissolved underwriting standards on home loans, we would not have had a subprime mortgage crisis in 2008.[27]

At the same time, other obstacles have piled up over the years. One is the swelling cost and shrinking value of a college education—yet another government-inflated bubble. A second obstacle is the loss of virtue and the breakdown of the family fed by other well-meaning but misguided policies. Then, too, the decline in factory jobs and the rapid disruption of industry have taken a toll. Many Americans are still misled—by media and academia—about how free enterprise works. They have bought into popular myths—that the American Dream is out of their reach, that we're about to run out of jobs and resources, that the system is rigged, so what's the use in trying?

And these are just the tremors of a greater earthquake that is only now getting started: the rise of "intelligent" machines. We must adapt if there is to be a third American Dream.

# 2

# RISE OF THE ROBOTS

## WILL SMART MACHINES EAT ALL THE JOBS?

I n the 2016 presidential election, Donald Trump's margin of victory over Hillary Clinton was wafer thin: Eighty thousand people in three states tipped the scales in his favor. He won in part because tens of thousands of blue-collar workers who pulled the lever for Barack Obama in 2012 went for Trump in 2016. The pain among these workers in the Rust Belt and elsewhere is real. Soon, though, the greater threat to their jobs will come not from China or Mexico but from machines that are finding their way onto factory floors and offices right here in the US of A.

As the agrarian age gave way to the industrial, the industrial has given way to the information age. The new economy, and the American Dream that corresponds to it, are not marked by farms or factories or houses but by ever more "intelligent" machines that can do much that we once thought was the unique province of man.

Technology can make our lives better and our work more fruitful. But it has always had the downside of making some jobs obsolete. Buggy-whip makers get displaced by cars. Eight-track tape factories get displaced by cassette factories, and then CD factories, which are then displaced by MP3 files that are not even produced in factories. Information technology tends to vaporize jobs that are easily automated. And the vaporizing is just getting started.

Derek Thompson, a senior editor at the *Atlantic*, worries that "technology could exert a slow but continual downward pressure on the value and availability of work—that is, on wages and on the share of prime-age workers with full-time jobs." He points to the loss of labor, the "spread of nonworking men and underemployed youth," and the "shrewdness of software."[1] Tech entrepreneur Martin Ford warns of the "rise of the robots"—of a future of mass joblessness and, as he puts it, lots of "unnecessary" people.[2]

In 2013, the hotshots at McKinsey & Company warned that by 2025 "robots may jeopardize from 25 million to 40 million jobs in developed countries and from 15 million to 35 million in developing ones," leading to swarms of "redundant people."[3] Other robotics experts predict a near future in which armies of humanoid robots will outnumber humans and be controlled over the cloud with smartphones.[4] Computer scientist Moshe Vardi warns that, in the next thirty years, half of the world could be out of a job.[5]

The fear of job-killing machines is nothing new. The short-lived uprising attributed to apocryphal figure Ned Ludd inspired weavers in early-nineteenth-century England to attack power looms in textile factories that put the weavers out of work. The Luddites' gripe was as much with the owners of the mills as with the less-skilled workers the factories employed. Mechanized factory work favored more specialized, less skilled, and less costly workers over artisans who had spent years honing their craft.

But this fear didn't begin or end at the Industrial Revolution. For thousands of years, we have built *labor*-saving devices: wheels and carts and wheelbarrows and cotton gins and steam engines and tractors. Most of these devices aided rather than replaced human labor. They created jobs for some and let the rest of us move up the value scale, as economists put it. Some of us still labor literally—in construction, mining, deep-sea fishing, and so forth. Others spend a couple of decades in school and then do "knowledge work." We become accountants, bankers, lawyers, surgeons, insurance adjusters, financial advisors, engineers, software designers, teachers, and writers.

In the information age, however, even the white-collar side of the street has started to sweat. Earlier, those in air-conditioned offices assumed that machines might replace laborers but would never touch the rest of us. A lot of us aren't so sure anymore. Earlier technology merely aided human labor. Information technology seems to *replace* not just human labor but thinking itself. Kayak and Orbitz replace travel agents. TurboTax replaces low-level accountants. Complex writing algorithms (sets of rules) replace financial reporters. A/B testing programs replace ad agents. Robots replace factory workers and roughnecks.

These worries lead to a wider fear that machines will replace us, or our children, plummeting our society into a harsh and jobless future.

## Machines Giveth, and Machines Taketh Away

This shift has already transpired with the icon of the information age, the computer. For the first half of the last century, the word "computer" was a job description for women who computed for a living. Indeed, the father of information theory, Claude Shannon, married a computer named Betty, whom he met at Bell Labs. The swap is now so complete that we only use the word to refer to a machine. To refer to a woman as a "computer" now would be an insult.

This trend toward smart machines has shaped our lives in countless subtler ways for decades. In the mid-1990s, Allstate Insurance began using machines to do underwriting that had been done by employees before. "During that process, two-thirds of 1,000 Allstate knowledge workers were able to move upstream to higher-skilled jobs in portfolio management, enterprise risk management, and agent relationships," reports *Fast Company*. But there was a downside: "The remaining one-third did not have the right skills to move upstream and ultimately lost their jobs."[6]

This story, like all such stories, doesn't say what happened to these former Allstate employees. For all the reporter can tell us, they now live in abandoned subway tunnels in Queens.

It's a similar tale in the world of stock markets and financial advisors. More than three of every four stock transactions today are automated. The venerable chaos of the trading floor of the New York Stock Exchange has started to look like the crowd at a mall that has seen too many winters. Even financial advisors, who spend most of their time with clients rather than computers, are slowly becoming obsolete as more and more amateur investors grow used to sophisticated trading platforms. Some analysts predict that in the next decade or so, the number of jobs in this pocket of the financial sector will drop by 50 percent.[7]

Rumors of the rise of the machines are leaking out. A 2016 poll by the Pew Research Center revealed that two-thirds of Americans expect much of the work now done by people to be done by computers and robots fifty years from now. But it's not a full-blown panic: Most of those polled make exceptions for their own jobs. If we trust the experts, though, these respondents are wrong. A 2013 study by two scholars at Oxford University reckoned that 47 percent of US jobs were at risk of what they called "computerization."[8] They expect a hollowing out of routine, middle-skill jobs.[9]

Amazon's huge fulfillment centers are at the bleeding edge. When Jeff Bezos launched the start-up as an online bookstore in July 1994, he and his employees fulfilled orders à la carte from a garage in Seattle, using handmade desks crafted from old doors and lumber. By the end of 2014, the company sold everything, including the kitchen sink—thousands of them.

For the 2014 Christmas season, the internet behemoth released a short video. It revealed some of the inner secrets of its newest distribution centers, populated with over fifteen thousand orange and yellow Kiva robots. (Amazon bought Kiva for three-quarters of a billion dollars in 2012.) Many of the robots hover along the floor like industrial-grade Roombas. They find and move large pallets of products. These are then sorted by mounted robotic arms before being whisked away by a labyrinth of conveyor belts. The process still involves a few humans. The "pick-and-place" robot arms can't remove every item—of various shapes and sizes—from shelves. So, in the video, one man loads packages, a woman works on a touchpad, another man operates a mini-forklift—a handful of carbon-based life-forms in a sea of silicon and steel.

When I first watched it, I found the video awe-inspiring. It was a testimony to human genius: Almost any product could be delivered to my house in one or two days, at cut-rate prices. I thought of how Amazon had boosted the purchasing power and leisure time of the average American. As an early subscriber to Amazon Prime, I knew that this technology had helped me avoid the mall for my Christmas shopping.

But the media saw a story about job-killing robots. They were hardly assuaged by the fact that the company had hired eighty thousand seasonal workers to keep up with the demand brought on by such a tight operation.[10] John Markoff of the *New York Times* was one of the journalists who sounded the alarm. He warned in his book *Machines of Loving Grace*[11] that the fulfillment center from Amazon's 2014 video was "clearly an interim solution toward the ultimate goal of building completely automated warehouses."[12]

Amazon, smarting from the outcry over its earlier video, tried to rebut the story. "Our fulfillment centers are a symphony of robotics, software, of people and of high-tech computer science algorithms—machine learning everywhere—and our employees are key to the process," a spokesperson said. "There has been no job loss associated with the use of robotics in our buildings and in fact due to increased efficiencies, some of our buildings utilizing robotics have the highest headcounts in our network."[13] This is good PR. But behind the scenes, Amazon is still trying to solve the robot-hand conundrum. They even host "picking challenges" where teams compete to find the robot that can master the art of putting products of all sorts directly into boxes.

Why, in the age of Siri and self-driving Google cars, would Amazon have trouble getting a machine to do what any four-year-old can do? Blame it on a killjoy challenge called Moravec's paradox, named after Carnegie Mellon robotics professor Hans Moravec. It's much easier to make a computer that can solve some tough mental tasks—to play chess or find the factors of 25,638—than to build a robot that can handle the work of muscle and bone that you and I perform every day.

When I pick up a wineglass, fill it with pinot noir, and hand it to my wife, the action relies on complex feedback among my mind, eyes, and fingers. I know how fragile the wine glass and wine bottle are, and adjust my grip based on input from my fingers. I rely on my sense of balance and direction. I can tell up from down and know not to turn the glass sideways after I've filled it with wine. I know to stop pouring before the wine overflows, no matter the size of the glass. I can easily hand it to my wife and decide to let it go once I can see and feel that she has a firm grip on it. I can't say how I do any of this. I don't follow a set of rules in my head. I just do it. But the computational and engineering resources needed to replicate these feats in a machine are so vast that we haven't managed to do it yet. Robots excel in structured environments, not unstructured ones.

The dilemma roughly corresponds to two types of knowledge, which the ancient Greeks called *episteme* (knowing that) and *techne* (knowing how). *Episteme* is *knowing that* in 1492, Columbus sailed the ocean blue. *Techne* is *knowing how* to hoist the sails and walk the deck on a ship while it crosses the Atlantic Ocean. The former is mere *knowing.* The latter is *doing.* For computers, *episteme* is a cinch. *Techne* is one tough mother. Remember that.

Because of Moravec's paradox, skilled and semiskilled manual labor is hard to automate. That means jobs in construction, welding, fine carpentry, masonry, plumbing, landscaping, hairdressing, and housekeeping will outlast assembly-line work. So, long before Mark Zuckerberg can purchase Rosie 1.0 to trim his hedges and butter his toast, Amazon will have stationary factory robots with supple grip tasked with putting glow-in-the-dark toilet paper and popcorn-scented pillows in boxes.

We should expect an automated Amazon fulfillment center in the next decade.[14] During Christmas 2016, Amazon had forty-five thousand Kiva robots in its twenty fulfillment centers. It needed less than a minute of human labor to ship your package.[15] In March 2017, a grinning Jeff Bezos tweeted a picture of himself piloting a thirteen-foot-tall humanoid robot.[16] I haven't even touched on Amazon's plans for drones for same-day delivery, which will undercut a key advantage of brick-and-mortar stores. Amazon is opening a few of those, too—without workers.

Most factory workers know how to drive, so many of them could become drivers for Uber or Lyft. Not a bad gig, but not a permanent one, either. By the time those platforms finish disrupting the limo and taxi industries, Uber and Lyft drivers will start to feel the pinch from self-driving cars. The Ford Motor Company is working with the two ride-sharing services and shooting for a launch date of 2021.[17] Uber has already delivered its first self-driving fleet to Pittsburgh, home of the famous robotics lab at Carnegie Mellon. The sensor-packed Volvo XC90s still need human monitors—for now.[18] The company is currently chatting about the next step: flying cars.[19]

Even before driverless cars swamp the streets of Manhattan, semiautonomous long-haul trucks will haunt the highways. Driverless cars must deal with the trials of urban environments: the potholes, jaywalkers, sanctimonious cyclists, homeless guys with squeegees, and limited space for navigational gadgets. To drive a big truck on a highway is simple by comparison. And unlike taxi drivers, truckers rarely have to deal with customers.

Truck automation will swallow far more jobs in far more states than the Amazon or Tesla robot factories. Right now, there are 1.8 million truck drivers in the United States, mostly men.[20] In 2014, NPR's Planet Money used census data to map the "most common job in each state, 1978–2014." In 1978, several western and midwestern states, from Montana to Iowa, still had more farmers than any other single profession. By 2014, in most states—from California to Texas to Pennsylvania and Maine—"truck driver" got top billing. Guess what job already had the top spot in Utah, Colorado, and Virginia? Software developer.[21]

That's the trend—from growing corn to writing code. But again, it's not a simple binary between outdoor and office, or blue- and white-collar work. Some blue-collar jobs will stay safe. Some white-collar jobs will get the axe. Already, few people are shocked by news that a computer could master insurance adjusting. But in recent years computers have learned to recognize complex visual patterns. They've even begun to master human language, a feat I used to think would take decades. The wake-up call for me came in 2011, with IBM's Watson.

## IF YOU THINK YOUR JOB CAN'T BE AUTOMATED, THINK AGAIN

Watson is a platform first developed to play *Jeopardy!*, the game show hosted by Alex Trebek. In February 2011, Watson was pitted against two previous human champions, Brad Rutter and Ken Jennings. At the end of round one, aired on Valentine's Day, Jennings and Watson were tied for first place. Watson then trounced both men in the next round, despite making some odd mistakes, and again in the second game, aired on February 16. The first victory, it seemed, was more than just beginner's luck.

When the IBM computer Deep Blue beat reigning chess champion Garry Kasparov in 1997, it was just a matter of brute-force calculation. It ran through millions of possible chess moves in response to the previous move by Kasparov, and picked the one most likely to succeed. That's the skill set that a fast computer with the right algorithm was bound to solve at some point.[22]

In the two decades since the victory of Deep Blue, computers have gotten much better at doing well-defined tasks. Watson went even further. It offered a glimpse of the computer generalist. After its *Jeopardy!* victory, doctors realized that Watson might help them diagnose illnesses based on patient symptoms.

A computer in place of a doctor? To become a physician, you need to perform well in college, then get a medical school degree, take an internship, and complete a residency. This doesn't seem like a field at risk for automation, but it turns out machines have an edge when it comes to one of a doctor's most important tasks: diagnosis. A recent study from Johns Hopkins estimated that as many as 40,500 American patients in intensive care die each year because they're misdiagnosed.[23] Despite years of training, doctors still rely far too much on hunches, habits, and cognitive biases such as "premature cloture." That's when doctors make up their minds too quickly and then fail to take account of new evidence. If they've been out of school too long, they may also rely on obsolete training.

MD Anderson Cancer Center started to test Watson even before its *Jeopardy!* victory had faded from the headlines. Memorial Sloan Kettering Cancer Center and the Mayo Clinic followed. Like a real doctor, Watson can ask questions about patients and get feedback from physicians. Unlike a real doctor, it can keep track of the millions of relevant articles in PubMed—including the torrent of new research published every year. It can quickly scan the symptoms of the more than ten thousand human diseases. And it can search for patterns in millions of MRIs, CAT scans, and X-rays from previously diagnosed patients.

"When Watson goes over the patient's case," explains medical futurist Bertalan Meskó, "it comes up with the list of suggestions for treatment and assigns a confidence value between very low and very high."[24] Physicians can review the reasons and background research that Watson used to arrive at its suggestions, and then decide what to do. Watson takes account of the feedback much like Google stores its users' choices to improve future searches.

Watson-like platforms will soon connect to the growing toolkit of electronic sensors. Already with AliveCor's Kardia app and accessories, you can take an EKG for less than a dollar a day, using your smartphone or Apple Watch, and send it instantly to your doctor. CellScope provides iPhone attachments that help diagnose moles, rashes, and ear infections. Other peripherals will test the gases in your breath to detect lung diseases.[25]

In 2016, Watson was even disguised as a teaching assistant for grad students at Georgia Tech. "Jill Watson" spent the spring semester answering student questions about papers and due dates. "She" even emailed questions to provoke conversations.[26] Expect more of the same for teaching assistants, customer service reps, and other routine, instructional jobs in which most interaction is over the phone or by email.

In fact, any work that involves scads of data and can be reduced to rules will go the way of the dodo bird, and with just as little ceremony. Take compliance officers. With millions of pages of government regulations, and thousands of new pages a year, all sorts of companies need these workers—from banks and hospitals to building contractors and retail chains.[27] In 2014 the *Wall Street Journal* claimed that the future was bright "for anyone entering into compliance as a career."[28] A mere two years later, Julia Kirby and Thomas H. Davenport noted in the *Harvard Business Review* that much of the work will soon be automated. "Compliance workers will either be looking for work or lonelier at work, and that stinks."[29] It sounds like hell to me to keep track of the latest dos and don'ts of the nanny state, but most of these folks would rather not lose their jobs.

Given these trends, you might think the best bet is to train for a career that calls for complex manual labor, so you can ride Moravec's paradox to retirement. That's not a bad plan for the next decade or two—maybe longer. But what happens when robots *can* physically do everything we do? When they don't just aid our physical labor but replace it?

Despite decades of false promises, general-purpose robots are now on the horizon. In 2016, Boston Dynamics, owned by Google parent company Alphabet, unveiled "Atlas," a humanoid robot that seems to have mastered basic bipedal skills. The company released a short video (of course) that shows Atlas going through a closed door, walking on snow through a forest, moving boxes, and even getting up on its own after being shoved rudely to the ground.

"This is really the end of manual labor," said angel investor Jason Calacanis on CNBC. "Manual labor is going to end in our lifetime, and in this video you can see how close we really are. It's a huge societal issue with jobs, but it's going to be a huge lift in terms of efficiency of companies that nobody expected."[30]

These are just a few of the highlights. But you get the gist: The future, say the experts, will in many ways resemble a sci-fi dystopia ruled by a tiny cabal of capital-hoarding trillionaires in charge of armies of robots and automated factories, trucks, cars, and drones, along with billions of unemployed people with nothing to do.

## The Death of Capitalism?

You should be worried, at least a little. The future job climate won't look like the present—and we know from surveys that people tend to wrongly think their jobs are safe. The disruption will surely be as profound as it was during the Industrial Revolution, when one form of life replaced another for almost all Americans. And it will happen not over the course of centuries but over the course of years. Amidst such dizzying change, it would be natural to worry not just about our jobs but about our very place in the universe.

That said, don't panic. If technology led to permanent unemployment for the masses, history would be one long, dismal story of expanding joblessness. Obviously it's not. In fact, and paradoxically, without the technological progress that led to all the job loss, the global economy could not sustain the billions of jobs and human beings it now does.

The real danger of these gloom-and-doom forecasts is when they're used to justify bad policies. In March 1964, a group called the Ad Hoc Committee on the Triple Revolution—scientists and activists—wrote President Johnson to warn him of a "cybernation revolution" that would give rise to "a separate nation of the poor, the unskilled, the jobless."[31] Except for archaic usages like "Negro," the manifesto could have been written yesterday. The group proposed a universal basic income to blunt the coming mass unemployment.

Shortly after, Johnson launched his "War on Poverty." The poverty rate had been slowly dropping for decades, and then stopped when these programs went online.

Thirty years later, Jeremy Rifkin prophesied "the end of work," "the decline of the global labor force," and "the dawn of the post-market era," right in the middle of a tech boom.[32] Now it seems every book or think piece you read about the imminent robot apocalypse, or "economic singularity,"[33] announces the death of capitalism and then proposes government policies to battle the job famine.

To counter this line of argument, economists tell a story about the late economist Milton Friedman. He was on a visit to China[34] and was taken to see a gargantuan project: the digging of a canal. He noticed that the workers were using shovels. "Why are the workers using such primitive technology, rather than tractors and backhoes?" he asked the Chinese official.

"By using shovels," the government official told Friedman, "the project is able to create far more jobs."

"Oh," Friedman replied. "I thought you were trying to build a canal! If you were trying to create jobs, why not use spoons rather than shovels?"

The point of the story is that economic progress is about finding ways to do more with less, to get more output from less input. The purpose of production isn't to create jobs; it's to create value in the form of goods or services for customers. Tractors replace oxen, ATMs replace bank tellers, forklifts replace a dozen burly men, trucks replace horses, and backhoes and excavators replace shovels and spades, because these provide more output with less input.

The upside is obvious. Technology makes our work more fruitful. And, contrary to the false predictions of Karl Marx, Friedrich Engels, and their acolytes, workers using the new tools fetch a higher wage than they could get without it. This also lowers the cost of the good in question and so boosts the purchasing power of everyone, including the poor. And as purchasing power and standards of living rise, new kinds of jobs emerge to answer the growing demand for new goods and services, new jobs that often are based on the new technologies.

Now, none of these perks erases the problem of *disruption*. When technology allows one person to do the same job as many, the many have their lives and livelihoods turned upside down. Remember, though, that the challenge of disruption isn't unique to now. Around 95 percent of the population got by on farming at the time of the founding of the United States, just as most people had for thousands of years before.

Imagine an American philosopher in 1776 who comes upon a primitive steam engine. He begins to ponder how this device will raise the country's farm output in the future. Since people need only so much food, he figures, there must be a limit to demand. At some point, perhaps only 1 percent of the population will be needed to produce enough food for the whole population. Yikes! Ninety-four percent of Americans would end up jobless as a result! Most American farmers in 1776 were poor and uneducated. The barriers to entry for them in other fields would be as imposing as the ice wall in *Game of Thrones*, especially since they would be leaving a way of life that had provided them with food. Surely, he concludes, the future will have throngs of jobless ex-farmers and starving horses wandering the streets like the zombies in *The Walking Dead*. (Okay, he wouldn't have thought *that*, but something like that.)

The point, of course, is that this is not what happened. Two centuries later, the American population is ten times larger, due largely to much better farming methods. Farmers produce more food with less labor, which brings the cost of food down for everyone. Instead of massive poverty and joblessness, most people now do something other than farm, and they have a much higher standard of living as a result. Less than 1 percent of the US population now works on farms. Most of the jobs of the other 99 percent didn't even exist in 1776.

## THE LUMP OF LABOR MYTH

Economists call this philosopher's mistake the Luddite, or "lump of labor," myth. The mistake is to assume there's a fixed amount of work or labor or jobs. If a power loom allows a man to do the work of a hundred weavers, and everything else stays the same, then ninety-nine weavers will find themselves consigned to the soup line. But everything doesn't stay the same. The machines drive down the cost of clothes for everyone. This leads in turn to a demand for more clothes since, all else being equal, when the price of a good or service goes down, the demand goes up.

So the lower prices create new markets for much cheaper clothes. That increases demand, which increases employment in a much more fecund textile industry, which spurs entrepreneurs to find even better ways to do the job. This is why manufacturing jobs in textiles and other fields exploded during the Industrial Revolution, and standards of living went up. James Bessen calls this the "automation paradox."[35] Technology can lead to more jobs rather than fewer.

This is the basic story of innovation since some caveman first pounded two flint rocks together to start a fire. Robert Bryce tells this tale of progress in his terrific book *Smaller Faster Lighter Denser Cheaper*.[36] No one in his right mind would deem such economic growth a net loss. It has brought food, shelter, clean water, communication, transportation, and medicine to billions of people across the world.

In sum, technological progress brings challenges as well as opportunities. Any analysis that ignores either one is blinkered.

If there were a fixed lump of labor, every time one person was added to the economy, either by turning eighteen or crossing the border to look for a job, unemployment would go up. But that's not what happens in developed economies that make it easy for entrepreneurs to launch new businesses. There are three times as many people and three times as many jobs in 2010 as there were in 1929. And the 2010 jobs are much more lucrative.[37]

The "lump of labor" myth persists because of the gap between the "seen" and the "unseen." We can see automated factories and unemployed workers. We don't see how more productive manufacturing raises everyone's purchasing power, since that perk is spread across the whole population. It's also hard to imagine the new kinds of jobs that will be created. Great entrepreneurs get a glimpse of it, but they're the exception, not the rule. All most of us can hope to see is the pattern, the historical trend of more and new kinds of jobs over the long term. That trend is real enough but not as tangible as the frustrated, out-of-work factory hand down at the local bar.

We should have due regard for that frustrated fellow. If we don't find a way to regard both him and the broader picture, however, we will wrongly think that the story ends with a throng of jobless factory workers standing on the corner, begging for bread.

This is the fate of all those "imaginative" writers who foretell a jobless future. I put "imaginative" in scare quotes since such stories spring from a *failure* of the imagination. We should dismiss their dire forecasts for this reason, and because they so often use their forecasts to justify a power grab by the state to prevent the sky from falling.

## How to Survive Disruption

"But this time it's totally different!" cry a hundred pundits at *Salon* and the *Atlantic* and the *New Yorker*. The shift now under way "will ultimately challenge one of our most basic assumptions about technology: that *machines are tools* that increase the productivity of workers," insists Martin Ford in *Rise of the Robots*. "Instead, machines themselves are turning into workers, and the line between the capability of labor and capital is blurring as never before."[38]

No. What's happening now has happened many times before: A new economy-changing technology bursts onto the scene, followed by apocalyptic predictions that never pan out. Remember, *what's different about our era is not that technology makes earlier forms of work obsolete but the time scale on which this is happening.* Previous revolutions were separated by thousands of years and often took centuries or even millennia to be fully realized. Some two thousand years separated the domestication of plants from the domestication of animals. The wheel came along—in some places—about four thousand years after animal domestication started. The Iron Age started roughly three thousand years after the wheel. It was another 2,700 years or so before the printing press came along, and even that invention took about four hundred years to spread around the globe. That's more time than it took for the next big disruptor, the steam engine, to arrive on the scene. In the next century, railroads, the internal combustion engine, and electricity emerged. In the early twentieth century, we developed mass production, and then, in the blink of an eye, the Information Revolution was upon us.

We're now in the throes of another revolution. We should prepare, not panic. To do that, we need to spurn the myths, reject the bad advice, and debunk the bad philosophy we get from the media, the academy, and even the public. We need to think more lucidly about the nature of technology, about how we interact with it, and how we differ from it. And then we need to exploit *la différence*. We'll turn to this in the next section.

## Augmented, Not Replaced

A closer look at current trends gives reason for hope, not despair. In 1997, when Deep Blue beat Garry Kasparov at chess, pessimists thought it would be the end of the game. *Newsweek* bemoaned the contest with the cover headline "The Brain's Last Stand." The worrywarts missed what Kasparov himself knew: Deep Blue was a *human* achievement. How quickly we forget that *we* build integrated circuits, motherboards, hard drives, fiber-optic networks, and software!

Despite the eulogies written after the match, chess didn't die. Twenty years later, chess masters now *work with* chess programs, acting as hybrids that Kasparov calls "centaurs." The result has been even more impressive freestyle chess. Rather than a permanent loss in an epic zero-sum battle between man and machine, man and machine achieve heights that neither could achieve alone. Man improves from the partnership. There are now many average chess players who use computers to do far more than the players could do otherwise. There are also far more chess grand masters than there were before the advent of chess-playing programs. And more players reach that empyrean realm much younger than in the past.

Overall, this is a better model of the near future than is a jobless dystopia. And in many fields automation will be less dramatic than the battle between Kasparov and Deep Blue. Think of a machine that becomes more helpful over time. "When we talk about how smart machines should be deployed in workplaces," write Julia Kirby and Thomas Davenport about their recent study on the subject, "we constantly emphasize the importance of *augmentation* rather than *automation*."[39] Rather than see computers and robots replace human work anytime soon, we should expect new and more fruitful work in symbiotic relationships with smarter, faster machines. We won't just lose out to robots. We'll keep thinking of new tasks to keep them busy.

Ironically, many manufacturing jobs are still in the United States because they are more augmented with technology than ones overseas. Say an American factory worker has ten times more output than his counterpart in China. Then it makes no sense to move the role to China, even if the Chinese worker is paid only one-fifth the wage of the American worker. There could very well be a net gain in jobs in some US manufacturing sectors, at least in the short run, because of this dynamic.

The first and second American Dreams were centered on the individual, the family, and the corporation. They were tied to places: farms, homes, cities, office buildings, factories. Literal labor and labor-saving devices dominated the first; mechanization and supply-side economies of scale dominated the second. The economics of information, of networks, and of "intelligent" machines will dominate the third.[40] But heralding a revolutionary new economic system is way off. The truth is, old-fashioned enterprise, trade, free markets, and rule of law will be as vital as ever. If you're not sure what this means, don't worry. I'll explain it in the following chapters.

This new economy has already created and destroyed whole industries. It will throw up new challenges and unprecedented prospects for all of us. The good news is that it's in your power to overcome the challenges and seize the prospects. The right strategy draws not on future mysteries or high-tech wizardry but on ancient wisdom. Building on the earlier revolutions in agriculture and industry, we are now passing into an era when we must focus on what most distinguishes us from animals on one side and machines on the other. We must hone virtues such as a willingness to fail, to learn from failure, to serve and work with others, and to exercise our creative freedom. We will need to focus on what is uniquely human, on our absolute advantage, on what no machine can replace.

# PART II

## REBUILDING A CULTURE OF VIRTUE

# 3

# THE HUMAN DIFFERENCE

## What Only We Can Do

If we can build machines that do everything we do, what work will be left for us? The answer to this question rests not on tech forecasts or efforts to reinvent human nature. The answer lies in what might sound abstract or outdated but will become even more crucial in tomorrow's economy: human virtue. Before we get into the details, though, we need to get clear on what a virtue is, and get past the *fatalist myth* that would prevent us from even getting off the ground.

A virtue is a good, *freely chosen* action that is repeated so much and so well that it becomes instinct. It's the fruit of a spiraling feedback loop: It starts with a belief—that you can change yourself. That belief informs a choice to act in a certain way, which directs you to certain outward actions, which in turn slowly changes who you are on the inside—making you more kind, helpful, courageous, diligent, careful, and truthful. Your mind, your will, your body, and your emotions are all wrapped up in the process.

To pursue virtue, you choose to act in a certain way, even though part of you doesn't want to. You say "Thank you" to the snooty attendant at the DMV and smile at the sketchy woman behind you in the grocery line who keeps shushing her kids—even though you'd like to give them both the evil eye. Act on such choices, bit by bit, and you slowly reshape your feelings and your passions. At some point you find that you *want* to do the very thing you had to force yourself to do in the beginning. In a sense, you will have become someone else.

You might imagine that virtue comes naturally to the saintly. But the man we now call "Saint" Paul told a quite different story about himself. "I do not understand my own actions," he complained. "For I do not do what I want, but I do the very thing I hate."[1] If you've ever tried to break a bad habit, like biting your nails—or something worse, like a drug or alcohol addiction—you know what he means. At each point along the path, there is struggle—with yourself, your desires, your tendencies, and your peers.

None of this is to say nature and nurture don't play a role. In his 2008 book *Outliers*, Malcolm Gladwell argued that success rests not so much on inborn talent as on cultural quirks, family background, and lucky timing.[2] Little of this is under your control. What you can choose, though, is how you practice and how much you *practice*. Gladwell draws on a study by psychologist Anders Ericsson. He boiled down Ericsson's research to a simple rule: Mastery of any skill takes about ten thousand hours of deliberate practice. We're tempted to believe that world-class experts are prodigies from birth. But years of grueling study and practice precede mastery, even for prodigies like Mozart. In fact, one of the key traits of prodigies is that they practice obsessively.

Alas, the rule isn't really a rule, as Anders Ericsson explains in his 2016 book, *Peak*. It's at best a rough average of what it takes for some experts to master some skills, but it's no magic bullet. Ericsson stresses the nonstop, deliberate part of the right kind of practice. To see gains in a skill, whether playing the violin or shooting three-point shots, you can't just work until it becomes automatic. You must keep pushing the envelope *after* it's instinctive. You must also use reliable methods. Ticking off hours of practice isn't enough.[3]

The right kind of repeated action, it turns out, rewires the brain, for good or for ill. Contrary to the story I heard as a child—that you're stuck with the brain you're born with—we now know about "neuroplasticity." For instance, if you work on similar math problems over and over and memorize the formulas involved, you will slowly internalize the process. Keep at it, and you can become an expert. Although some skills are best acquired early, our brains can still change in adulthood.

On the dark side, vices are acquired in much the same way. For example, the persistent viewing of pornography triggers "a cascade of neurological, chemical, and hormonal events," which sooner or later leads to addiction. That leads to the desire for more and more extreme forms of pornography, in a vicious feedback loop.[4] "A man may take to drink because he feels himself a failure," George Orwell observed, "but then fail all the more completely because he drinks."

Such addictive behavior harms the frontal lobes of the brain, which weakens impulse control. In other words, we can lose the freedom to control our passions that we once had.[5] In the same way, recent research suggests that telling little white lies seems to numb the brain so that it's easier to tell big whoppers later.[6] This may be one reason why it's easy to "pick up" a vice. We acquire a vice simply by giving in to base temptations, but can only attain a virtue through focus and hard work.

Some people may be naturally gifted for certain skills, such as grasping theoretical physics or sprinting. No matter how much he practiced, comedian Jim Gaffigan would never beat a well-trained Usain Bolt in the hundred-meter dash.[7] Still, Gaffigan could become a lot faster if he spent years practicing sprints and avoiding donuts. And even in cases like this where nature has a strong vote, experts are not born. They're made.[8] Usain Bolt didn't descend from a cloud with wings on his feet. He trained for years with a top Jamaican coach and a single-minded zeal to become the fastest man on the planet.

Okay, but what about virtue? Can it be inherited? Anyone with children knows they don't all start out with the same disposition. My daughters have a friend, Theresa, who has a preternaturally sunny temperament. We've seen it on display at track meets when it's 95 degrees and 95 percent humidity. She cheers on other students and adults as naturally as most kids breathe. One day she missed lunch and went almost all day without a meal. Most children would have been snapping heads off. Theresa got so hungry that she . . . started to laugh, and laughed so hard that tears poured from her eyes. Clearly, she has far more than the entry-level package for kindness and cheer.

On the nurture side, she also enjoys good health, good parents, kind siblings, a good church, good friends, and a good neighborhood where petty crime and drug use are rare. As social settings go in the United States, she's easily in the top 3 percent. Still, for her kindness to be a virtue, Theresa will need to practice it freely when she'd rather be cruel. She will need to take her above-average nature and nurture and persistently pursue virtue.

In contrast, many people have far less in the way of nurture. Somewhere in Washington, DC, there's surely another Theresa. She is raised by a poor, single, drug-addicted mom in a corrupt environment that has perfected the art of crushing the human spirit. She goes to a bad school rife with crime and thuggery. This Theresa has the cards stacked against her. She could easily fall into a vicious circle, like the one George Orwell described, drinking because she felt like a failure and then failing because she took to drink. She will have to work against her surroundings, and maybe even her natural tendencies, to beat the odds of her birth and lead a happy, successful life.

## Fighting the Fatalist Myth

And it's here that we must stress what the debate over our economy and the future of work almost always leaves out: free will. It's our mysterious power to choose from alternatives without being compelled to do so. If we don't have free will, then we can't develop vice or virtue. Everything I say about how to succeed in the information economy would be null and void.

I can't prove that you have free will, but I don't need to. You experience it at least as directly as you experience any observation from the senses or inference from reason. You assume you have it. If you believed chemistry and physics dictated your every thought and action, why would you bother to read this book?

Our legal documents and institutions also assume that we have this power. Heck, every three-year-old knows the difference between choosing ice cream and gagging on Brussels sprouts under duress.

Setting aside (for now) the philosophical question of free will, the *fatalist myth* is the widespread claim that the American Dream is wholly out of reach for many Americans. This pernicious lie comes from grievance-mongers who insist that society is not just flawed but hopelessly unjust. It coaxes you to nurse every slight, to insist your failure is always someone else's fault, to not even bother trying. Far too many academics and media megaphones preach that message. For example, a short-lived University of Wisconsin speech code claimed that it's racist to say, "Everyone can succeed in this society, if they work hard enough," since supposedly it really means, "People of color are lazy and/or incompetent and need to work harder."[9]

Sloth is, of course, a color-blind vice, and many people of color have been dealt hands from the bottom of the deck: poverty, fatherless homes, lousy schools. But what if racism were still so widespread that minorities had at best a perilous and steep path to success? How would it help them to reinforce a sense of helplessness? To tell them that hard work is a waste of time? Such a message doesn't fix real injustice. It keeps minorities down and prevents them from even imagining the truth: that despite the steep obstacles they encounter, a life of virtue gives them the power to succeed.

To seek virtue, you must first commit to the idea that it *is* within your power to succeed.

You must also watch out for a subtler form of the fatalist myth. You may believe that you have free will but still adopt a fatalistic attitude that holds you back. In her book, *Mindset: The New Psychology of Success*, Stanford psychologist Carol Dweck calls this a "fixed mindset."[10] If you think that your intelligence, creativity, character, and chances of success were pretty much settled at birth, you've got a fixed mindset. In effect, you accept your freedom in theory but deny it in practice.

If, instead, you think you can cultivate virtues by hard work, careful choices, and deliberate practice, then you have a "growth mindset." You don't just believe that you have free will. You act to change yourself for the better.

Dweck spent twenty years doing research on children and adults. She found that a simple contrast between these two mindsets was a strong predictor of success or failure in later life. People with a fixed mindset fritter away time trying to prove their innate abilities. This makes them risk averse. They blame God or their parents or society or the man for their failure. They downplay the value of practice. After all, if I have to study for hours before a math final, doesn't that prove I'm not a math genius?

People with a growth mindset do the opposite. They ask questions, admit their ignorance, and do whatever it takes to succeed. If they fail, they figure that they just haven't mastered the skill yet, not that they can't.

As a result, these mindsets can become self-fulfilling prophecies. If you doubt you can improve your lot in life, you won't bother to do so. If you think you can, you're far more likely to try and to succeed. Seems obvious, but it's nice to have some research to back it up.

The good news, Dweck says, is that the growth mindset can be learned. You might have had a fixed mindset for your whole life. But you can decide right now to adopt a growth mindset—although you'll still need to make it a habit.

So here's the basic picture. Nature, nurture, and happenstance are the background. Free will is the foreground. We're born with a basic tool kit. At birth and by instinct, we breathe, nurse, cry, and exercise a few other bodily functions that keep parents occupied for two to four years. We're also born with the *potential* to walk, speak, read, write, do arithmetic, use smart phones, say "please" and "thank you," look both ways before we cross the street, cross our *t*'s and cross-examine witnesses, think clearly and think through our actions, roll with the punches and roll our eyes at our parents, and so on. But we still must *learn* to do all these things. We may learn them more or less well, depending upon our surroundings, our natural endowment, our actions, and our freely chosen mindset.

Virtue is not about where you start. It's about the good you become by your actions, starting with what you've been given.

Why does this matter? Because virtue above all else determines whether we will flourish. If we cultivate our freedom in the right way, we will exploit not just our comparative advantage over machines but our absolute advantage. That way, machines will augment and enhance our work rather than replace it entirely.

In the United States, minimal virtues plus basic health are all you need to avoid poverty. You live in one of the freest and most prosperous countries on the planet. You're not likely to die from thirst, starvation, or the countless water- and airborne diseases that tormented our ancestors. Given this blessing, if you're thankful, courteous, thrifty, punctual, honest, and hardworking; graduate from college or trade school; seek employment where it may be found; wait until you're married to have kids; stay married; don't commit felonies; and don't abuse drugs or alcohol, you're sure to end up far better off than most people in history and easily in the top 10 or 15 percent of the global population.

Of course, the American Dream is about more than just staying out of the poorhouse. And there are rough waters ahead. That's why, along with these basic virtues, we also need to nurture several others. You've heard of Stephen Covey's *7 Habits of Highly Effective People*, right? The story of the future is about the five virtues of happy and successful people, each of which matches a feature of the information economy. These are the killer apps of the third American Dream:

- *Courage*—the willingness to risk failure
- *Antifragility*—the ability to learn from failure and suffering
- *Altruism*—acting for the benefit of others
- *Collaboration*—working with and learning from others
- *Creative freedom*—mastering yourself and the skills needed to create value for others

In the next several chapters, we'll look at why we need them, how to acquire them, and how they can lead to our happiness.

Along the way, we'll expose the myths and roadblocks that threaten to stop us from achieving the American Dream, and show how to overcome them.

Though the life of virtue must be a life of struggle, its reward is not exhaustion but true happiness, as we'll see later. "Happiness is secured through virtue," wrote Saint Thomas Aquinas. "It is a good attained by man's own will." Those words ring true even in today's uncertain economy.

And since happiness involves a willful struggle, it must begin with courage. "Courage is not simply *one* of the virtues," C. S. Lewis said. It's "the form of every virtue at the testing point . . ." And so, it is with courage that we begin.

# 4

## FEAR NOT

### Courage in an Age of Disruption

Brad Morgan was born in the second half of the twentieth century, but was still attached to the first American Dream. He grew up in the pastoral plain of central Michigan, with its rich black soil plowed and flattened by receding glaciers at the end of the last ice age. His dream in life was to own and operate his own farm.

If there's a body type for farmers, Morgan has it. He's stocky, with a low center of gravity, calloused fingers, and forearms grown thick from years of lifting rather than typing. Unfortunately, he was born too late to make a ready go of that way of life. By the time he was a teenager, industrialized farming had raised farm yields to historic levels and made it hard for small family farms to succeed. If Morgan had done a market evaluation, he might never have taken the plunge.

As fate would have it, though, Morgan spent the first five years of his career renting a small farm near Evart, Michigan. He eventually scraped together enough to get a loan to buy the farm. Things looked good at first: In the early years, he led the region in milk production per cow. In 1999, however, milk prices plummeted and the market's invisible hand almost delivered Brad's farm to the bank.

Brad could have given up at that point, but he had another idea: What if he could turn the manure from his dairy cows into compost that other farms would buy? He hired some agricultural scientists from Michigan State to do what he might have called a "feasibility study" if he had gone to Harvard Business School or even gotten a college degree. The scientists told him, yes, he could turn his manure into compost. There was one hitch: It would cost him far more to produce the compost than he could sell it for.

"Well, that didn't make a whole lotta sense," Brad later recalled. A risk-averse man would have put out the FOR SALE signs after getting such an assessment. But Brad had enough of what some economists call "local knowledge"—concrete experience gained from working with cows, soil, fertilizer, and manure—to suspect he knew something that the bookish experts did not. He started tinkering, and before long he developed a way to compost manure far faster than anyone thought possible.

He then called in a soil expert—not for business advice but technical expertise. The agronomist helped Morgan tweak and re-tweak the formula until he had developed high-quality compost that could be made in record time. Soon he was hauling in dairy manure by the truckload. "We're speeding up this process from what everybody thought would take two years," Morgan's son later explained, "and we're doing it in sixty days."

Any entrepreneur knows that the story doesn't end there. No product, no matter how revolutionary, succeeds unless there's a market for it. The universe's greatest mousetrap is useless if no one wants to catch mice or knows about the contraption.

But that would not be a problem in this case. Morgan knew that many people were seeking organic compost over chemical fertilizer.

That's one of the reasons he took the leap in the first place. But at first it had been an expensive luxury good. Morgan had found a way to produce it at a competitive price.

His marketing started off slow and local: He pitched his "Dairy Doo" to nearby gardeners, farmers, and golf courses. But in the age of the internet, it didn't take long for word to get out. Morgan Composting, Inc., now has a full-time agronomist on staff, hosts seminars for other aspiring soil farmers, and posts video highlights online.[1]

Brad Morgan did everything in the right order. He worked, saved, and invested. Although he was good at what he did, he still failed at his first plan to be a dairy farmer. But by building on what he had learned, he faced down necessity and possible financial ruin, and found a way to turn waste—literally—into wealth.

Morgan is an interesting case study, because his success story spans all three phases of the American Dream. He first tried his hand at a family farm but couldn't succeed against much larger dairy businesses that enjoyed huge economies of scale. Then, rather than move to the city and reach for the second American Dream, he moved straight to the third. He courageously yoked his own intuition with scientific knowledge—knowledge he acquired despite lacking a college education—to try what would not have occurred to farmers in other times and places.

In the 1950s there might not have been a market for Dairy Doo. And even if there had been, it would not have been easy to promote. Chemical fertilizer made far more economic sense. But, fortunately for Morgan, a postindustrial demand for natural fertilizer has been growing in the developed world for the previous few decades as people have started to worry about environmental damage from chemical fertilizers. And this all came together just as the internet, the nervous system of the information economy, was becoming popular with the public. Without this new way to market his Dairy Doo, his business might have stayed a very local concern and never become sustainable.

Failure is a common part of the story of new business ventures, especially at economic inflection points. Many people lack hope, assume the future is jinxed or the system is rigged, and give up at the first sign of failure. But Brad Morgan, in the face of present and likely future failure, cast out into the dark and tried what the experts told him could not work. That's courage. It's not the absence of fear but bold action in the face of long odds. "Courage," John Wayne said, "is being scared to death but saddling up anyway." Sadly, courage seems to be in dwindling supply.

## Have Americans Lost Their Mojo?

Every family that ever left its ancestral home and boarded a ship or plane for America showed courage, though the courage might have been born of desperation and a lack of options.

In the mid-1800s, most of the Irish were dirt-poor, persecuted tenant farmers who lived in huts made of mud and stone and paid rent to British landlords. Their diets were centered around the humble potato. When a fungus began to ravage Irish potatoes in 1845, many subsistence farmers no longer subsisted. By 1851, over a million Irish had died from starvation and related diseases, and one and a half million had fled to England and the United States.[2] Here, most of them landed in big East Coast cities like New York and Boston, where their fate was often just a little better than the starvation they had left behind. Today, however, Irish Americans are so fully assimilated that they don't even make up a distinct ethnic group. The Maguires, our friends and next-door neighbors, are no more ethnically distinct than their neighbors, the Richardses.

The point isn't that the Irish had as many obstacles as every other group in America. Nobody who knows the history of American slavery or of Native Americans could think this. The point is that bitter poverty and anti-Irish prejudice didn't keep Irish immigrants from forging ahead.

The American Dream has always called for a willingness to leave behind the known for a risky, unknown future. "Indeed, until quite recently," wrote Timothy Noah in 2013, "what most distinguished Americans from other peoples was the high percentage of us who were willing to move from anywhere to anywhere to seek a better financial toehold."[3] Many Europeans live within a few score miles of their ancestors' graves. This has been far less true for Americans, for whom Horace Greeley's words "Go West, young man" became a rallying cry to seek opportunity wherever it could be found.

The current crop of Americans, however, is far more risk averse than earlier ones. In light of the trend among millennials to return to the nest, Derek Thompson suggests in the *Atlantic* that Greeley might offer different advice today: "Move back home, young man."[4] Or, as Timothy Noah put it, "Stay put, young man." In 1975, 71 percent of all thirty-year-old Americans were married, had a child, were out of school, and lived on their own. In 2016, only one in three had reached those benchmarks.[5] It might be wise for twentysomethings to move in with Mom and Dad after college for a short time to save money, start a business, or pursue a new career path. But many of them seem to be on the path to nowhere.

Travel is far easier and safer now than it was in the past: No one need risk death on a mountain pass. And it doesn't entail that we leave family and friends forever. So you'd expect Americans to be more mobile than ever. But according to census data, we move far less often now than at any point in the last half century.

"Americans are less likely to switch jobs, move to another state, or create new companies than they were 20 years ago (or 100 years ago)," Thompson reports. Indeed, a recent survey finds that 61 percent of unemployed Americans are "not at all willing" to "move to another state to find work." Only 4 percent of those polled had already moved.[6]

Why the sea change from a bolder, more mobile America to a less mobile, more timid one? Noah and Thompson both argue that

Americans have quit moving not because we've gone soft but because of . . . inequality. The working class has been priced out of the cities, the argument goes, because others are being paid too much. This drives up house prices in desirable city centers. As a result, writes Thompson, "people aren't moving toward productivity. They're moving toward cheap housing."

Yes, fussy zoning laws, housing policy, and supply and demand have driven up housing costs in large cities. I know firsthand. We lived in urban and suburban Seattle for years and now live in the Virginia suburbs of Washington, DC. Housing is three times the average cost in these urban hubs. House prices are especially high in California. There the ultrarich pass extreme environmental rules, which puts the places out of reach to everyone else.

But this *inequality myth* (which comes in many forms) ignores two obvious facts.

First, if you want to get onto the first rung of the ladder of success, you don't need a big, pricey metro area. You may just need a spot with low unemployment that isn't allergic to newcomers. Five minutes on Google will give you a range of choices with low cost-of-living and rock-bottom unemployment rates.

Second, inequality doesn't explain what everyone who has passed through a big metropolitan area in the last hundred years has seen firsthand: Plenty of recent immigrants somehow manage to find their way to major urban centers and thrive there. Have these *Atlantic* writers never taken a cab or Uber in a major city or metro area suburb?

In the DC suburb where I live—in the county with the highest median income in the United States—there's a small shopping area called Great Falls Plaza. It's anchored by Food Lion, Rite Aid, and a clock tower (really). It holds about eighteen other shops. Korean immigrants own the do-it-yourself frozen yogurt place, Cold Spoon. Next door is New Era Eyecare, which employs immigrants. Next to that is Miyama, a sushi place owned by Japanese immigrants. (Half-price rolls on Monday and Tuesday!) Next to that is

Shebang, the kitschiest hair salon south of the Mason-Dixon Line, owned and operated by a married couple from Vietnam. Next to that is a garish nail and waxing place called Nails. It's also a Vietnamese operation. Next to that is an unassuming dry cleaner called Laundry run by Chinese women. Next to that is Health Relax, a booming massage place owned and operated by a Chinese family that can barely speak English—which is great, because who wants a chatty masseuse?

I could go on—there's also a tae kwon do gym—but you get the point. Every one of these people left their homes and crossed an ocean or a continent to live in a land that speaks a different tongue. What do they know that so many native-born Americans do not?

This willingness to move to where the jobs are—or can be—characterizes both skilled and unskilled immigrants in the United States. A 2014 study of ninety-seven US cities found that low-skill Mexican immigrants were more likely than native-born low-skill Americans to pick up and move. Reporting on the study, the *Washington Post* explained that "cities with job growth among low-skill Mexican-born immigrants also saw growth in that population. Cities with job losses saw their Mexican-born immigrants move away. There was no pattern though, for the low-skill native-born, who either did not migrate or tended to migrate for family reasons."[7]

In 2014, *National Review*'s "roving correspondent," Kevin Williamson, saw this pattern up close. He visited the poorest county in the United States: Owsley County in eastern Kentucky. His article about it in the December issue stirred up a hornet's nest of outrage. His advice to its poor residents—"Move!"—somehow proved he was heartless. Williamson painted a dystopian portrait of a "Big White Ghetto" in which Appalachians of Scotch-Irish ancestry fritter away their lives on drugs, booze, and a life determined by the "draw." That's the monthly government food stamp disbursement, which recipients then trade for cash at a discount on the thriving black market.

Every social dysfunction associated with the inner city—save for violent crime—is in full bloom in Owsley County. And much of it is fed, not by a recent recession, but by well-meaning antipoverty programs. "Welfare has made Appalachia into a big and sparsely populated housing project—too backward to thrive, but just comfortable enough to keep the underclass in place," Williamson concludes.[8]

In another piece in the *Atlantic*, "The Free-Time Paradox in America," Derek Thompson sees the same symptoms emerging among "twentysomething male high-school grads." This demographic used to be the most dependable working cohort in America, Thompson notes. "Today one in five are now essentially idle. The employment rate of this group has fallen 10 percentage points just this century, and it has triggered a cultural, economic, and social decline." These guys don't starve on the streets. "Three quarters of their additional leisure time is spent with video games. . . . And these young men are happy—or, at least, they self-report higher satisfaction than this age group used to, even when its employment rate was 10 percentage points higher."[9]

In 1930, British economist John Maynard Keynes predicted that automation would allow his grandchildren's generation to work only fifteen hours a week—with Wednesday through Sunday as a weekend.[10] An idle underclass is not what Keynes had in mind. In fact, contrary to Keynes's forecast, the well-off tend to work long hours, while the poor have more free time. In 2015, NPR interviewed Keynes's nearest relations. His grandnephew worked fifteen hours *a day* as a professor until he retired. Keynes's grandniece works a more laid-back fifty-hour week as a psychotherapist.[11] Such work hours are uncommon among the underclass.

Thompson offers three theories to explain why "overall leisure has increased, but it's the less-skilled poor who are soaking up all the free time, even though they would have the most to gain from working":

1. Attractive work is declining while cheap entertainment is rising.
2. Social forces cultivate a conspicuous industriousness (even workaholism) among affluent college graduates.
3. Leisure is getting "leaky" (that is, technology such as computers and smartphones allow us to sprinkle leisure activity throughout the day).

There's truth to all these. But there's another cause that Thompson doesn't mention. Modern prosperity plus a large social safety net have a cost: They rob many people of the circumstances that in earlier times *forced* people to be courageous and take risks. If you face famine or debtors' prison, a long journey across the ocean seems appealing in comparison. If, instead, you can live with your parents, work odd jobs on the side, and still get a check from the government, you're less likely to move to a strange city—let alone a strange country—and work hard at a boring job so that your future kids can live a better life.

Perhaps there was nothing uniquely great about the Greatest Generation. That cohort was simply compelled by a Depression and then a civilization-threatening war to scrimp, save, ration food, work hard, and fight Nazi Germany and Imperial Japan. For many in more recent generations, a well-meaning safety net has become a giant spiderweb that traps recipients in a form of developed-world poverty unlike the poverty suffered by most people for most of history.

My point is *not* that we need to fight another world war or shred every safety net to recover our courage. Rather, we must cultivate courage as a virtue rather than a necessity. If we can come together around some commonsense policy reforms that will encourage rather than discourage bravery, so much the better. However we manage it, if we are to achieve greatness, we must become more willing to risk failure.

## Embracing the "F" Word

Failure has always been a main character in the story of enterprise. It draws even—perhaps especially—the most successful firms into its maw. It's easy to forget that Apple, one of the world's greatest companies, has had its share of flops. Do you remember Apple's 1996 game console Pippin? I don't, either. I do recall the Newton, a PDA that claimed to be able to decipher handwriting but was so bad it was mocked on an episode of *The Simpsons*. Steve Jobs put it out of its misery when he returned to Apple in the late '90s.

At the other extreme was Apple's Power Mac G4 Cube, which was cutting-edge but cost a fortune. The Macintosh Portable was on the vanguard way back in 1989, but weighed sixteen pounds(!) and cost $6,500, which is about $13,000 in 2018 dollars. Worse still was Apple's infamous Lisa computer, priced at $9,995 in 1983, or almost $25,000 at current prices. Apple buried a bunch of these costly albatrosses in a landfill in Utah.[12]

The trail of failure is even more crowded among entrepreneurs and inventors. Steve Jobs, who founded Apple with Steve Wozniak, was a college dropout. He had serious personality issues and had to resign from his own company in 1985 when he was thirty years old. He then launched NeXT Computer and bought Pixar from George Lucas. After years of losses, Apple bought NeXT for its operating system in 1996. Jobs returned as interim CEO a year later, and Apple started turning a profit a year after that.

Sir James Dyson tested more than five thousand prototypes in trying to develop a new, bagless vacuum cleaner.

Every schoolchild learns that Thomas Edison ran through ten thousand tests of the lightbulb before he found one that worked. But Edison didn't invent the electric light or even the incandescent bulb. He took key ideas from a long line of inventors who had tinkered with electric lights since 1802 in fields as diverse as glass-blowing, chemistry, and electrical engineering.[13] But even the gauzy tale of ten thousand failures gets the gist right. Edison invented a lightbulb that was stable and cheap enough for farmers and maids to afford. But it didn't spring from a unique flash of genius while he sat under an apple tree. Instead, it emerged slowly from a seventy-five-year quest that involved hundreds of people and was riddled with dead ends and blind alleys.

Books on enterprise often romanticize failure, as if it's the secret sauce that allows success later.[14] Yet surely it would be better to succeed at your first, deliberate strategy. You don't zigzag in a race if you can see the finish line straight ahead.

Failure hurts. Just ask any honest entrepreneur, such as Sallie Krawcheck. She ran Merrill Lynch during the 2008 financial crisis after it was bought by Bank of America—and now runs her own start-up, Ellevate Network. She insists that her new job is more stressful than her old job. I've been involved in several nonprofit start-ups and can confirm this. The risk can be terrifying.[15] As a strategy, trial and error is crazy.

So, why do business books offer a million versions of the idea that failure is a key to success? Because failure is far more *likely* than instant success. No matter how well you plan, you don't *know* the future. So you're much more likely to succeed *at some point* if you can handle failure.

This has always been true. But failure is a much more prominent part of the story now because of the rate of change. Remember: In a dynamic economy, more creativity means more destruction. More companies and industries appear and then disappear, and cause their employees' fortunes to rise and fall as a result. You must steel yourself for both. You must, if necessary, be willing to try new things, move to strange places, teach yourself new skills, acquire new knowledge.

Of course, having the courage to fail is only part of the story. You must train yourself to learn from, and to improve with, failure. If you do that, you'll be more than tough. You'll be antifragile— the virtue we turn to next.

# 5

## KEEP GROWING

### Antifragility in an Age of Exponential Change

B rad Morgan, the failed dairy farmer turned compost entrepreneur, had courage. But a mere willingness to fail is no guarantee of success. For failure to really be useful, you should become stronger because of it.

Since we can only act in the present, without knowledge of the future, we can't help but make mistakes. Even when we happen to make something that other people want, we may not foresee how it will be used. This is why persistence in the face of failure is so vital. Do this well enough, and you can turn necessity into knowledge. As Clara Shih, the founder and CEO of Hearsay Social, says, "It's not failure. It's data."[1]

In his far-ranging book *Antifragile*,[2] Nassim Nicholas Taleb describes a feature of systems—economies, natural processes, organisms—that is often overlooked. Quick: What's the opposite of "fragile"? Maybe you thought of "robust" or "hardy" or "strong." If a teacup breaks easily, it's fragile. If, in contrast, you can drop it on your granite countertop and it bounces but doesn't break, it's strong.

But that's not quite the opposite of fragile. To be fragile is to be easily damaged by perturbation or shocks. To be robust is to be highly resistant to shocks. Taleb argues that there's a third choice: antifragility. To be antifragile is to improve with shocks, to gain from disorder, to have more upside than downside, to thrive on unpredictability and chaos. Pop culture anticipated Taleb's idea: Comic-book hero Iron Man gets a power boost rather than blowing up when he gets struck by lightning, and movie monster Godzilla gets stronger when assaulted by power lines.

Antifragility is more than just adapting to change.[3] It involves real improvement. Taleb's most memorable examples are drawn from mythology: the Phoenix versus the Hydra.

The Phoenix, before it was a city in the Arizona desert, was a mythological bird that is born anew from the ashes of its predecessor. Since it arises but doesn't improve with each iteration, it's merely robust. The Hydra does it one better. The nine-headed serpent of Greek mythology has one immortal head and eight that will grow back from their stumps. Cut off one of its heads, and two will sprout in its place. That's antifragility, a trait that no doubt frustrated Hydra hunters.

College students are fond of quoting Nietzsche, usually when they're about to do something stupid: "That which does not kill me makes me stronger." Well, no. Plenty of things can harm you without killing you. Somebody lops off your arms and legs but stanches the bleeding. Does that make you stronger? How about a degenerative but nonfatal disease? You can still breathe, but you will be left weaker. How about a tapeworm? Or losing three nights' sleep? Or forgetting to study for your final? There are plenty of nonlethal events that don't make you stronger.

In recent years, though, we've had the opposite problem. Social psychologist Jonathan Haidt argues that we are raising our children to be fragile.[4] Pampered by indulgent parents and then steeped in an academic "victimhood culture,"[5] millions think they really are victims. Some people are harmed by others, of course. But for everyone else, victimhood has become a *fragility myth.* The grit of Americans who survived the Great Depression and World War II has been replaced with hypersensitive twenty-somethings who need counseling and cry for "safe spaces" if they feel dissed by the librarian. If you spend your time nursing grievances, real or imagined, you'll be crippled by rather than learning from the school of hard knocks.

To see why this matters, let's look at a real-life example of antifragility.

Scott Adams has this virtue in spades. He's best known as the creator of the *Dilbert* cartoon. As it happens, *Dilbert* is just the most successful of Adams's many ventures, only a few of which have panned out. His book *How to Fail at Almost Everything and Still Win Big* is literally a comedy of errors, detailing the many bad ideas Adams pursued over the course of his career. "Everything you want out of life is in that huge, bubbling vat of failure," he tells readers. "The trick is to get the good stuff out."[6]

Adams grew up in a tiny town in upstate New York. But already at small Hartwick College he was trying and failing. He had an idea to make tennis shorts with a Velcro-lined pocket where players could store rosin. He talked to a lawyer and contacted sporting goods companies, with no success.

There were other misfires. Tons of them. He screwed up his first job interview with Xerox by claiming that his desire to argue would make him a good salesman. He and his college friend wrote a beginner's guide to meditation that sold a grand total of three copies.

Some of his other ideas made more sense. In the early 1980s he used his savings to buy a computer. As he puts it, he "spent almost every night and every weekend for two years trying to teach myself enough about programming to create a space-themed, arcade-type game." He bought ads in the backs of computer magazines but sold "fewer than twenty copies." That's not much to show for a year's worth of work.

Adams used up all his free time for a year on yet another space-themed computer game that went nowhere.

Then he wrote a computer program designed to test if the user had psychic abilities. You don't need telepathy to guess how that turned out.

After graduating from college, Adams moved to where the jobs and sun were—California—where he worked for eight years at Crocker National Bank. He rose to junior management and then hit the "diversity ceiling." So he moved on to Pacific Bell for eight more years, where he hit the same ceiling again.

But Adams's ventures hadn't stopped just because he got a day job. He once spent a year's worth of free time building a program called Zippy Ship. It was supposed to make it easier to transfer files from one modem to another. Later, he and a friend tried to create a program that would make home delivery of groceries easier. He was too far ahead of the curve on that one, so it didn't pan out.

At some point Adams took a flyer on something he'd thought about for years: cartoons. There was nothing in his career to suggest this would be his biggest success. He had never been to design school or showed any clear affinity for fine art. In fact, his first shot at the craft was just what you'd expect: His drawings were amateurish, and no newspaper wanted to publish them.

He kept at it, though, and one day he got a lucky break. He sent some samples of what would become *Dilbert* to a cartoon agent. She wasn't amused by sarcastic banter between dweeby cubicle workers in the bowels of some faceless corporation. But her husband was. He happened to see the sketches in her car, identified with the dull office life of the characters in the cartoon, and gave it two thumbs up. His wife thought the comic might appeal to readers stuck in the same subculture. So she helped get *Dilbert* placed in a few newspapers, where it gained a following. It slowly found its way into hundreds of dailies around the country.

Just to be safe, though, Adams held on to his dull day job for years, until it became clear that he could make a decent living long-term as a cartoonist.

The story doesn't end there. He kept having ideas for new ventures. Once he had managed to build up some risk capital from *Dilbert*, he spent millions of dollars developing a vitamin-and-mineral-fortified fast food called the Dilberito. He even got it placed in grocery stores, 7-Eleven, Costco, and Walmart. The venture failed anyway. Product placement was part of the problem. Gastronomic distress was another. "Because of the veggie and legume content," he explains, "three bites of the Dilberito made you fart so hard your intestines formed a tail."[7]

This is just a sketch of some of Adams's misfires. But notice how his many failures led, in a meandering sort of way, to his greatest success. Everything he learned became fodder for *Dilbert*. They also led to more obstacles, more failure, and more success.

Thanks to the comic, Adams became a highly sought-after speaker. That was put in jeopardy when he developed spasmodic dysphonia, which he describes as a sort of "weird social laryngitis."[8] Anytime he tried to talk in a social setting, he could only squeak out every third syllable or so. He tried every known treatment. Doctors told him that the condition was incurable. He chose not to believe it. Instead, he set up a Google alert for "spasmodic dysphonia" so he would find out every time the term appeared online. In due course, he found a doctor who surgically severed the nerves that linked his brain to his vocal cords, on the theory that the body would reconnect them. He underwent the surgery and, after a long rest, his normal voice came back.

Then there was the pinkie problem on Adams's business hand. This was a syndrome called focal dystonia he developed early on from the repetitive drawing of cartoons. He found one of the planet's brightest medical experts on the syndrome and asked him, "What's the cure?"

"Change jobs," the doctor told him. "There's no known treatment."

Most people would have taken this as a sign to quit drawing cartoons. Adams took it as a sign that he needed to find a cure for the ailment—which he did. It was a self-cure—the first known case. He had his strong belief in mind over matter confirmed as a result.

As is clear with Scott Adams, antifragile people have another, related virtue: perseverance. Psychologist Angela Duckworth calls this "grit." Like Carol Dweck in her book *Mindset*, Duckworth has done years of research on grit that shows just what you would expect: People who press through, learn from their mistakes, and don't easily give up are more likely to succeed and to flourish.[9]

None of this means the risk of failure is a sure road to success. It's possible to just fail and keep on failing. In their book *Creative Destruction*, Richard Foster and Sarah Kaplan argue that to succeed in business you and your firm must change at the rate of the market.[10] You don't want to be too far ahead of or behind the curve. Lots of online retail ventures, including some that Scott Adams tried, failed because they launched before people felt safe buying stuff online. Others failed because they merely tried to copy what someone else, like Amazon or Zappos, already did well. The trick is to be open to change, change at the right time and at the right speed, while learning from failure. Then you're more likely to ride the learning curve toward success, rather than careening down into the abyss of failure.

Antifragility was critical to Adams's career, even though it started way back in the leisurely 1970s, before the age of the PC, commercial internet, and smartphones. This virtue will be even more vital tomorrow. In the next few decades, we will witness more technological change than a European Methuselah would have witnessed if he had been born in AD 1000 and lived until 1969. He would have grown up in an age of feudalism, simple farming, and hand-illuminated manuscripts. He would have died just as man first landed on the moon.

That's a lot of change for one "lifetime." But imagine that much change in a tenth of the time, and you'll get some idea of what lies ahead. Entire cities oriented around factories filled with workers will either have to transform or become rusty ghost towns. Over-specialized college degrees will become obsolete ten years after graduation. All manner of jobs we thought were fit only for humans will be handed over to machines. Jobs no one had ever dreamed of will become the hot new thing and then die a decade later. This may sound like hyperbole, until you realize that we have entered the age of exponential change.

## THE STAGGERING POWER OF EXPONENTIAL GROWTH

In a 1965 article, Gordon Moore, an engineer and cofounder at Fairchild Semiconductor who went on to cofound Intel, noticed something odd. He observed that the number of transistors that could be crammed onto an integrated circuit—what ordinary folks call a "computer chip"—doubled every year.[11] The semiconductor industry was still in its infancy, but he speculated that the trend could very well continue for the next decade. Ten years later he tweaked the prediction to a doubling of computer power every two years. For over forty years now, computer power has doubled on average every eighteen months. (Caltech's Carver Mead later dubbed the prediction "Moore's law," and the name stuck. But it's not a law. It's a trend that may or may not continue.)

Moore was describing a type of "exponential growth," with 2 as the exponent. The classic illustration of this kind of growth comes from a tale of an Indian man named Sessa who invented the game of chess in the sixth century BC.[12] He traveled to the imperial city of Pataliputra to show off his invention to the emperor. The emperor was so pleased with the game that he asked the inventor to name his own reward. Sessa made a seemingly modest request: some rice for his family. He proposed that the emperor merely place one grain of rice on the first square of the chessboard, then two grains on the next square, then four on the next square, and so on, doubling the number one square at a time, until all the squares of the chessboard had their allotted grains of rice.

There are sixty-four squares on a chessboard. So that's sixty-three doublings, for a total of $2^{64-1}$ grains of rice. Nothing much happens at first. One grain is put on the first square, then two, four, eight, and so on. Even at the halfway point (thirty-two squares) there are only four billion grains. That's about as much rice as a farmer might harvest from a single farm. No problem for an emperor. But then things start to get out of hand: two farm harvests, then four, eight, sixteen. On and on it goes. Slowly it dawns on the emperor that, to complete the order, he would need a Himalayan heap of rice—eighteen quintillion grains, to be exact.[13] Realizing that he's been had, the emperor orders the inventor's head removed from his shoulders.

The lesson is that while exponential growth seems normal at first, almost leisurely, at some point it will start to get crazy (even if you don't lose your head). Plot the doubling function on an X/Y graph with increments of, say, 1,000. It starts off with a line that is mostly horizontal, since it takes ten doublings to break the 1,000 barrier. But then it quickly reaches an inflection point, or elbow. From there it curves sharply upward and becomes almost vertical— like the history of innovation and industrial growth we discussed earlier. Remember that.

Exponential growth takes us by surprise, because the kind of growth we're used to is the fractional and linear kind. Fractional growth is what we see in the stock market and in our children's height over the course of a year. Kids after their first birthday might get 5 or 10 percent taller per year until puberty ends. With linear growth, a real estate agent might go from two customers to three customers to four customers to five customers. Our minds handle this sort of growth easily, since we experience it all the time. Exponential growth, especially fast exponential growth, blows the mind.

But it's a real thing, in the real world. As we noted above, Gordon Moore noticed in the 1960s that the number of transistors that could be fit onto an integrated circuit went up exponentially year after year. It's easy to assume that the trend is due to the quirky details of crystalline silicon and integrated circuits, and doesn't apply elsewhere. But it does. In the 1990s, futurist Ray Kurzweil looked at how computers developed over the course of the twentieth century. He found that the same exponential trend held further back in time, for five different types of (artificial) computers, based on unrelated physical processes.

The first artificial computer in the early twentieth century was electromechanical: wheels, gears, pegs, punch cards, and so forth. This was soon replaced with a relay system, with wires, electromagnetics, and switches. That was replaced with vacuum tubes, which were replaced with transistors—basically tiny switches—which were replaced with integrated circuits with ever tinier transistors in a mad dash to the nanoscopic bottom.

A century ago, Henry Adams anticipated this idea in *The Education of Henry Adams*, with his "law of acceleration." Kurzweil argues that Moore's law is just one example of what he calls the law of accelerating returns. Exponential growth, he claims, has been happening all along. Whether he looks at the evolution of stars or of writing—from "goatskins to downloads," as he puts it—he sees exponential change everywhere. No one noticed it earlier because it's only become obvious in technology in the last few decades.[14] History until very recently was in the first half of Sessa's chessboard. We're now in the second half.[15]

Setting aside Kurzweil's conjectures, though, the clearest signs of exponential growth are in IT—the information-dense parts of the economy. IT wasn't even a category at the US Bureau of Economic Analysis until 1958. We see this type of growth not just

## Moore's Law—The Fifth Paradigm

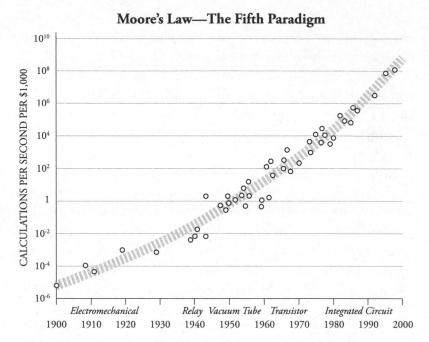

Courtesy of Ray Kurzweil and Kurzweil Technologies, Inc.

with computer processors but in data storage devices, fiber-optic cables, networks, digital cameras and phones, wireless technology, and digital fabrication tools (more on that later). Kurzweil's big book *The Singularity Is Near* is filled with charts that show the accelerating pace of change of the US phone industry, cell phone subscribers, mass use of inventions, dynamic RAM (random access memory), and on and on and on.

The economic effects are staggering. All such technologies start out really rare, really expensive, and really bad. Only a few, elite early adopters can use them. Then, with mass production, they get better and cheaper. At some point they become nearly universal and free. This is true with technologies as diverse as microwave ovens, refrigerators, and stereos,[16] but it's much more dramatic with digital tech. It took around fifty years from the time the telephone was invented until one-fourth of the population were calling their grandparents at Christmas and Easter. A century later it took only a decade for a fourth of the population to adopt cell phones, and even less time for the internet to become ubiquitous.[17]

Apple released the first iPhone in June 2007. By September 2012, about half the population—and two-thirds of young adults—had a smartphone. Most of this tech didn't exist in 1970 at any price. And the computational power? As Kurzweil put it in a 2013 interview in the *Wall Street Journal*: "A kid in Africa with a smartphone is walking around with a trillion dollars of computation circa 1970."[18] In 1961, it would have taken $8.3 trillion to buy the same computing power you get for 8 cents in 2013. That's more wealth than existed in 1961.

All this to say: The growth in the IT sector dwarfs the growth in all other parts of the economy.[19] If you want to find fresh opportunities, target those places where IT touches the world. This is more open-ended advice than simply "Learn computers." The fresh prospect you seize may be upstream or downstream from IT. When the gold rush began in 1840s California, the prospects weren't all in prospecting. Some sold picks and shovels to the prospectors. Others opened saloons and supply stores. There was also rising demand for the secure transport of gold, and for many other services. If all that was true of a gold rush, it's all the more true of the IT revolution, which will reshape the economy far more than any gold rush did.

But be warned: These areas of the economy will also be the most volatile. They are like the seams between tectonic plates where volcanoes erupt. To survive, you'll need to learn to surf waves of lava.

## BEATING THE FRAGILITY MYTH

Alas, just when we most need to become antifragile—to learn quickly and continually in the face of failure—we have schools and universities turning the next generation into fragile hothouse flowers. The *fragility myth* has given rise a national cult that must soon either reform or get left behind.

As usual, a little history helps us frame our current quandary. In the past, wealth preceded formal education rather than giving rise to it. For centuries, formal education was a luxury good. Think of a wealthy medieval family whose spiritually sensitive fourth son could take up the life of a monk or priest, where he would have access to precious manuscripts. That pretty much summed up formal schooling. The vast peasantry of Europe in the Middle Ages and early modern period knew nothing of sixteen years of sedentary study from age six, prior to work. Most children grew up working on farms or in family trades. The lucky ones snagged apprenticeships. As recently as 1820, the average American had a mere *two* years of formal education, compared to thirteen years today.[20]

That's a great blessing, but now we have a problem. We've inherited an educational system built by and for a previous age. It did an okay job a century ago, when much of the country had little formal schooling and was moving from country to city life. But now it's sluggish and outdated.

What's more, college has become the key recruiting ground for every bad idea, especially in the humanities. One literature professor at the University of Chicago describes a discipline that has descended into what she calls the "thrill of destruction." Students, incited by their professors, spend their time protesting ever more elusive grievances about sex, race, class, privilege, and cultural "appropriation." At some point this can even pass over into psychological disorder.[21]

The results are hyper-fragile students. "A 22-year-old can go from raising children to being a child by crossing the street onto a college campus," writes *National Review*'s Kevin Williamson.[22] Unfortunately, victimhood culture now starts in many high schools and is then weaponized in college.[23] Every day brings a new story of delicate snowflakes who mark off "safe spaces," denounce ever tinier "microaggressions," announce trigger warnings, and issue surreal demands for faculty to submit themselves to seminars that resemble the Maoist "struggle sessions" in the Red China of old.

This hyper-fragility infects even our nation's privileged elites. We read of:

- Yale students who lose their minds over hypothetical Halloween costumes.
- Princeton students who stage sit-ins because the Woodrow Wilson School is called the Woodrow Wilson School.
- Rutgers students who enroll in "Politicizing Beyoncé" at $5,000 a head.
- Bryn Mawr students who line up to take "Queens, Nuns, and Other Deviants in the Early Modern Iberian World" for $7,400.
- Brown students who cough up $8,000 a pop for "Global Macho: Race, Gender, and Action Movies."[24]

The children of elites can afford such cotton-candy poison, although they are harmed by it. But the students who suffer most are those who aren't backed by family wealth. They desperately need to learn that they can succeed, and then learn something useful to do so. For them, our outdated system functions like a conspiracy designed to keep them in their place. In an economy marked by exponential growth, we must rethink what education is and adopt a model of learning that's intentional, self-directed, and continuous.

At Catholic University's business school, we ask executives what skill they look for most among recent graduates. They tell us, over and over: Send us students who can write a coherent sentence. At most colleges, studying English doesn't develop good writing skills; it prevents it. To get a BA in English literature at UCLA, you must take courses in gender, race, ethnicity, disability, or sexual studies, imperial transnational or postcolonial studies, and critical theory. But you don't need a course on Shakespeare.[25] If someone is paying for a degree like this, I would recommend that they stop at once and transfer—or at least drop the major and do something worthwhile. It's not just a huge waste of time and money. It makes students more fragile and more stupid.

I would be in complete despair if it weren't for the fact that pampered students are nothing new. In *Liberal Parents, Radical Children*, Midge Decter wondered how a generation as noble as hers could raise such a silly one. "We proclaimed you sound when you were foolish . . ." she wrote to the younger generation. "[While] you were the most indulged generation, you were also in many ways the most abandoned to your own meager devices."[26] Decter wasn't writing about millennials. Her book was published in 1975. She was writing about baby boomers, the children of the "Greatest Generation."

Maybe today's delicate daylilies will grow up, spread seeds of creativity, and usher in a new era of American bounty. But unless they toughen up, they won't fare well in the job market—except for the lucky few who have trust funds or get the odd job of corporate agitator or community organizer.

In this time of light-speed creative destruction, we must learn from tough breaks, job churn, and failure. We should plan to do several things during our career. Don't imagine a career spread out over adulthood as either a single full-time job or even a series of such jobs. We should not assume that we can finish our education at age eighteen or twenty-one, and depend on that for the next forty-five years. What students don't prepare for in their formal education, they'll have to learn later, on the job or on their own time.

Most of the work of the future doesn't exist yet, so you can't specialize for it. Sure, tech skills are valuable, and many of them can be learned on the cheap (more on that in a bit). A degree in engineering, science, or business still promises a good rate of return.[27] You won't go hungry if you avoid too much student debt,[28] get good grades at a good school, graduate with a BS in a high-demand field such as computer engineering, and move to where the jobs are.

But don't imagine that a high-tech economy requires us all to become coding wizards, any more than being a NASCAR driver requires you to be a mechanical engineer. Instead, you should develop a suite of skills that allows you to adapt quickly.

Some people only generalize. Others hyper-specialize. Here's a better strategy for the college-bound: Combine the most general skills with a cutting-edge specialty. Become logical, literate, and numerate, since these underlie every other intellectual skill. For example, get a BA in philosophy from a department that takes logic seriously, plus a minor in coding, a summer seminar in business writing, a self-directed certificate in app development, and an internship in social media. That would be far more useful than a degree in literature and a summer job protesting the minimum wage.

And as we'll see later, an apprenticeship in fine carpentry or welding would do more for you and for humanity than a BA in sociology—unless you're a very good student and plan to get a PhD in the field.

Even for the college-bound, some competence in a manual trade is priceless. I did low- and medium-skill construction work on and off for years. It gave me skills and an outlook I could never have gained from books. For one thing, it taught me that I didn't want to remodel schools and houses as a career—although I could if I had to. And when my family was young and dollars were scarce, it came in handy to know how to use a hammer, drill, screwdriver, nail gun, plumber's wrench, and miter and coping saw.

If you're not in school, you still have lots of options. That's because the very technologies that disrupt education also give everyone historic chances for *continual* education.[29] Think of Scott Adams. He got a degree in economics from Hartwick College, and an MBA from Cal Berkeley that he picked up slowly while he worked at a bank—and graduated near the bottom of his class. Yet all his greatest successes involve self-taught skills.

Your life should be one long apprenticeship. Like a good app that stays forever in the development stage, you should keep your mind in "perpetual beta." Every year until you die, learn a new skill or a new subject, or at least keep yourself up-to-date. Don't expect this trend to let up. Take command of your continuous education. If you're in your forties, you've already learned, as an adult, how to use laptops, search engines, smartphones, touch screens, apps, and social media platforms.

Fortunately, any motivated person with an internet connection can learn IT skills through sites such as Galvanize and General Assembly. The latter even provides a three-week coding boot camp. Heck, you can get the knowledge equivalent of an advanced degree from an Ivy League college at little to no cost, through websites such as Udacity, edX, Khan Academy, Coursera, and iTunes U. Udacity even promises, "Get a job or your money back!" How many times have you seen that in a college catalog?

Scores of colleges, including elite ones such as Stanford and MIT, offer MOOCs (massively open online courses). You can get superb musical training on the cheap through websites such as JamPlay. (I've used it.) You can learn a foreign language with free smartphone apps such as Duolingo and Babbel. Through College Plus, college students can get a useful and accredited bachelor's degree, mostly via a home computer, for under $10,000.

We're still in the early stages of this new type of education, and we can only guess at the crater it will leave behind. This we know: Our current system costs way too much: Student debt is now $1.3 trillion dollars. And quality is declining: 98 percent of research published in humanities journals is not cited even once in the relevant literature.[30] Yet many colleges provide neither a soul-expanding liberal arts education nor marketable skills.[31]

At the same time, there are new technologies that not only bypass the old systems, they can deliver the goods at little to no cost. In one corner, an old, corpulent, hypertensive boxer who should have retired in the last century. In the other, a muscular, long-armed, lightning-fast brawler just coming into his own. It's gonna get ugly.

Here's what I predict. For centuries, colleges have provided knowledge, culture (the traditional goal of liberal arts), credentials, and social networks.[32] The elite schools with multibillion-dollar endowments won't go anywhere. They offer prestige and connections over and above whatever knowledge they impart to students. They're also best situated to take advantage of new technologies.

At the same time, no law dictates that the same entities must deliver all those goods. Expect them to be unbundled in the coming years. Platforms will give rise to new and cheaper choices for education, such as Minerva Schools at KGI, which combines liberal arts, small student communities, and live online chats with professors.[33]

Among the other 95 percent, both K–12 and college, some schools will adapt and survive. Those with strong religious or educational missions that move quickly to offer both in-class and online options will weather the storm.

Expect more traditional and online learning to be integrated in the years ahead. Many of our better public school teachers already use videos from Khan Academy, the free online tutorial website started by Salman Khan, to teach the children under their care. The teacher becomes the hands-on tutor. That's because Khan explains subjects, especially math and science, far better than the average teacher. Also, students can watch the tutorials over and over without taxing Khan's patience.[34]

The bad and overpriced schools will die—unless government subsidies keep them on life support.

Expect messiness, job loss, failures, and false starts in the transition.[35] The result, we may hope, will be new, more diverse, and more effective ways to deliver the functions now bundled together in higher education.

There's a "Matthew Effect"[36] with these technologies. The well-off and educated take advantage of them, while the poor and un-educated do not. The real scarcity now is not the chance to learn but the gumption and drive that have always been necessary but that, until recently, were not enough. At a personal level, though, there's only one question: Will you ignore these opportunities, or exploit them?

# 6

## DO UNTO OTHERS

### ALTRUISM IN A DIGITAL AGE

Danielle Tate looks like she was born for business. When I first met her at Paul bakery in the tony Tysons Galleria in Tysons Corner, Virginia, she was dressed down with a black sweater, dark jeans, and high-heel shoes. But her customary uniform is a red power dress that matches her irrepressible energy. I had just listened to the audio version of her book *The Elegant Entrepreneur*. It mixes sage advice to women on how to start a successful business, literate references to business theorists such as Michael Porter, and tales of trial and tribulation from her own career. She narrated and produced the audiobook herself after raising the funds in a Kickstarter campaign.

Although she looks like the textbook image of an MBA, Danielle doesn't have a business degree. In fact, even as she graduated from college, she had no plans to enter business. She calls herself an "accidental entrepreneur." Her lifelong goal was to go into medicine, and she even graduated a year early from Bedford High School in

Bedford, Pennsylvania, so she could get started. Danielle majored in biology at McDaniel College in Westminster, Maryland, and took a medical internship at Howard Hughes Medical Institute in Chevy Chase one summer. She fell in love with cardiology. During her senior year, she applied to three highly selective medical schools: Georgetown, Cornell, and Baylor. Unfortunately, Danielle didn't get accepted to any of her choices. She was devastated.

"What about moving back home?" I asked her, since that common strategy for millennials with a college degree and no plan B.

"No way. That's the one thing I didn't want to do."

So instead of heading back to Bedford (population 3,500) after graduation in 2003, Danielle moved to Columbia, Maryland—between Baltimore and Washington, DC—and took a job with Canon selling printers and fax machines. She was good at it but didn't enjoy it.

"This involved cold calls to businesses," she said with a sigh. "I was once escorted from a building for solicitation."

"That sounds just like an episode of *The Office*," I said.

"Oh, I've never seen that," she said.

*How is that possible?* I thought, but didn't ask.

"We don't really watch TV."

About a year later, she moved on to Ventana Medical Systems to sell a complex tissue-staining platform used to diagnose cancer. She put 1,300 miles on her car every week, sprinting around the Northeast to meet with pathologists and histologists. Unlike the common office fixtures she had sold at Canon, her new product was a highly specialized piece of equipment that cost between a quarter of a million and half a million dollars a pop. But Danielle's natural vivacity paid off, and she soon won a prize for being top salesperson: a Harley-Davidson Fat Boy motorcycle.

Is this a story about a woman who didn't get into medical school and found her purpose in medical technology? No. The main story has nothing to do with medicine. The true watershed of Danielle's career came when she decided to get married. She had met her future husband, Culin Tate, soon after she moved to the DC metro area. Once they decided to get married, she found herself overwhelmed with the countless details that most women impose on themselves when they plan a wedding. Sure, some of these to-dos are fun: picking out the dress, the cake, the church, and the invitations, selling your Harley-Davidson to pay for new furniture, and so forth. But there is also the blasted government bureaucracy involved in changing your marital status.

Danielle, like most American women, planned to change her name. No big deal, she thought. She checked the Maryland DMV website, found the official form, printed it and filled it out, and took it in. But after a long wait in line, she learned that the form—you know, the one on the DMV's very own website?—was outdated. They gave her a new one to fill out. Since she still worked full-time driving hither and yon, she had to leave, fill out the form, and come back later. Then, on her second visit to the DMV, she learned that the form needed to be certified by a county clerk. So she had to leave again, get it certified in another office, and return to the DMV yet a third time.

The very thought of this raises my blood pressure. But the ordeal gave Danielle an idea. "If TurboTax can make it possible for ordinary citizens to do their taxes," she asked her fiancé, Culin, "why hasn't someone created a service that makes the painful thirteen-hour name-changing ordeal easier?"

"You should do it," he told her. The thought bounced around in Danielle's head for a few months, slowly taking the form of a plan. How would she make it happen? The last computer class she had taken was in middle school, and it was deadly boring. As it happened, Culin's old fraternity brother Mike Bradicich was good with databases. So, with start-up capital of $15,000 dollars—$5,000 from her savings, $5,000 from Culin, and $5,000 from Mike—they set out to engineer a way to untie the name-changing knot.

During 2005, Danielle worked on the service's launch while still holding down her other full-time job. Soon, though, she realized that the name-changing service would never get off the ground if she treated it as a side project So, she took a deep breath and quit her lucrative job with Ventana.

At the end of 2006, her business finally launched.

MissNowMrs.com is an online service that allows women in all fifty states to bypass the thirteen-hour bureaucratic maze. The cost: $29.95 plus a half hour of work. So far, more than 350,000 busy brides have decided that's a good trade.

Did Danielle merely figure out how to make some cold hard cash off a bunch of harried brides-to-be? That's how a critic of capitalism might see it. But here's a much better way to view it: Danielle Tate found it frustrating to change her name when she got married, and realized that millions of other women might like a service that made the process much easier. So she channeled her own frustration and creative energy to provide just such a service. These women pay thirty dollars to use the service because the service is—wait for it—worth at least thirty dollars to them. The only way to cast this as a tale about greed is simply to define greed as any act that ends up benefiting oneself, which is silly. MissNowMrs.com is the textbook example of a win-win game.

Tate's is the basic story of most successful entrepreneurs—and by extension, most successful businesses and employees—in a market economy. They don't succeed through greed or self-absorption. Rather, they anticipate the needs and wants of others, take risks to fulfill that need, and learn from the success or failure that follows. To create value for others is, in the root sense of the word, altruistic, since "altruism" comes from a Latin word that means "other." In a market economy, if you provide a good or service—LASIK eye surgery, a car wash, or an easy online service to change one's name—you're acting altruistically, whatever else you might be up to.

Call it whatever you want, but it's one of the most overlooked facts about capitalism.

## The Greed Myth

You have probably heard just the opposite: that business and enterprise are all about greed. And, to be fair, champions of "capitalism" share as much blame as do the critics for this *greed myth*. Indeed, the twentieth century's most widely read cheerleader for capitalism was an eccentric atheist who denounced religion, embraced selfishness as a virtue, and derided altruism as a vice.

Ayn Rand was born in Russia in 1905 as Alisa Zinov'yevna Rosenbaum. She immigrated to the United States in 1926, just as communism secured its stranglehold on the Soviet Union. Her hatred of the system she lived under in her youth was etched into her mind, her writings, and even her strange personality. The release of her novel *The Fountainhead* in 1943 made her famous, and *Atlas Shrugged*, published in 1957, cemented her legacy.

It's telling that one book of Rand's essays, a primer of her philosophy, is called *The Virtue of Selfishness*.[1] In it, she argued that greed was the basis for a free economy, and altruism was its enemy. "Capitalism and altruism are incompatible; they are philosophical opposites; they cannot co-exist in the same man or in the same society," she said.[2] In her novels, she created characters who expressed her philosophy of "man as a heroic being, with his own happiness as the moral purpose of his life, with productive achievement as his noblest activity, and reason as his only absolute."[3] Indeed, she went so far as to claim that she was "not primarily an advocate of capitalism, but of egoism."[4] Her egoism was so strident that Rand did not accept that parents were obliged to care for their children.

Rand tended to define terms eccentrically, making some of her ideas sound worse than they were. Take the word "altruism." She defined it as acting for the benefit of someone else at your own expense.[5] So defined, altruism for Rand could only ever be a zero-sum game: If I act to intentionally help you, it harms me. But she didn't define self-interest or even selfishness that way. Although she believed that one could, indeed *ought* to, act selfishly and for one's own benefit alone, she also thought that when great entrepreneurs act selfishly, they often unwittingly help others.

Thus, despite Rand's praise of selfishness, her literary heroes don't act like Ebenezer Scrooge or Rich Uncle Pennybags, the tuxedo-clad guy in *Monopoly*. In *Atlas Shrugged*, John Galt is a brave wealth creator who pursues his vision despite great obstacles, including an evil state bent on destroying him. Although Rand despised the Christian idea of self-sacrifice, Galt is suspiciously Christ-like. He preaches a message of salvation, founds a community, and challenges the status quo. Insofar as Galt's character connects with readers of *Atlas Shrugged*, it's because he contradicts the greedy stereotype that Rand's philosophy leads them to expect.

Nonetheless, when combined with the anti-business biases of many journalists, playwrights, and academics, the Randian caricature of capitalism has created a straw man of the business world. Critics are more than happy to prop up Rand's straw man so they can knock it down. It's also led to a skewed take on the father of modern economics, Adam Smith. His view of business and enterprise is far richer and subtler than even many economists realize. The good news is that getting Smith right will help us understand an important factor for success in the future of American work.

## SELF-INTEREST DOES NOT EQUAL GREED

Adam Smith was a Scottish moral philosopher who in 1776 wrote the most famous book in the history of economics, *The Wealth of Nations*.[6] He is a patron saint of what we now call capitalism. But far from sucking up to the business class, he warned that "people of the same trade seldom meet together, even for merriment and diversion, but the conversation ends in a conspiracy against the public, or in some contrivance to raise prices."[7]

Even more, Smith never attributed the happy outcomes of trade and business to the virtues of businesspeople. "It is not from the benevolence of the butcher, the brewer, or the baker that we expect our dinner," he wrote, only to be quoted by every economics textbook ever written, "but from their regard to their own interest."[8] Nevertheless, thanks to the invisible hand of the market, such an individual will "promote an end which is no part of his intention."[9] That end often helps society overall.

Notice that this isn't Rand's "Greed is good" shtick. The Scottish philosopher didn't goad butchers, brewers, and bakers into becoming more selfish.[10] His point is that you're usually on safer ground if you can appeal to someone's self-love instead of their kindness. The butcher, for example, is more likely to give you meat if it's a win-win trade than if you come to him as a beggar.[11]

Smith wasn't naïve about the motives of merchants, but he knew the difference between self-interest and true selfishness. Greed is a vice, he granted, but mere pursuit of your self-interest is not. Every time you take a breath, take a shower, take your vitamins, or take a nap, you pursue your self-interest. Not only is that okay, in most cases, you *ought* to do these things.

In fact, proper self-interest is the basis for the Golden Rule— Jesus's command to "do to others as you would have them do to you."[12] If my conscience is properly formed, then I should use my concern for myself as a guide in how I treat others. This makes perfect sense, since I know best what I need. And since we're social beings (more on that in the next chapter), our self-interest includes our friends, families, neighbors, coworkers, coreligionists, and others.[13] When I work hard at my job, I don't just pursue my narrow interest. I pursue the interests of my family, my bank, my community, and my employer. I choose my house and my neighborhood and my car not just for myself but for my children.

Smith's point is that in a free market each of us can pursue ends within our sphere of competence and concern—our "self-interest"— and yet a prosperous order will emerge that vastly exceeds what anyone intended.[14] No central planner, however wise and well-informed, could ever achieve anything close—as we learned over and over again in the twentieth century.

At the same time, Smith thought, the "natural system of liberty" can *channel* greed, which makes the system fit for real, flawed human beings. "In spite of their natural selfishness and rapacity," he argued, businesspeople "are led by an invisible hand . . . and thus without intending it, without knowing it, advance the interest of the society . . ."[15] Notice that he says "in spite of." His argument isn't that the butcher should be selfish. It's that *even if* the butcher is selfish—even if the butcher would love to sell you a spoiled veal cutlet—the butcher can't make you buy his meat in a free economy. If he tricks you, he'll suffer from the nasty review you'll post on Yelp. The greedy butcher, in other words, must look for ways to set up win-win scenarios. Even to satisfy his greed, he must meet your needs. That's making the best of a bad situation, and of a bad butcher.

## EMPATHY CAN MAKE YOU RICH

With MissNowMrs.com, Danielle Tate *discovered* an unmet need in the course of her own bad experience. She *anticipated* a market for a name-changing service by guessing that there would be lots of women just like her. That's empathy. She then took a courageous risk: She put up seed money and quit her secure job to create a service and then to cultivate the market for it. Here as elsewhere in enterprise, initiative and invention preceded supply. Supply preceded demand and indeed created it. Danielle didn't just look at an existing market and find a way to fill it. She imagined a market for a service and then *created* the service—and, in a sense, the market too. As Thomas Edison said, "I find out what the world needs. Then I go ahead and try to invent it."

She acted, in other words, for the good of others. Such altruism is only the tip of the virtue iceberg for our poster-child entrepreneur.

Before entrepreneurs can invest capital, they must first accumulate it. So, unlike gluttons and hedonists, entrepreneurs set aside rather than consume much of their wealth. Unlike misers and cowards, they courageously risk rather than hoard what they have saved, providing stability for those who become employed as a result. And unlike the sour skeptic, they have a kind of faith in their neighbors, in their partners, in their society, in their employees, and "in the compensatory logic of the cosmos."[16] Through this cluster of virtues the entrepreneur gains personal success by meeting the needs of others. It's this cluster of virtues, not the vice of greed, that is the essence of what Father Robert Sirico calls the "entrepreneurial vocation."[17]

To achieve the third American Dream, leave behind the straw man image of the greedy capitalist and nurture this type of altruism. If you're self-absorbed, or reflexively suspicious, or cautious to the point of miserliness, you have soul-searching to do. You may think technology will allow you to succeed as a misanthrope, but don't count on it. Like Danielle Tate, successful entrepreneurs anticipate and meet the needs of others.

Beyond that, many of today's safest jobs are for "people persons."[18] Managers, sales reps, physical therapists, fund-raisers, pastors, priests, counselors: Robots won't take these jobs anytime soon. And the best and easiest way to show interest and concern for others is—get out your highlighter for this—to *be interested in and concerned for others.*

The good news is that our economy offers far more chances for mutually beneficial outcomes than earlier economies did. Danielle Tate's website service is just one example of this, since so much of it is automated. To really get what's happening, we need to understand the second feature that distinguishes our information economy from the industrial one that preceded it: It's digital.

## We're All Digital Now

The 2010 print edition of *Encyclopedia Britannica* had thirty-two volumes, weighed 129 pounds, and cost $1,395. It is a big, bulky, dusty thing. The online version is not—because it's digital.

The word comes from the Latin word *digitalis*, which means "finger." When applied to technology, it refers to the translation of something into discrete units, such as the binary of zeroes and ones, or a physical quality such as on and off. At its most basic, to digitize an encyclopedia is to convert the words on the pages into zeroes and ones. These are then stored and transmitted in a technological environment rather than in a book. As Erik Brynjolfsson and Andrew McAfee put it in *The Second Machine Age*, "Digitization . . . is the work of turning all kinds of information and media—text, sounds, photos, video, data from instruments and sensors, and so on—into the ones and zeroes that are the native language of computers and their kin."[19]

That you could compress a huge encyclopedia onto a tiny thumb drive makes no sense if you focus on the paper and ink. The way to get the trick is to focus on the information. The purpose of those thirty-two volumes of the 2010 edition of the *Encyclopedia Britannica* isn't to cut down trees and turn them into reams of paper. It's to store and convey information for English readers.

Think of a ninth grader working on a paper on William Shakespeare. If she has the encyclopedia nearby, she could pull down the *S* volume, look up "Shakespeare, William," and learn that Shakespeare's contemporary Ben Jonson, a poet and dramatist, said that the Bard of Avon "was not of an age, but for all time." The information about what Jonson said about Shakespeare is *not* the book, or the paper, or the ink, or the letters.

*Okay, big deal*, you might think. Here's the point: There's a difference between (1) the information, (2) the language it's coded in, and (3) the medium that transmits and stores it. The *same* information can be stored and conveyed in different media: electrical signals, laser-inscribed patterns on a CD, a magnetic structure in a hard disk, and so forth. This tells us that information isn't identical to any of the physical media it rides on. Same goes for different languages. Sure, if you translate a text from one language to another, you may lose some nuances and even add shades of meaning here and there. If it's an artful poem, you'll lose a lot. But information is not the same as the language it inhabits. Otherwise, no one would ever try to translate text from one language to another. Here's what this means: Medium and language are distinct from message.

All the same, digitization does do some strange things to the information it stores and conveys. If you capture Yo-Yo Ma's performance of a Bach suite in digital form, suddenly it's what economists call "non-rival." That means it can now be in two places at once, or three or four or a million places. And to replicate it costs next to nothing.[20]

Strictly speaking, all information is non-rival. If I know the periodic table of elements, or the score of last night's Cowboys' game, that doesn't prevent you from knowing the same. There's no zero-sum game when it comes to information. Thomas Jefferson saw the point in the eighteenth century when he wrote, "He who receives an idea from me, receives instruction himself without lessening mine; as he who lights his taper at mine, receives light without darkening me. . . . [I]deas . . . [are] incapable of confinement or exclusive appropriation."[21]

In Jefferson's example, to teach and remember the idea may cost time and money. But my knowing it does not keep you from knowing it. The information itself is non-rival. It would be easy to have missed this, though, because until recently most of the ways we stored and transmitted information *were* rival.

To write and edit the encyclopedia articles cost time and money. Due to economies of scale on the supply side, the publisher can get the cost per set down with huge print runs. Still, the cost to print, store, transport, and deliver each additional set—the "marginal cost"—is pretty high. They're heavy. They take up a lot of space, paper, ink, glue, and cardboard. And if the company sells out of a print run, it will have to go back to the printer to print more sets.

Also, these are rival goods. You can't have the same encyclopedia set in your library that I have in mine. You could borrow my set and use a copy machine to make your own set. But that would be dopey even if it weren't illegal. The copy would not be as good as the original. Copies of copies would be even worse. And you'd spend far more on paper, ink cartridges, time, and printers than if you just bought your own set outright.

Now we see the contrast between a physical copy and a digital copy. To produce the online version of *Encyclopedia Britannica* in the first place is also quite expensive. But it's trivial to store, sell, and transport new sets. The DVD version is a mere $46.44. If you're connected to the internet, however, you can get a lot of its content free, or just subscribe to the premium service for $75. There's little cost to maintain it and zero or near-zero cost for each additional set. Each "marginal" copy of the encyclopedia is nearly free to produce, deliver, and store. Even more, these copies can be everywhere at once—at least, everywhere the digital stream can reach. This feat can only happen because the information isn't stored as letters inscribed with ink on pages but in bits, the basic units of digital information.

It's hard to exaggerate how much the printing press and mass production of books changed civilization five hundred years ago, even though books were still somewhat costly, rival goods. It shifted civilization from the spoken to the written word. Half a millennium later, we find ourselves amidst another epochal shift: digitization. We happen to live just when the information, storage, and transmission of book equivalents have become non-rival and dropped to almost zero marginal cost. We have little idea how profoundly this will change civilization worldwide in the next few decades.

This is digitization, and it's happening all around us. Two hundred years ago, fine orchestral music could be heard only in the presence of an orchestra. That meant that most people never heard it. Now, thanks to digitization, countless millions of MP3s—digital audio files—are available at near zero marginal cost.[22] Do you think that this change is no big deal? Then you haven't spent enough time thinking about the lot of 99 percent of humanity who, for most of history, had little access to high-quality music. (I'm not counting the guy with the stringed thing down at the local tavern.)

It's the same story with books, maps, movies, pictures and videos, accounting help, travel guidance, newspapers, magazines, and job boards—much to the chagrin of print, audio, and video media. Even in non-media fields, the information explosion gives customers far more control. In car sales and residential real estate, customers have far more information and negotiating power than they ever had before.

If you take the time to do some online research, you won't be the victim of a shifty used-car salesman or real estate agent. Read the Carfax report on that used Chevy you see on the way to work, and the car salesman won't be able to fool you. Compare house prices on Redfin and scan neighborhoods with street view on Google Maps, and you'll have almost as much information as the real estate agent who tries to convince clients that popcorn spray on ceilings is about to make a comeback. Read the descriptions and reviews on Amazon, and you're much less likely to buy a book—or pants, shoes, or a scooter—that's not exactly what you expected it to be.

And if you get married and want to change your name, you can do it with little time and cost and without having to endure a maddening ritual at the DMV.

## INFORMATION ABUNDANCE

Economics is often defined as the study of the allocation of scarce resources. Once digital goods have been created, however, they aren't scarce. They're abundant and can be easily stored, copied, delivered, and scaled up. "Information is costly to produce but cheap to reproduce," wrote Carl Shapiro and Hal R. Varian in their 1998 book *Information Rules*.[23] "Making things free, perfect, and instant might seem like unreasonable expectations for most products," observe Erik Brynjolfsson and Andrew McAfee, "but as more information is digitized, more products will fall into these categories."[24] The economics of this abundance—the economics of our future— look quite different from the usual economics of scarcity.[25]

Because Danielle Tate created an automated, online service, millions of women can access MissNowMrs who could not have if the service were delivered in person. What if she had trained fifty experts as name-changing tutors and then advertised their services? The company's offerings would have cost much more time and money, and been available only at certain places. If all fifty tutors were busy, new customers would have to wait in line before they could get a tutor. Those customers could wait down at the DMV for free. It's unlikely that such a business would ever have gotten off the ground. Until the service could be made non-rival, most women just had to change their names on their own. Which is what they did.

For most users, the MissNowMrs process is wholly automated. Since the company prizes customer service, they do have about six full-time staff to answer questions, but even that is semi-automated. Customer service reps have a binder that lists the top one hundred questions. Unsatisfied customers get a full refund. Those are costly luxuries. But with internet technology Danielle Tate could find a price point low enough that it's an impulse buy for frustrated brides-to-be. In this way, she created not just a service but a market that didn't exist before.

## No Zero-Sum Game—in Myth or Reality

Again, historical contrast helps put things in perspective. Primitive life was much more prone to zero-sum games. Think of two hunter-gatherer tribes competing over hunting grounds on the same small island, or a family farm that produces just enough to feed the farmer and his family. It would be hard for such people to imagine abstract possibilities about the benefits of trade and specialization. They're too acquainted with nature, red in tooth and claw. Alas, many people in modern societies still buy the *zero-sum-game myth*, even when it clearly distorts the picture of the real economy.

There has never been a greater time for win-win games. The chances for mutually beneficial exchange go up as technology makes us more productive and gives us time to do things far beyond what we need just to keep ourselves alive. A country filled with family farms that have plenty left over after feeding themselves can then trade for other goods and services it needs. A global economy with safe waterways and giant container ships offers still more ways to trade. And in a digital world, the chances to create value for others are endless because our creations can take flight on the far more capacious jet streams of information.

This isn't limited to software and app design. Any good or service that we can convert to bits, in part or in full, will enjoy this benefit. This includes not just text, images, audio, and video—streaming and archived—but also graphic design, advertising, record keeping, editing, news and periodicals, education and tutorials, long-distance communication, non-athletic game competition, banking, and commerce. This is to say nothing of the new world of additive manufacture, of converting bits to atoms, which we'll discuss later. There has never been less reason to believe the zero-sum-game myth than now.

## SCADS OF INFORMATION

The smallest unit of digital information is the bit. If you flip a coin and it comes up heads, that is one bit of information. There were two possibilities—heads or tails—and the flip reduced them to one actuality—heads. There are 8 bits in one byte ($2^3$ bits). A megabyte is roughly a million bytes ($2^{20}$ bytes).[26] A gigabyte is a billion bytes ($2^{30}$ bytes). A terabyte is a trillion bytes ($2^{40}$ bytes or 40 Blu-ray disks). Above that is a petabyte ($2^{50}$ bytes), then exabyte ($2^{60}$ bytes), zettabyte ($2^{70}$ bytes), and yottabyte ($2^{80}$ bytes, or the storage capacity of 45 trillion Blu-ray disks). There are no official names beyond that. Yottabyte is the largest data size the General Conference on Weights and Measures named back in 1991.

We're still in the exabyte era, so we're good for now. But we won't stay here long, because the amount of data is growing . . . exponentially. According to IBM, by 2015 we were creating 2.5 quintillion bytes of data every day, with 90 percent of the data created in the *previous two years*.[27]

## BOTH FREE AND PREMIUM

But don't digital copies destroy the market for the originals? Not necessarily. Most of us recall the music industry's terror when Napster first made it easy to share audio files. There have been huge disruptions in the decade and a half since then. Still, digital goods didn't eradicate the demand for the real thing. They seem to have done the opposite. Take music. Yes, digitization has wiped out certain delivery vehicles for music: There's no market for 8-track tapes. Yet, as the marginal cost of music approaches free—and access becomes near universal—the demand for live music has gone up, not down.

The spike started around 2001, when iTunes and iPods were first released, and has really picked up speed in the last decade. (The first iPhone came out in 2007.) The prices for some music festivals have more than doubled in that time.[28] In 2015, the progressive rock band Rush had its fortieth and final tour. My lifelong friend, Marshall Dawkins, and I had vowed to go to a Rush concert together just before they retired. We met in Dallas, near the beginning of the tour. The price for two silver VIP tickets? Five hundred dollars. It was totally worth it, even though music in concert rarely sounds as good as it does in a digital recording played on nice speakers. A lot of people seem to value unique experiences with friends, family, and other fans in the presence of the actual musicians. They will pay a lot for that experience, even if they could hear a high-quality recording of the music free.

In a more prosperous future, we should expect *more*, not fewer, jobs and industries that provide unique encounters—in food, travel, entertainment, theater, art, music, and other realms we haven't yet imagined.

## Don't "Follow Your Passion"

Of course, digitization will not usher in a magical world that rewards navel-gazing with gifts of rainbow-sherbet-pooping unicorns and hundred-dollar-bill money trees. You still need old-fashioned virtues to succeed. You still must provide value to someone else.

If you were raised in the last thirty years, decades' worth of commencement speakers and self-help gurus have told you to follow your passion and disregard anyone—stodgy parents, anal-retentive teachers, left-brained peers—who tells you otherwise. "If you are passionate about it, pursue it, no matter what anyone else thinks," advises one husband-wife motivational team. "That's how dreams are achieved."[29] "Build your own dreams," says American businessman and motivational speaker Farrah Gray, "or someone else will hire you to build theirs." To succeed, Steve Jobs said, you should do what you love.

This all sounds wise, but it's a better fit for valedictorian speeches than it is for the realities of a competitive job market.[30] Call it the *follow-your-passion myth.*

Taken as career advice, "follow your passion" implies one of three things:

1. What you want to do right now will match what someone will pay you to do.
2. People *ought* to pay you to do whatever you want to do.
3. People should be *forced* to pay you to do whatever you want to do.

The first assumption is dumb. The second is dumber. And the third is evil.

Sure, it's a free country. If your idea of the good life involves writing blog posts about the extraterrestrials that control the UN, go for it. If you long to catch butterflies, or dress up Pekinese puppies in little sweaters, or play Halo 5 in your sweats for fifteen hours a day, have at it. Just don't expect anyone to pay you, unless there's a market for one of these pursuits waiting to be filled. Otherwise, it's a self-indulgent hobby.

The follow-your-passion myth also assumes that our "passions" are fixed—that we just find ourselves with them, perhaps inscribed in our genes or etched on our brains. In the real world, our interests wax and wane with our experiences and choices. They rarely provide the grist that sustains a career over the long haul.

In the eighth grade, my older daughter passionately drew pictures of cats in long, fancy dresses. She expended her cognitive surplus with Prismacolor pencils and sketch paper, scribbling ever more elaborate kitty gowns and blanketing her walls with these sartorial masterpieces. Her mom and I valued them. We also knew they had no economic value, apart from the long-shot chance that her efforts would lead to a career as a dress designer. Within a year, in any case, she changed her mind and started to draw castles.

When I was a kid, I had many passions that I thought would lead to great riches. For a while I wanted to be a heart surgeon, then an inventor, and later a rock musician (the latter one still lingers). I watched a TV show on heart surgery, read some books about the human heart, and bingo!—I had a passion for cardiology. Later on, I got a subscription to *National Geographic World*. The magazines came with poster inserts of oceans, whales, sharks, and dolphins. I hung them on my wall and soon imagined life as an oceanographer. The problem was, I lived thirteen hours from the nearest ocean and thought the career would allow me to live in pods on the seafloor, swim with dolphins, and discover long-lost treasures.

These passions weren't wholly frivolous. Music was a major part of my life for years, but I always doubted it was a viable career path. Perhaps I could have been a heart surgeon or oceanographer, but only if I had gotten good enough to help others, not because I had followed my fleeting passion.

Mike Rowe of the long-running series *Dirty Jobs* skewers this myth in a popular video from Prager University. He compares the rare musical stars such as Lady Gaga to the many thousands of passionate but deluded souls who show up every year for *American Idol* auditions, just because they lack friends honest enough to tell them that they can't carry a tune. Rowe offers, in contrast, "the dirty truth": "Just because you're passionate about something doesn't mean you won't suck at it." If you base your career plan on a passion, Rowe argues, you might fail to find work that is truly meaningful.

And what do you do if you aren't passionate about anything? This is a growing epidemic among college graduates. Should they just join the welfare rolls, or maybe lobby for a mandatory income paid for by someone else?

In one episode of *Dirty Jobs*—a show that was itself the result of happenstance—Rowe tells the story of Les Swanson, a multimillionaire septic tank cleaner from Wisconsin who explains "the secret to his success."

"I looked around to see where everyone else was headed," Swanson told Rowe, "and then I went the opposite way. Then I got good at my work. Then I began to prosper. And then, one day, I realized that I was passionate about other people's crap."

That, my friends, is much closer to the secret of the American Dream in any age than a thousand treacly tidbits from that guy on the TED stage who tells you to follow your bliss. In *Dirty Jobs*, Rowe focused on the work of skilled and semiskilled tradesmen. Over and over, he found stories of people "who followed opportunity, not passion, and prospered as a result." This truth is hardly unique to the blue-collar sector. It's sound advice for anyone who hopes to achieve the new American Dream.

Les Swanson didn't start out enthralled by excrement. Did he just toughen up and learn to do what he hates? No. Studying how best to clean septic tanks is surely in one of Dante's circles of hell. No sane person would commend it as an adventure in itself. If no one needed his service, Swanson would have hated it. It was the fact that he found a way to *meet the needs of others while meeting his own and his family's* needs that gave the work meaning. Passion wasn't so much the foundation of his career as its outcome.

In the same way, Danielle Tate wasn't transfixed by computers, HTML code, internet tech, the sociology of name changing (a real but deadly boring subject), or the DMVs in all fifty states and the District of Columbia. Remember, her passion was biology and medicine. It was only after med school rejection, two jobs, and three irritating trips to the DMV that she discovered how hard it was to change her last name.

Tate focused on all these subjects because they were the means to her chosen end: to help other women avoid the frustration she had endured. A successful entrepreneur must be willing to study mountains of boring stuff to solve a problem for other people. A preexisting passion has little to do with it.

As a rule for success, "Learn to love what you do" is much better advice than "Do what you love." But it doesn't answer every question. What if you end up in a job you find you despise and surely always will? What if you have a cruel boss and coworkers? What if the product or service you provide violates your conscience? What if you thought you'd found a good career fit but then realize you stink at it no matter how hard you try? Do you just have to suck it up? In some countries and centuries, the answer would have been "Yes, sorry, you don't have a choice." But most of us have far more options.

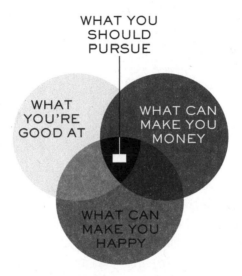

Shannon Henderson, based on Prager University

Don't just follow your passing passion or wander aimlessly until you find one. Look for ways to channel your skills and interests, whatever they are, into an area of unmet need. That's altruism. It's not just for aid workers and the Sisters of Charity. Search, by trial and error if you have to, until you find an overlap between *what you think you might do well* and what other people *need* or *might want* if it existed. (Search for wholesome needs. There's already a glut of vice in the world—and it's no sure path to success.) When you find the overlap, then work to fulfill that need better than your competitors do.

Cultivate this altruistic desire to meet other people's needs, and the passion—and, more important, the happiness—will come. That passion and happiness will, in turn, make you better at what you're doing. This may start as a sheer act of the will—like Les Swanson cleaning septic tanks in Wisconsin and Danielle Tate calling every DMV in the country. But keep at it and the work will grow into a habit, then a passion, and eventually a virtue.

# 7

## NO ONE IS AN ISLAND

### COLLABORATION IN A HYPER-CONNECTED AGE

While writing this book, I've worked to launch a new TV series called *A Force for Good*, in partnership with the Catholic channel EWTN and the Busch School of Business and Economics at the Catholic University of America. When we set out to shoot the pilot episode, one of our first tasks was to develop a logo with a color scheme and branding. I've been involved in logo projects before. They can drag on for months, even if you already know a good designer. We had two weeks, so we decided to use an online service called 99designs. It promised at least ninety-nine logo options for $799, with a money-back guarantee if we didn't get one we liked.

The service began by having me answer a series of questions on an online form: What samples of preexisting designs did we like? What colors do we prefer? Who's the target audience? Do we want our logo to look warm, academic, high-tech, or whimsical? Once I'd answered these questions, our project was made public to a global army of designers. Soon designs started to come in from strangers in the Philippines, Spain, China, Japan, France, the United States, and elsewhere. At first, I didn't get any logos I really liked. But once I started to rate the options and interact with the designers, things took off. Since the designers could see one another's logos, they fed off one another, creating a series of better and more appealing designs. (Still, I made sure to note who originated ideas and who copied.) I was also able to put logos to a vote from among chosen colleagues at key stages in the process. Within two weeks we had dozens of basic concepts for a total of 317 options.

This never could have happened without a platform that linked us with eager designers from all over the world, created an open competition, and established a system of trust between us and the contractors vying for our business. Let's assume I could have gotten on Craigslist and found the guy who ended up winning. Even so, I would never have paid $800 to a designer in Spain I'd never met, in the hope he'd create a good logo for our American TV show. And without the feedback and competition from other designers, the eventual winner might never have landed on the design that was right for us. None of this was possible until recently. But in our hyper-connected world, we already take it for granted. What's more, it opens countless ways to achieve the third American Dream: to create value with and for others.

It's not just the digital nature of our economy that creates more prospects for win-win interactions. Its hyper-connectivity does so as well.

## Tapping the Wisdom of Crowds

In his 2005 book *The Wisdom of Crowds*, James Surowiecki describes how a large, diverse crowd of amateurs can guess the number of jellybeans in a jar or answer questions from *Who Wants to Be a Millionaire* better than a small, uniform group of experts.[1] Ask enough people how many beans are in a jar, find the average guess, and it will be eerily close to the right number. These aren't blind guesses. Each person makes an independent judgment based on what he or she can see. Some will guess high, some will guess low, so finding the average—a simple algorithm that filters the guesses—washes away the random errors. Surowiecki thus shows that H. L. Mencken was shortsighted when he said, "No one in this world, so far as I know . . . has ever lost money by underestimating the intelligence of the great masses of the plain people." On the contrary, there's money to be lost by failing to recognize and harness the gifts of plain people that, until the day before yesterday, could not be tapped. And money to be made by doing the opposite.

The greatest algorithm for tapping the wisdom of mere crowds is surely Google. I remember when I first used the early search engine AltaVista in 1996. I would type in "Dante's Divine Comedy" and watch in amazement as scores of indexed pages scrolled down and off the bottom of the screen. AltaVista indexed some 20 million webpages, nearly ten times more than its competitors. The downside was that I might spend fifteen minutes sifting through pages to find what I wanted. With "Dante's Divine Comedy," for example, I was just as likely to get an ad about a bar called Dante's or a comedy club called Divine Comedy as to get an article about the epic poem. Sites like AltaVista, Ask.com, and Infoseek worked by sending "spiders" to crawl around the dark highways and byways of the internet. They then created indexes of webpages based on word similarities, much like an ordinary index. They provided some order, but the internet still seemed like an amorphous expanse of data.

Once Google came along, these also-rans felt clunky. Google seemed to know just what I was looking for, and to get ever better at anticipating my questions. Was I "feeling lucky"? Yes, more and more, I was.

What set Google apart? It was that its searches weren't based on dead indexes. Instead, its algorithms harnessed the choices of millions of human users to improve the searches. Today, this process is called "machine learning."

Larry Page and Sergey Brin, the founders of Google, landed on their strategy while doing graduate studies at Stanford. They, too, were frustrated with the then-current generation of search engines. Page came up with the idea of modeling a search system on the same rule that scholars had used for decades to rank academic papers: how many times a paper is cited by other papers. Rather than count footnotes and citations, Google's algorithm counted hyperlinks to decide how relevant each page was to each search. If a thousand diverse webpages link to the same webpage about Dante's *Divine Comedy*, it's a safe bet that it will be relevant to other people who type those three words into Google. This is Google's cleverly named PageRank system—named after Larry Page, though most users assume it refers to webpages.

This positive feedback between Google's search rules and the choices of people—the creators of webpages and people who do Google searches—created a much better search engine. Which brings us to the bigger point: Google is not just a clever piece of software built by smart people. *It's a hybrid of well-built technology with the networked, intelligent choices of millions of people.* Human fingerprints are all over it. It's easy to forget that part of the story and notice only the simple white Google page, computers, server farms, and fiber-optic cables. Call it "machine learning" if you like, but not much happens without the purposeful choices of the designers and users. Together, however, those users and the networks that connect us are remaking our world, both at work and at play, and giving rise to new prospects, new professions, and new industries.

Page's strategy was brilliant. But what if he only had a few users and just a tiny slice of the Web? In that alternate universe, Google search algorithms would have gotten little benefit from what's called a *network effect*. This refers to the way some things, such as beehives, mass transit, and insurance plans, can improve as the number of users increases. The common example is a telephone. The greatest salesman in the world, it's said, was the guy who sold the first phone. To go from one to two phones is a huge improvement, if you have a phone, the other person is someone you want to talk to, and a phone line can connect you both. The value of a phone network goes up fast as the user numbers increase.

In 1993, George Gilder described this effect—which he called Metcalfe's law, in honor of Ethernet coinventor Robert Metcalfe—by saying that the value of a network is proportional to the square of the number of connected users in the system ($n^2$). So, if a network has two users, the value is 4. If they add a third, the value of the network is 9. If there are 4 users, the value is 16, and so forth. No need to sweat the details, which are controversial in any case. The basic idea is that the value of a network goes up *exponentially* as the number of nodes goes up linearly. In English: Add more folks to the network and it will get way better and more valuable, really fast.

With a positive network effect, the whole is far better than the sum of the parts. As it gets better, more people will want in on the action and join the network, and that will make it even better. This is called, as you might have guessed, the bandwagon effect. We see it every day with smartphone map apps such as Inrix and Waze. These use the GPS-enabled phones of users to create a detailed map of traffic patterns, which then allows users to find the best route to their destination. The more users, the better the data received.

Of course, people have always worked together. Even great geniuses—*especially* great geniuses, such as Isaac Newton—depended on the work of others. Newton drew on the observations of Johannes Kepler to develop his laws of planetary motion. "If I have seen farther than others," he wrote to a rival, the natural philosopher Robert Hooke, "it is by standing on the shoulders of giants."[2]

Every firm, too, is a group of men and women who depend on one another. They work together toward a common end. In a well-functioning market, in contrast, prices coordinate the choices of people with different ends. Until recently, global markets have been by far the largest ways for people in different countries with diverse interests to coordinate their actions. The result? Bananas, under-wear, and gasoline are distributed far better than if the details had been controlled from the top.

Before the rise of network technology, however, our ability to *collaborate* was quite limited in time and space. Take research—a quite modest form of collaboration. Even in the 1990s, to glean the work of other scholars, I had to scour dusty journal indexes in aca-demic libraries. This was more or less the same way Newton kept track of the work of Kepler, Leibniz, and Hooke. Now I can find what I'm looking for in a few seconds.

It's the same story on the publishing side. Back when I used journal indexes, I was also one of a group of editors of a journal. We all had email accounts and laptops. Still, the easiest way to get the thing finished was for all the editors to huddle in a room and hand floppy disks back and forth to one another.

I'm now the executive editor of the Stream, an online news and commentary site. Because of a content management system, Skype, and Zoom, the whole thing runs smoothly even though I'm in my sweats at home in Northern Virginia, two colleagues are in DC, another half dozen or so are together in Texas, others are in Seattle, Columbus, Pittsburgh, Atlanta, and Phoenix, and our contributors are all over the place. In fact, I can see right on my computer who is on the clock and what they're working on.

As we saw earlier, it still matters where you live when you're try-ing to find a job and launch a new enterprise. At the same time, network technology permits more and more internet-enabled jobs to be done anywhere. My literary agent started his career in Man-hattan—of course. As his family grew, however, he chose to move a few hours north and buy a house in Vermont. He still comes into New York City from time to time for meetings. But so much of his work is done over the phone and email that, once his career matured, he didn't need to keep paying Manhattan prices. Since I work from the DC area, it was a long time before I realized he'd moved to Vermont.

As we'll see, when it is networked properly, *information technology vastly amplifies our ability to work together, to trust others, benefit others, and benefit from the work of others.* Computers are just one part of an electrified and more and more integrated light-speed network that includes servers, clouds, websites, and database programs; global-positioning and communications satellites; health, traffic, and weather sensors; appliances; smartphone sensors such as cameras and accelerometers; and, soon, smart clothes, private and commercial drones, networked appliances, houses, robots, and driverless cars and trucks.

In the next decade or so, there could be 200 billion machines in this "internet of things." All of them will be connected to much faster, broader, and more efficient networks than we have now.[3] These things will link us, their human users and creators, in profound new ways.

We've already gotten a tiny taste of this with the first truly global social network: Facebook. Facebook is so valuable because so many people are on it, sharing pictures of their latest meals, news, updates, and cat fail videos. It sits atop layers of other network technologies. By 2016, over one billion people—that's one-seventh of the global population—checked Facebook every day, even though the Chinese government still blocked its country's 649 million internet users from accessing the site.[4]

## WHAT NETWORKS DO

It's not just about cat fail videos. Networks are about new ways to connect friends, customers, clients, employers, collaborators, co-workers, and folks who have not yet met but have common interests. Networks connect the disconnected, harness their work and creativity, and tap assets that until recently sat idle. The economic impact of our hyper-connected world is perhaps easiest to see in the many "peer-to-peer" platforms that have appeared in the last decade, such as Uber, Lyft, and Airbnb. Writers often identify these companies with the "sharing economy." But the word "sharing" makes it sound like it's all fun and games. As James Surowiecki comments in his *New Yorker* piece "Uber Alles," "Sharing, it turns out, is often a hell of a lot of work."[5] If you expect these platforms to usher in the Age of Aquarius, you'll be disappointed. They matter not because they are harbingers of utopia but because they allow hordes of ordinary people to easily turn idle property into assets, to become freelancers without a lot of prep work, and to create value along the way.

I commute into Washington, DC, once or twice a week. Most of the cars, including my own, can hold five people, but contain exactly one person: the driver. The cars spend most of the day and night idle—parked in a garage, driveway, or on a street. It's the same story everywhere. Americans spend over a trillion dollars a year on new and used cars. You don't have to be freaked out about peak oil and climate change to notice the wasted time, energy, and untapped car capacity. But how to link would-be passengers with would-be providers? That only became possible with the advent of GPS-enabled smartphones, apps, and platforms built on top of them.

What Uber and Lyft do for cars, Airbnb and other such services do for vacation dwellings. Lots of us have extra space in our homes or would love to be able to rent out space to sane non-criminals when we're out of town. Until recently, though, there was no large-scale way to do this. Since it was launched at the height of the financial crisis in August 2008, Airbnb has brought millions of rooms, apartments, and houses into the vacation rental market.

These peer-to-peer platforms make four things possible.

First, they allow underused, expensive "durable goods" to become wealth-producing assets for their owners. Uber and Lyft do this with private cars and drivers, which compete in a market previously reserved for yellow cabs and limousines. Airbnb and like platforms compete with the hotel market a bit. But so far they have mostly created a new market for inexpensive vacation housing at prices and in neighborhoods not well served by hotels.

Second, these platforms create a "trust protocol"[6] or "digital trust infrastructure."[7] Few of us would want to rent out our houses for a weekend to, or ride across town with, a perfect stranger without the regulated brand of a hotel or cab company, even if we had a way to find strangers willing to do so. Because of peer-to-peer networks, this now happens millions of times a day all over the country.

Trust is vital to any trade. Low trust leads to what economists call a high transaction cost. A transaction cost is like sludge in the gears of commerce. The more sludge, the worse the trade car will run. A lack of trust is why merchants in bazaar markets in many poor countries take only cash exchanges at time of purchase: There isn't enough trust for mail order, checks, or credit cards. That drastically limits opportunities for such merchants. They can't sell over eBay or Etsy, or take credit cards from tourists.

For this reason, the wider the bonds of trust, the greater the economic prospects. In healthy market economies, strangers trust one another much more than do people in tribal groups, who often distrust even nearby tribes.[8] As Americans, we mostly take this for granted. Widespread trust can only be sustained, however, if most people in a market act in a trustworthy manner. Some may step out in faith, but not in blind faith off a cliff with smirking predators below.

And even in the best economies, most people have a policy of trust-but-verify rather than naïve trust. After all, there's always the risk of crooks and free riders. That's why some markets, such as the ones for hotels and taxi services, still have high transaction costs, usually in the form of complex regulations. Peer-to-peer platforms largely solve this problem. They not only link customers with providers but lower the hazards of trust between them. They register both parties to the exchange through the system with personal and financial information.[9] Then they use a rating system to encourage both parties to make good on their end of the bargain—much like the systems pioneered by eBay and Amazon did two decades earlier. (Some also have a well-engineered escrow service. 99designs holds the prize money for winning designs until clients have made their choice.)

The upshot is that, if you have a habit of puking in Uber cars, for instance, it won't be long before no driver will accept your hail. Your one-star ratings from the drivers of the cars you puked in will ensure that. Same goes for the drivers who are rude to their customers. The drivers will get bad ratings and will soon get booted from the system. A digital trust infrastructure provides countless ways for perfect strangers to buy, sell, and exchange goods, services, and information, across town or across the planet, in an instant, with very little fuss and bother.

Third, these platforms allow hundreds of thousands of micro-entrepreneurs to get some or all of their income by providing the service. Most who profit from these services have middling incomes, and can now make money using idle resources they already have. My Uber drivers have included former cabdrivers, retirees, a single mother who sold insurance, a part-time EMT, immigrants, and a college student writing his senior thesis—about Uber.

Fourth, such platforms have very low barriers to entry. To become a yellow cab driver in Manhattan before the age of smartphones, you first had to memorize the byzantine map of the five boroughs. Then you either had to buy or gain access to a medallion and an approved car—which cost hundreds of thousands of dollars! Compare that with Uber. If you have, say, a five-year-old Toyota Corolla and a good driving record, and know how to use a map app, it only takes about two weeks to become a driver for Uber X, which competes with cabs. There's also a higher-end Uber Black option that competes with limos and an even cheaper Ride Share option that competes with shuttles.

And imagine how much easier it is to fix up and rent out a room for vacationers through Airbnb or another vacation rental service than to open a new hotel.

Uber, Lyft, Airbnb, and platforms like them are *two-sided networks* that can scale up quickly. That's because they enjoy economies of scale on both the supply and demand sides.[10] (Henry Ford's car assembly plants enjoyed economies of scale only on the supply side.) Here's how it works. Word gets out that Lyft is in town. Early adopters use it instead of hailing a cab because of a promotional offer. They find that it's better, easier, and cheaper than hailing a cab. They tell friends about it, who sign up too. The growing customer base—that is, more demand—leads more drivers to sign on. That keeps costs down, which leads to more customers, which brings prices up, which brings in more drivers, which brings prices down, and so on.

As usual, these new creations also destroy. Uber and Lyft have caused panic in markets like New York City, where yellow cabs with costly (government-issued) medallions had long enjoyed near monopolies. The medallions still cost a fortune, but their value in recent years has tanked due to the competition.[11] The drivers for Washington Flyer, the taxi monopoly at Dulles Airport outside DC, fought Uber and Lyft for a while. But at some point many started moonlighting for the ride-share companies. If you can't beat 'em, join 'em. Washington Flyer will either get better or get displaced by Uber, Lyft, and other competitors.[12]

Another benefit to this system: The market for ride services is now much larger than it was when yellow cabs and limos ruled the roost. This soon will create a surprising surplus. Between ride-sharing apps and self-driving cars, millions of commuters will be able to do real work from cars. Americans burn up seven billion hours on their commutes every year. Right now, an entrepreneur somewhere is trying to figure out how to tap into this coming surfeit of labor.

This is just a sampling of the prospects that abound in the peer-to-peer ecosystem. Look for growth in parking and delivery services, banking and financing through blockchain technologies such as Bitcoin,[13] and start-up resources through crowdfunding platforms like Kickstarter, Indiegogo, and GoFundMe. These offer the first, modest glimpses of the countless new ways to create and share value in our hyper-connected world.

## THE POWER OF AMATEURS

These days, many of the most popular products succeed *precisely because they allow new ways to creatively share and collaborate among ordinary people.* The grand prizes tend to go to those platforms that turn customers into collaborators.[14] They help amateurs—not just the bohemian elites whom Richard Florida celebrates in his *Rise of the Creative Class*—create value.[15]

Think of how visual media has changed in the last few decades. When I was a small child, our TV had three networks—ABC, NBC, CBS—and a local PBS affiliate that played *Sesame Street.* When I was in elementary school, we got cable, which meant better reception and a few more channels. But the basic pattern was still the same: A few experts produced all the content and broadcast it in one direction to millions of passive recipients. Visit Rockefeller Center in New York City, home of NBC. You'll find idealized Art Deco architecture, complete with a gold statue of Prometheus, and nearby a lone statue of Atlas holding up the world.

Nowadays, in contrast, we all walk around with HD video cameras and audio recorders in our pockets. We can record half an hour of video, edit the results on our computer, and upload the finished product to Facebook and YouTube—for nothing. Most of this content is "user generated," a prospect that no TV network contemplated twenty years ago. The earlier swarm of passive customers have become not just consumers but producers, collaborators, distributors, and critics—what futurist Alvin Toffler calls "prosumers."[16] The rank amateur now has power that was undreamed of a few decades ago.

Sure, most of what is produced is bad.[17] If everyone is doing something, the law of averages must have its say. With filters and rating systems, however, it's easy to find the diamonds in the dung. We can sort music, images, videos, and everything else through ever more sophisticated filtering programs. These include not just search engines but the "recommendation engines" employed by Google, Amazon, Netflix, Spotify, iTunes, and every other digital media platform. These help guide our choices based on past choices. As digital goods proliferate, the filters will become ever more refined.

My younger daughter followed filter cues on YouTube and soon got turned onto science by two popular channels: the King of Random and the CrazyRussianHacker. Over the years, I've enjoyed audio podcasts, such as EconTalk by Russ Roberts, by searching my interests at iTunes. Few if any of these could have built an audience on radio. They're much too quirky and academic. Russ Roberts's nuanced interviews can go on for an hour—with no breaks! But digital networks, unlike the older forms of broadcast, make it easy for people with obscure interests to find what they want on the "long tail" of the information superhighway.[18]

I bet you've never seen the YouTube channel called Glitter Rainbow Toys. These are videos of a woman with an odd accent and glittery fingernail polish opening new toys and models and then showing viewers how to use them, all the while narrating the experience. She won't get a reality TV show on CBS. Yet one of her many videos has garnered over 50 million views—from a global army of little girls who have figured out how to navigate YouTube. I'm not the target audience. Still, this woman provides a value to her fans and makes money for her effort.

What's my point? It's this: The avenues for value creation for ordinary people are now beyond measure and prediction. You can succeed in the new media with almost no start-up capital or official credentials. Remember Daniel and Kelli Segars of Fitness

Blender, whose story opened this book? They knew nothing about video production or editing. They didn't need a $100,000 movie camera and degrees from USC film school. They didn't need film. They didn't need commercial sponsors or an agent or a licensing or broadcast deal.[19] Just a cheap video camera, a computer, an internet connection, and a service that other people wanted.

## FINDING THE NEEDLE IN THE GLOBAL HAYSTACK

Way back in 1999, Rob McEwen, the CEO of Goldcorp—a gold mining company—attended a conference about the open-source Linux operating system. It gave him what the industry and his own geologists thought was a crazy idea. His company owned a mine in Canada that in theory held a lot of gold, but until that point the company hadn't been able to find much of it. McEwen decided to release on the internet all the company's confidential geological data about the mine—fifty years' worth of data. Rather than keep relying on its own geologists, the company issued the "Goldcorp challenge." It offered prize money totaling $575,000 to teams with the best proposals for where the company should search for gold. A panel of experts picked the top five proposals. Two of the five winning teams were from Australia, and one had never been to Canada or seen a gold mine.

It worked! Four of the five proposals have so far helped the firm strike gold.[20] The formerly small Canadian company now has assets of over $20 billion and more than fifteen thousand employees around the world.

Man has searched for and mined gold for thousands of years. Yet a company at the dawn of the twenty-first century can still tap into a major new seam and create new jobs for miners by harnessing a network to find the expert needle hiding in the global haystack.

Many traditional companies now use prizes and networks to

solve their toughest problems. It's true, as economist Ronald Coase argued, that firms can reduce transaction costs by internalizing some operations.[21] But it's also true, as Bill Joy once said, that "most of the smartest people work for someone else." And a smart crowd, properly networked and channeled, can often make discoveries that even a firm's smartest employees miss. In 2001, a team from the drug firm Eli Lilly launched InnoCentive, a "marketplace for minds."[22] The company offers cash rewards for solutions to tough engineering and science problems. Major corporations with thousands of employees in research and development, like Procter & Gamble, liberally use InnoCentive to tackle problems they can't handle in-house.

Colgate-Palmolive used an InnoCentive challenge to find a better way to get toothpaste in tubes. An engineer from Canada, Ed Melcarek, "proposed putting a positive charge on fluoride powder, then grounding the tube."[23] It only took him a few hours to think up. He won $25,000 for his effort. Notice how different this is from working with an internal research team. In the latter scenario, a corporate executive might try to find an expert who could later solve an unknown class of problems, and then hire that person. In an open challenge, the right expert "self-selects" the specific problem based on his or her knowledge and interest, and then solves it.

So far, there have been over 2,000 such challenges and more than 62,000 submitted solutions. Some 380,000 users from almost every country in the world are now registered with InnoCentive. Many have PhDs in a science-related field, but no official credentials are required to compete. Prestige and connections count for nothing. If a clever amateur or amateur team finds the solution, they can, and often do, beat established academic scientists at their own game.

We've only scratched the surface, but it should be clear: There have never been more chances to work with others, and to benefit from that work.

## The Myth of the Rugged Individualist

For the same reason, the third American Dream—the sharing and creating of value itself—belongs to the collaborators. As a virtue, collaboration is related to the virtues of humility, prudence, and altruism. Imagine a man, Jack, who is puffed up with false pride and so thinks he can do far more than he really can. That's not a formula for success. Humble and prudent Jill, in contrast, knows her gifts as well as her weaknesses. Prudence helps her see the world as it is, and act accordingly. So she focuses on what she can do best—her competitive advantage—and seeks partners for the rest. Tomorrow's economy favors the Jills, not the Jacks.

Then there's altruism. When we act altruistically, we help others and may also help ourselves. When we collaborate, we accept whatever good things others have to offer and happily work with them for our own or common ends. How is this a virtue? Because collaboration calls for humility and a willingness to learn from others. It requires you to embrace and exploit the fact that you depend on others for your life, your knowledge, your accomplishments, your prosperity, and, yes, your happiness. If you're a know-it-all who wants to be known as the smartest one in the room, this virtue will be a challenge.

Doesn't this violate the vision of the "rugged individualist" that for so many people epitomizes the American Dream? We imagine the late eighteenth and nineteenth centuries as a time when intrepid farmers, ranchers, and prospectors headed west. These were solitary pioneers who sought the proverbial gold ring. In the late nineteenth and early twentieth centuries, the rugged individualist often took the form of a railroad, industrial, or banking magnate: John D. Rockefeller, Henry Ford, Andrew Mellon, Andrew Carnegie, Cornelius Vanderbilt, or a banker such as J. P. Morgan. Today, we think of tech virtuosos such as Steve Jobs, Bill Gates, Larry Page, Sergey Brin, Jeff Bezos, and Mark Zuckerberg.

Part of the genius of the American Experiment is that it defends the individual against the tyranny of the state, the tribe, and the majority. But by itself, individual*ism* is unbalanced. Our old friend Ayn Rand, for instance, depicted the entrepreneur as a solitary being who strives to get ahead without reference to the needs of others. In this way, she channeled the American *myth of the rugged individualist.*

That's what it is: a myth. Most of those who migrated west were *families*, not lone cowboys. And even the cowboys worked in teams. When Alexis de Tocqueville visited America in the early nineteenth century, he hoped to learn its secrets. What he saw were not hermits and loners but groups of people who formed voluntary associations wherever they went, with almost no help from a far-off government. Read his *Democracy in America* and you get a sense of how communal Americans really were.

Surprised? You shouldn't be. We're social creatures. Even Robinson Crusoe needed the skills he'd gained from his childhood in York; the goods from his wrecked ship; his servant, Friday; and his pet parrot to survive on an island. No one can literally be self-made. We are born to and raised by parents (ideally). We live in neighborhoods and cities and countries, whose customs and cultures shape our habits and outlooks. We are taught by teachers. Even as adults, we need others: Long bouts of loneliness can wear down our bodies.[24]

Individualism can be a cartoon stereotype that overlooks the richness of human life. Its overwrought rhetoric matters, too, because it can lead some young people to flirt with socialism. They recoil at the myth of the rugged individualist and look for something more, well . . . social. Enter socialism, stage left. It sounds nice. It has the word "social" in it. But in the twentieth century, both socialism and its cousin fascism confused true society with a metastasized state. Italian dictator Benito Mussolini offered the most chilling formulation of the idea: "All within the state, nothing outside the state, nothing against the state."

But society does not equal the state. The state, in its proper place, is a creation of a society that keeps it in check. That's why the

American founders did not check despotism with anarchy. They established a "more perfect union": a constitutional republic that gave the central government certain enumerated powers and insisted all other powers be devolved to the states and the people. They also set up firewalls to keep those powers in check—through separate branches, a Bill of Rights, federalism, and so on.

As Lord Acton said, "Liberty . . . is the delicate fruit of a mature civilization." And it can only be sustained with constant vigilance. Unbalanced, utopian ideas always crop up at moments of great social change. Marxism emerged from the ferment of the Industrial Revolution in Europe. Just as Marx thought that a new order must emerge from the ashes of what he called "capitalism," writers now speak of the glories of "crowd-based capitalism," "the gift economy," "peer production," "the end of hierarchy," and "the eclipse of capitalism."[25] We read about the dawn of a hybrid economy that mixes sharing and commercial elements.[26] We see odes to "collectivism,"[27] "digital socialism," and the current favorite, the "sharing economy," which the experts say will replace capitalism in some utopian future. This *post-capitalist myth* sits in the opposite corner from our rugged individualist.

Much of the literature relies on false contrasts—"gift" versus "greed"—and on caricatures of the market economy debunked in the previous chapter. Far too much of it accepts the Randian stereotype of capitalism and then reacts to it, rather than asking if there's a third option.

Leaving aside these flaws, though, two key insights in this literature remain.

First, new technology creates vast new ways for people to exercise their creativity for fun, without a clear economic incentive. Just look at the rising ocean of free content at Creative Commons, Flickr, YouTube, Wikipedia, iTunes, and social media platforms like Facebook, Instagram, Pinterest, and Snapchat. Much of the content on these platforms is produced just for the heck of it. They are, in effect, hobbies amplified by networks.

Then there are the countless open-source projects like Apache, Linux, Wikipedia, Firefox, and Minecraft. These platforms generate economic value, but they are very hard to reduce to economic motives. It's foolish to assume that we do everything for financial gain. Not everything is about the bottom line. Creating value with others is often its own reward, perhaps because it's in our nature to do so.

Second, the literature on networked tech rightly highlights that innovations arise from groups, not lone individuals. The greatest inventions that we identify with geniuses usually emerge from creative communities. They build upon rather than sweep aside previous creations.

President Obama found the clumsiest possible way to make this point when he told a crowd of businesspeople during the 2012 presidential campaign, "If you've got a business, you didn't build that." Of course they did. But they could not have done so without the work of countless others who preceded them, and without a society of laws and institutions that made it possible. Steve Jobs on a desert island would surely have starved to death. Even today's best-known entrepreneurs have often had cofounders—Paul Allen and Bill Gates, Steve Jobs and Steve Wozniak, Larry Page and Sergey Brin. "No man is an island, / Entire of itself," wrote John Donne. "Every man is a piece of the continent, / A part of the main."

That's why the growth of ever richer and faster networks should make us sanguine about the many innovations still to come, rather than lead us to conclude that all the growth and invention are behind us.

All these technologies are disruptive, and many of them will make their inventors fabulously wealthy. But they also offer historic chances for regular people not only to serve others but to benefit from the work of others.

It might look like these prospects are limited to the digital world. But as we'll see in the next chapter, networks multiply the choices in the analog world of stuff as well.

# 8

## BE FRUITFUL

### CREATIVE FREEDOM IN AN AGE OF EVER MORE INFORMATION

Marcus and Kelly Daly met in the late 1990s while working for a landscaper in Seattle. Several years earlier, Marcus and his friend had bought and moved into what Marcus describes as "a dilapidated Korean grocery store with a Laundromat on the other side." They gradually remodeled it, an undertaking that allowed Marcus to pick up the basics of carpentry.

By the time Marcus and Kelly got married, though, their funky urban neighborhood began to look like a bad place to raise a family. "The hypodermic needles on the sidewalk went from being a concern to being a threat," he told me. Shortly before their second child was born (they now have eight), they hatched a plan to move to rural Vashon Island in the Puget Sound to do a bit of farming and build wooden boats to sell to the locals.

They found a mostly finished octagonal house with a simple workshop on five acres. But upon moving there in 2001, the Dalys quickly encountered hurdles. "I realized that it would take me at least two hundred hours to build one boat," Marcus said. Add the cost of materials, and he would have needed to charge $10,000 a boat to break even. Whatever the market on the island was for wooden boats, it was well below that price point. As a result, the couple spent their first few years as landscapers.

In 2003, Kelly had a miscarriage. She and Marcus wanted to find a way to dignify their loss, so Marcus decided to make a small casket himself—and the modest act brought some measure of healing.

Then, on April 2, 2005, Pope John Paul II died. During his televised funeral in Rome, Marcus noticed the pope's simple wooden casket, which stood out from the baroque grandeur of St. Peter's Basilica. The only decoration was on its cover: an inlaid Marian cross. That's a cross with an elongated right arm and a capital letter *M* underneath it to signify the presence of Mary, Jesus's mother, at his crucifixion.

John Paul II had touched both Marcus and Kelly at different times in their lives. When Marcus was "floundering" in his twenties, as he puts it, the pope inspired him to renew his faith. Later, in 2002, Kelly—along with Marcus—witnessed the elderly pope soldier through a grueling World Youth Day appearance in Toronto. He spoke boldly to hundreds of thousands of teenagers, even as he shook from advanced Parkinson's disease. The pope's courage stirred Kelly, who was not Catholic. She entered the Catholic Church the following Easter.

From these seeds, an idea started to grow. "I found out that because of a 1995 ruling by the FTC, anyone could build a casket," Marcus explained to me. The rule allows customers, in a highly regulated industry, to shop around and supply their own caskets.[1] It was designed to give some control to grieving customers of funeral services, who, because of a lack of experience, often spend too much. Marcus realized he could build wooden caskets without traversing the regulatory briar patch that often ensnares small businesses.

Marcus now spends most of his days in the workshop next to his house, building wooden "Marian caskets" much like the one John Paul II was buried in. They come in either oak or pine, with an inlayed Marian cross, and an option to add carved text drawn from the Divine Mercy prayer on the sides ("Holy God, Holy Mighty One, Holy Immortal One, have mercy on me"). On the high end is the Divine Mercy Oak for $2,350, or Divine Mercy Pine, for $1,950. Kelly lines the caskets with simple muslin fabric and makes a small matching pillow stuffed with straw, since Jesus was born in a stable. The result is a rustic simplicity that contrasts with the glossy caskets common in most American funerals.

Funeral services are expensive, and a casket is often the costliest item. Still, you can buy fancy, polished, wood-and-metal, plush satin-lined caskets for around $2,000 online. So why would someone spend more on a simple, handmade one? Why is there a market for Marian Caskets? Won't a robot factory soon make Marcus Daly's work obsolete?

No. Because his customers aren't buying a commodity.

If I want a tank of gas, and every gas station around is the same except for price, I'll go for the lowest price. But man does not live by price—or commodity purchases—alone. If we did, we would just bury loved ones in cheap body bags. People buy caskets because they want to honor their loved ones' remains and respect their memories. That's why, even if the government offered a free cardboard coffin, few families would use one. People prefer not to be exploited in their hour of need, but they also want a dignified funeral and burial.

Marian caskets appeal to devout Catholics not because they're a bargain but because their unique, handmade form resonates with Christian beliefs like the uniqueness of every person, the value of the body, the devotion to the Divine Mercy prayer, the memory of a beloved pope, and the livelihood of Jesus, a humble carpenter.

Yet Marcus did not always see all this as the unique appeal of his caskets. "How did you market your caskets when you first started?" I asked, figuring he had planned to cater to like-minded Catholics.

"I was very naïve about the business side of things," he confessed. "I thought that wooden, handmade caskets would tap into the growing interest in natural, sustainable products, especially in the Northwest. I didn't realize that most secular environmentalists weren't that interested in traditional burials. They were much more likely to go for cremation."

"But what about the Divine Mercy prayer?" I asked. "Doesn't that make your caskets appealing to Catholics?"

"Actually, we didn't start putting the prayer on caskets until 2011," he admitted. And only later did the Dalys change the name of their business from Vashon Island Coffins to Marian Caskets.

"So what percentage of your customer base is Catholic?"

"I'd say about 99 percent."

Seems obvious after the fact, but Marcus Daly stumbled on a key selling point of his product through trial and error.

This, in a nutshell, is why robots will *never* replace all human labor. For some things, we value the fact that they are handmade, that the supply is limited, that each one differs slightly from the other. For some goods, as labor has become rare, it has become not simply an input—that is, a cost—but an output. The proof: We freely pay *more* for variable and man-made than for standardized and machine-made. In the age to come, such goods won't cease to exist. They'll have a vastly expanded market. Those who find ways to create value in these ways will prosper.


## Options, Options, and More Options

The unique value of human creativity is obvious when it comes to handmade caskets with inlaid prayer text. But the unsung heroes of this economic shift are networks, which allow the personal touch to find its way into the nooks and crannies of global markets. Take a trivial example. Right now, I can go on eBay and buy any conceivable kind of silk tie for about six dollars. I have 47,941 choices. These ties are machine-made in garment factories in China. I could wear one to a meeting and none would be the wiser. But I never buy these ties. Instead, I search for ties that are new without tags or pre-owned but pristine, such as Charvet ties made by hand in France.

Even at a discount, these ties may cost ten times more than the ties from China. Am I irrational to search for and buy them? And what about the men who buy Charvet ties at Neiman Marcus for—gulp—$245? Are they crazy? Maybe. But clearly there's a market for such ties or they wouldn't exist.

Why the market? Well, some men notice the subtle differences between the Chinese factory-made ties and European handmade ones, just as some people discern oaky or pomegranate undertones in a glass of wine. A high-end tie brand like Charvet signifies quality. And since they're handmade, their supply is limited. Until recently, to get one of these ties, you had to either go to the store in Paris—at 25 place Vendôme, in the 1st arrondissement—or drop a load of cash at one of the few authorized retailers, such as Neiman Marcus.

That is, until eBay created a global aftermarket for them. Thousands of small merchants can find the ties and sell them to picky professors who can't afford $245 ties but are happy to nab them a few months after they come out for far less money. This is another example of what a hyper-connected market affords. Mastering the handmade tie market takes a lot of fashion fussiness, so it sits way out on the long tail of the tie market. In another age, it would have sat so far out there it would have been lost. But eBay has taken a highly specialized, narrow market, and opened it up to anyone with an internet connection. There are artisan-tie merchants who owe their livelihoods to eBay shining a light that far out on the long tail of commerce. It has also opened the supply of mass-produced ties with "Made in China" tags to the 99 percent of humanity who couldn't care less about fancy French cravats.

Think again about the Dalys' enterprise. The market for Marian Caskets on Vashon Island (population 10,000) is niche almost to the point of vanishing. In 2015, the island was reported to be the most liberal place in the country.[2] My family and I lived there in 2013, and I would guess that the number of daily pot smokers on Vashon exceeds the number of churchgoers—let alone Catholics. Marian Caskets would gather moss if limited to the island. Happily, the internet has expanded the market to the lower forty-eight states. Even though Marcus and Kelly have barely tapped into that market, this development has allowed them to turn their micro-niche product into a real business.

Etsy, the online platform for handmade and vintage products, is another example of this new kind of market. Headquartered in gentrified Brooklyn, Etsy exudes a hipster, locavore aesthetic and culture. Its founder, Rob Kalin, referred to it early on as "an anarchist artist collective." Others have waxed eloquent about the platform as a "post-capitalist workplace."[3]

By whatever name, Etsy shows how technology can vastly expand rather than destroy the market for handmade and artisanal goods. As Amy Larocca puts it in *New York Magazine*, "Some people like to make things, other people like to buy things that others have made, and now, thanks to the internet, these people could be brought seamlessly together . . ."[4] Mr. Local, meet Ms. Global. Etsy not only links small artisans to a global market—in 2016 there were 1.6 million sellers and some 24 million buyers—it practically erases their start-up costs. Etsy gets 20 cents for every item listed as well as a 3.5 percent cut on transactions. In exchange, Etsy connects the Spanish maker of a silver-plated "Octopus Tentacle Septum Nose Ring"[5] to the five customers in Portland, Oregon, who want it.

Brooklyn's Etsy now has stiff competition from Seattle. In 2015, Amazon got in on the action with its virtual storefront called

Handmade at Amazon. Who knows how this will wash out? But the safe bet is that the market for handmade goods will grow, not shrink.

Ditto for small-scale agriculture. In the past century, small farming could rarely compete with giant industrial farming. This process came at a cost: hundreds of thousands of smaller family farms. Still, it helped all of us over the long term. We got more food at much lower prices, and more time and resources for other pursuits beyond famine prevention.

What no one expected is that as the price of food dropped, the desire for organic, locally grown products would reemerge, first as niche luxury items and then as more widely enjoyed indulgences. Necessity no longer compels most of us to engage in farm labor, the backbone of the first American Dream. Yet these endeavors have reemerged for moral and aesthetic reasons. Whatever the merits of this, the market for such farm goods will surely grow rather than shrink for two reasons. First, some folks will pay a lot of money for it. And second, technology makes it easier to match sellers to buyers. The burgeoning market for micro-brewed beers, grass-fed beef, pampered pork, free-range chickens, specialty cheeses, small-batch whiskey, urban gardens, and locavore farmers' markets is proof.

Yes, twenty years from now, upper-middle-class Americans may have robot housekeepers. Machines may handle most farming, trucking, factory work, and hazardous mining. But here's a prediction: As many goods and services become nearly free, the monetary value of the unique human touch will go up. Our economy will be filled not just with artisanal goods but artisanal *services*. Personal butlers, footmen, housekeepers, chefs, gardeners, midwives, nannies, personal assistants, tutors, and athletic trainers will become high-paid employees for the wealthier among us. I for one would much prefer a human nanny for my future grandchildren. But they might have to settle for a robot.

Long story short, the whole world will not be converted to bits. Don't despair at the thought that all handmade goods and human services will disappear into the ravenous jaws of robot factories. Prepare.

## "The Long Tail of Stuff" and the Commodification Myth

In fact, the options are already expanding beyond mass-produced on one end and handmade on the other. For over a century, farms and factories became bigger and more centralized to exploit greater economies of scale. There are huge start-up costs to build, say, a book printing shop, and the setup of a new book for offset printing is also costly. These costs are fixed, whether you print one or a million copies of a book. So the more copies printed, the more the start-up costs can be amortized over the print run.

Let's say you have a print shop, and it costs you $10,000 to set up for a new book and $1 for paper and ink for each book. If you only print one copy, all the start-up costs must be recovered in that one copy. So you'd need to make $10,001 on that book to cover costs, which makes no economic sense. If you print five hundred copies it will cost you $10,500. You'd need to make $21 per book to cover costs, which is still too high. If you print ten thousand copies, though, it will cost you $20,000. Now the printing cost per book is a mere $2. If you sell all ten thousand copies for $20, you'll make a nice profit. So the more copies, the more spread out the start-up costs will be, and the smaller the marginal cost of each additional copy. That's an economy of scale. The same logic works for cars, toasters, underwear, men's suits, airplanes, Cabbage Patch dolls, and whatever else can be manufactured.

For the same reason, a mass-produced men's suit will be much cheaper than a bespoke suit with every swath tailored to the body of one man. The trade-off is that factory-made suits will be sized for the average man—the crowded middle part of the bell curve of the market, not its ever-narrowing long tails. The five-foot-ten-inch fellow with a forty-inch chest and thirty-six-inch waist is built for factory-made suits. A six-foot-five-inch bodybuilder with a forty-eight-inch chest and thirty-two-inch waist will look ridiculous in an off-the-rack suit. Mass production means standardization. "You can have any color you want," promised Henry Ford about the Model T, "as long as it's black."

False prophets have warned for decades of a dystopian future where the whole world is homogenized, standardized, and mass-produced in sweatshops. Let's call it the *commodification myth*. None of these ersatz sages foresaw the demand for specialty goods we mentioned above, or DIY manufacturing that is just now arriving onstage. Between big, automated manufacturing on the one hand and boutique, handmade crafts on the other, there's now a growing movement of small-batch manufacturing. The rise of 3-D printing and scanning, laser cutting, CNC milling, and the like gives us a glimpse of what *Harvard Business Review* in 2013 called the "designed by me" era.[6]

Three-dimensional printing, which comes in many forms, is "additive" fabrication: Tiny pieces or layers are added a little at a time. This contrasts with subtractive manufacturing in which tools are used to remove material such as wood or metal. Just as a regular printer is used to print 2-D text or pictures on paper, 3-D printers convert a CAD (computer-aided design) file into a 3-D object. A 3-D scanner does the same job as the text scanner built into many of our home printers, except the scan is of a three-dimensional object. The scan is then converted into a digital file you can manipulate on a computer screen and then fabricate on a 3-D printer. The scanner, computer, and printer may be in the same room or in countries thousands of miles apart.[7]

Until recently, these tools were the domain of tinkerers, hobbyists, and inventors. They're a bit like the Homebrew Computer Clubs in the 1970s, when techy nerds were transfixed by computers while everyone else played Frisbee. The fact that boosters still use the term "maker movement" is a sign that it's not yet mainstream. (Nobody talks about the "smartphone movement.")

That said, my sense is that small-scale manufacturing is past the Homebrew stage and into the Apple II stage, when computers became friendly to the masses. Hundreds of thousands of people now attend Maker Faire conferences around the world every year. Good 3-D printers that use ABS plastic can be had for less than the cost of a personal computer: from $500 on the low end, to $2,500 for the MakerBot Replicator 2X. If anything like Moore's law is at play with these tools—and it is—expect them to get much better, higher resolution, faster, easier to use, and cheaper in the next decade.

That doesn't mean that large-scale manufacturing (and farming) will go the way of the dodo bird. After all, 3-D printers, CNC routers, and the like are all used in factories, which still enjoy scale advantages for many goods and batch sizes. The current Tesla factory uses these devices. The gigafactory the car company is building in the Nevada desert will have many more. Architects and engineers in large and small firms have used 3-D printers and CNC routers for years to create simple models and prototypes to test their designs before moving to large-scale production.

Right now, it's as hard to predict how these tools will change society as it was to imagine the future uses of computers and networks in the late 1960s. In 1969, the major computer companies put their heads together and tried to guess what a home computer would be used for. "The most common prediction," notes Chris Anderson, "was that it would be used for recipe-card management."[8] There's that future-blindness again.

Here are two safe bets, though, based on what we already know: (1) There will be far more small-scale manufacturing on the periphery for more and more niche markets. And (2) the gap between inventor and entrepreneur will shrink. This will allow far more people in far more places to create not just digital files but material goods for use, for sale, and for fun.

To make a million standard-issue cars, you still want big, robot-filled factories to keep costs down. That's why mass production won't disappear, especially since robotics is still in its infancy. Instead, we should expect more and different kinds of manufacturing at different size scales. To make two or ten or a hundred cuff links for quirky or astute buyers, DIY manufacturing beats mass production. There's no setup cost, no complex supply chain to manage, no union to haggle with, no need to hire engineers and machinists to construct injection molders and program a platoon of pick-and-place robotic arms. The only thing a 3-D printer needs to do its job is a digital file to tell it what to build. It's optimized for variety rather than standardization, for unique one-offs, customized products, and small batches. Designs are modified on a screen, so costly machines don't need to be retooled or refitted.

In his excellent book *Makers*, Chris Anderson refers to this small-scale production as "the dark matter in the marketplace—the Long Tail of Stuff."[9] The internet and search engines have already solved the riddle of how to find and market products that appeal to a smattering of consumers spread far and wide: small-farm organic foods, hand-carved Marian caskets, pristine but pre-owned Charvet ties—on and on the list goes, and grows faster than we can track.

Most people are not yet aware of this. I know only one family with a 3-D printer. The United States may reach the tipping point next week, or next year, when someone will find the killer app for DIY manufacturing and every Tom, Dick, and Harry will want in on the action. But we will reach it. Expect the "digital natives" who have grown up with smartphones and touch screens to lead the way.

This is good news. We can't all start a profitable YouTube channel or build a best-selling app. Besides, for the most part, we still live in the world of stuff. We have bodies, live in houses, drive cars, and eat food. Any economy limited to the world of bits would be unfit for us.

The phrase "information economy" can sound bloodless: emails, video games, websites, and Facebook news feeds, a realm in which "software is eating the world," as tech venture capitalist Marc Andreessen put it in 2011.[10] Many tech writers portray it as all about "converting atoms to bits"—a metaphor I've used as well. But that's only part of the story. Picture, instead, an ever-widening landscape where we convert atoms to bits, and vice versa. It's a place where we make the material world around us ever more meaningful and connected. (See the endnotes for more details about how to tap into this new world.)[11]

In this new realm, Marcus Daly draws on the know-how he developed over years of hard work. He saws and carves and sands a niche casket from wooden planks, and markets it over a stable channel to the world. A networked group of coders uses tools created by others to design a CAD file for metal jewelry. They then upload it to Thingiverse (Thingiverse.com). A jeweler in California searches and finds the file at Thingiverse. He modifies it and then uses it to print his own unique jewelry using a fabricator created by still others. And so it goes, billions of times every day, as little creators freely share, modify, and transform an ever more information-rich world.

To really see why this does not portend a future where robots will replace us, it helps to know what information is, where it comes from, and why it matters for us in the material world.

## What Is Information?

"Everyone thinks he knows what information is," tech guru George Gilder wryly observes. We use the word every day. Try to define it, though, and it slips through your fingers. "Information is what we know. Information is change in what we know. Information is how we communicate," Gilder writes, and he's just getting warmed up:

> Information is on the Internet. It is growing exponentially. It is data or messages or media or music or money or recipes or websites or pixels or packets. It is memory. It is imagination. Information is in the cloud. It is in the air. It is weather or *Weltanschauung* or winks across a room. It is shrugging shoulders or pointing fingers. It is bits and words and bytes and gigabytes and zettabytes. It flips and flops, on and off, everything and nothing.[12]

Gilder sums up the problem: "Through the middle of the twentieth century, scientists could describe information no more definitively than they could define matter."[13] To grasp our economy and the difference between man and machine, however, we need to define it.

Let's start at the beginning. The noun "information" comes from the Latin verb *informare*, which means to instruct or train in some subject. The Greek words for "form" included *morphe*, which refers to the shape of something, and *eidos*, from which we get the English word "idea."

For the Greek philosophers Plato and Aristotle, the *eidos* referred to the essence of a thing—*what* it is, its nature or form. They illustrated what they meant with a marble statue. Michelangelo takes a lump of marble and forms it into the shape of a man, David. The sculptor has the idea, the form, of the statue in his mind, and then in-forms a block of marble with that idea. The result is a statue rather than a nondescript lump of marble. In a similar way, the cheetah is, well, a cheetah, rather than just a lump of atoms. And you are, in essence, a human being, rather than merely a sack of water and cells.

All of this mental furniture hides in the shadows. But the concept of information took on a more technical sense in the mid-twentieth century with the work of American engineer Claude Shannon. Standing on the shoulders of intellectual giants such as Kurt Gödel, John von Neumann, and Alan Turing, Shannon developed the core concepts of what is now called information theory. His work is built into the very bowels of our computer and communications technology.

The details of Shannon's work are complex and, frankly, confusing. If you want to dive deeper, see the endnotes.[14] But his basic insight is that information is . . . surprise. We can determine the information content of a communication by the amount of "surprisal" it contains. If I ask you to guess heads or tails, and then flip a coin, and it comes up heads, you will have one bit of information—

not much, since little surprise is resolved. You knew it would be either heads or tails.

On the other hand, ten flips and ten results will have far more information in Shannon's sense. I just flipped a nickel ten times and got: tails, heads, heads, heads, heads, heads, heads, heads, tails, heads. That's surprising. There's little chance you could have guessed that ahead of time. It looks like too many heads, right? If I'd tried to make up the sequence, I would have distributed the heads and tails more evenly.

Information is what could not have been predicted with certainty beforehand, like that sequence of coin flips. If I tell you what you already know, I haven't given you any new information. Information is *news*.

## THE VALUE AND LIMITS OF SHANNON'S ACCOUNT OF INFORMATION

It makes sense that Claude Shannon would settle on his way of describing information. Bell Labs, where Shannon worked, sought to improve the way messages were sent over channels, such as phone lines or radio transmissions. Bell Labs is named after the inventor of the telephone, Alexander Graham Bell. Its parent company, AT&T, is the acronym for American Telegraph & Telephone. Shannon wanted a way to quantify a communication from the perspective of the carrier. His formulation allowed that.

Think of information as a choice between alternatives: yes or no; 0 or 1, on or off. The answer to one such binary choice contains one bit (short for "binary digit")—the basic unit by which we measure the amount of information in a signal. The more choices combined in a string, the more bits.

Shannon studied how best to transmit messages across a channel and to overcome the problem of noise. "In Shannon's scheme," George Gilder explains, "a source selects a message from a portfolio of possible messages, encodes it by resorting to a dictionary or lookup table using a specified alphabet, and then transcribes the encoded message into a form that can be transmitted down a channel. Afflicting that channel is always some level of noise or interference. At the destination, the receiver decodes the message, translating back into its original form."[15]

So there's a predictable, orderly channel, such as an electromagnetic wave at a specific radio frequency. A station modulates the radio wave—think of it as imprinting it with a barcode—and transmits it through the air to a radio receiver, which then demodulates the signal. This is only possible because the wavelength of the wave hasn't changed from one end to the other. The channel is simple and predictable, and so it can carry a complex and unpredictable message. If a radio wavelength varied randomly, it would be noisy and useless. Communication requires that the receiver be able to distinguish the signal from the channel and that the noise doesn't blot out the signal.

Change in the signal itself is noise or interference. You want to keep noise to a minimum to best preserve the message a channel carries. Note, however, that the *meaning* of the message from sender to receiver is of no interest to the telephone engineer. He can just define information in terms of surprise, in terms of the amount of uncertainty resolved, and be done with it.[16]

That's an obvious drawback: Shannon's definition does not distinguish mere randomness from *meaningful* sequences in written or transmitted messages.[17] Both the typing monkey and Shakespeare writing *Hamlet* will generate scads of information. "Shannon information," then, doesn't pick out what we normally mean when we talk about information.

## Information as Meaning

Shannon got us well down the road by showing us how to quantify sequences of discrete symbols in terms of bits. This was a historic breakthrough. For the first time, we had a way to *measure* information along one dimension, to capture the immaterial in the material. Every time we refer to the storage capacity of our hard drive or smartphone or the speed of our Wi-Fi or landline, we pay homage to him.

Shannon gave us a powerful new spotlight, if you will. But meaningful information is a much vaster landscape than can be illumined in that small circle of light. To see why this matters for the third American Dream, we need to grab a bright torch and explore outside the circle. It helps if we look at information from several angles.

Information is like movement from a sea of unrealized possibilities to one concrete reality. Let's say you take an old friend you haven't seen in years out for lunch. There are twenty items on the menu—shrimp étouffée, a nine-ounce filet mignon, Parmesan-crusted sole, lobster bisque, a handful of other main dishes, and then half a dozen dessert options. Those options are the range of uncertainty. You have no idea what your long-lost friend prefers. It's equally likely from your perspective that he would pick any item on the menu. He picks the pricey filet mignon, the expensive lobster bisque, and the Baked Alaska—the costliest dessert on the menu—since you're paying. Surprise! You now know far more than you did before your friend ordered. That's information—which, alas, would have been nice to have had before you picked the restaurant.[18]

Information is also about specificity. If a woman tells her doctor that she wakes up in the middle of the night, and the doctor says, "That must be frustrating," she's received no information. If he says, "That sounds like a physiological response," she still hasn't gotten much. If he says, "That sounds like a hormonal response," she's gotten more info. If he does blood work and a sleep test and then tells her, "You're going through perimenopause, your estrogen levels are dropping, and that's causing you to wake up in the middle of the night," she's gotten a lot more information.

We're zeroing in on what information is. To fully understand it, though, we need to distinguish simple order on the one hand, complexity on the other hand, and meaning on still another. (Sorry, we need three hands for this.) Think of the order—the simplicity—of a repeating set of numbers or letters: 1111111111 or ABABABABABAB.[19] Those sequences contain very little information or complexity. To speak in the language of software, they're highly "compressible." That is, we could produce them over and over with a simple instruction: "type '1' and repeat" in the first case, "type 'AB' and repeat" in the second.

The literal opposite of such order is chaos, like that random sequence of coin flips. Chaos is a type of complexity. There's no way to compress a random sequence with a simple rule. Ditto for a random sequence of dots and dashes. It has far more "information" in Shannon's terms than a simple, repeating signal of dots of the same length. But if you were a telegraph operator who had just listened to that long string of random dots and dashes, you wouldn't feel any the wiser. You wouldn't feel more *informed*. What else do we need to capture what we mean by "information"?

What we need is meaning itself. The difference between a random sequence—which is merely complex—and a genuine message is that the latter conforms to a meaningful pattern. Take this message: "I'll see you when I get home tonight at 7:15. No need to go to the store. I already bought the beer." The message is in English. The letters form words. The words have specific meanings. And the order of the words conforms to the rules of English grammar and syntax. The sequence carries a meaning not present in the letters themselves. A message contains not only Shannon information but what we can call "complex *specified* information" or "*specified* complexity."

That's a lot to swallow, so let's refer to sequences of complex specified information as simply *messages*. (Information goes far beyond mere strings of letters and numbers, but let's take this one step at a time.)

The information in messages is not simple and repetitive. Nor is it merely complex and random. It's a third thing, a tertium quid. And it's information in this sense that matters.[20] Not random dots and dashes. Not a nondescript lump of marble. *Meaning*. Unless we add that missing third ingredient—meaning—to the recipe for information, the pie won't bake.

Two final points: First, information channels and transforms and releases the possibilities of matter.[21] *But information is not a physical object alongside other objects.* MIT mathematician Norbert Wiener, whose own work on information was overshadowed by Shannon's, put the matter bluntly in 1948, the year Shannon wrote his famous paper on the subject. "Information is information, not matter or energy," he wrote. "No materialism that does not admit this can survive at the present day."[22]

Which brings us to a final, related point: Meaningful information is always associated with *conscious minds*. The "creation of new information," discerned information theorist Henry Quastler, "is habitually associated with conscious activity."[23]

Indeed, agents acting for a purpose are the *only* known source of such information.[24] *Here*, then, is the payoff. When we talk about the wonders of the information economy, we're not talking about our ability to send random symbols through the air and across fibers of glass. Our vast and connected infosphere is not populated by armies of typing monkeys. Its promise is that it allows us to create, share, mix, recombine, and store more and more meaningful goods and services more easily, more quickly, and more cheaply. An information economy, then, is not an economy where mindless machines take over. It's an economy shaped by and fitted for us. It's an economy where human minds, creativity, and freedom predominate. It's an economy where we purposefully in-form the material and social world in more and more elaborate ways.

We won't become obsolete in the future. We'll be essential—as long as we focus on what only humans can do. Only we can *create* meaningful information of value to others. To do that, we must exercise creative freedom.

## SELF-MASTERY: THE TRUE FREEDOM

Our emerging economy and the third American Dream are optimized for those who exercise the virtue of creative freedom.

Wait—what? How is that a virtue? Haven't I said all along that, unlike machines and brutes, we are *by nature* free to do what we choose with our time, skills, and resources? Here we need a few key distinctions. These will help us better identify what *kind* of freedom gets rewarded in our economy.

We all enjoy a minimal type of freedom, called freedom of indifference. That means that it's up to you whether you eat chocolate, vanilla, or strawberry ice cream. You are also free not to eat ice cream. Or your vegetables. Neither the federal government nor the laws of physics compel you one way or the other.

As Americans, we also enjoy plenty of political freedom. Few of us fear that government agents or marauding bandits will kidnap us in the middle of the night. For the most part, government doesn't dictate where we live, the career we pursue, or the church we attend. We enjoy, in short, a wide measure of autonomy and freedom from undue coercion.

This is as far as some people go in thinking about freedom. They imagine that freedom just means getting to do what we want to do—as all children, some libertarians, and at least one Supreme Court justice believe. "At the heart of liberty," opined Justice Anthony Kennedy in one majority opinion, "is the right to define one's own concept of existence, of meaning, of the universe, and of the mystery of human life." If I get to smoke pot whenever I want and have sex with whomever I want and run naked wherever I want and pretend I'm

Napoleon to whomever I want—if I can "live without limits," as the inhabitants of HBO's *Westworld* put it—then I'm free.

But this confuses liberty with libertinism. Let's call it the *libertine myth*. In that sense of the word "freedom," the zombies in *The Walking Dead* are free, provided they don't run into one of the healthy people still able to defend themselves. Most of the time, those zombies pretty much do what they want, when they want. And yet, somehow, that ain't livin', is it?

What's needed for true freedom is the virtue of *self-mastery*.

Think of a little girl who has never touched a piano. She doesn't know the difference between middle C and the Dead Sea. She can sit down at her family piano and plunk on the keys as long as she wants. So she's "free" in a narrow sense. But is she free to *play the piano*, to play Mozart or Liszt or Rachmaninoff? Of course not. She can't read or play music at all. She's a slave to her ignorance and clumsy fingers. Why? Because she hasn't submitted to years of disciplined practice. She hasn't gotten the rules for excellent piano playing into her mind, her fingers, and her bones. Only after such disciplined self-restraint of mind and body will she be truly free to play the piano. Only then can she exercise creative freedom.

That's the kind of freedom I'm talking about. I'm also talking about my older daughter, who is seventeen as I write this and has just learned to play Rachmaninoff's daunting Prelude in C-sharp Minor. Ten years of hard work stood between the little girl with butterfingers and the pianist she is now. She is now free to play the piano, and has just reached the point where she can not only perform music but *create* it.

The set of note sequences is a vast, meaningless expanse of potentiality. To exercise true creative freedom a pianist must extract music from a cacophony of noise, just as Michelangelo had to extract his *David* from a nondescript lump of marble. Or, to put it another way, Michelangelo had to exercise his creative freedom to inform the marble, transforming it into his famous statue.[25]

"Creativity loves constraints," said the American architect and designer Frank Lloyd Wright. The same is true in art, poetry, music, literature, sports, software programming, engineering, and every other human pursuit. Unfortunately, this lesson comes hard to us, because we so often use "freedom" to mean almost its opposite. "The counterfeit of freedom," writes Princeton professor Robert George, "consists in the idea of personal and communal liberation from morality, responsibility, and truth. It is what our nation's founders expressly distinguished from liberty and condemned as 'license.'"[26]

The English writer Theodore Dalrymple makes the same point in an essay called "Your Limits Are Your Freedom":

> The sages of Israel, like the wisest men and women in all cultures—from Socrates to the Buddha, from Jesus to Gandhi—recognized that the most dehumanizing form of slavery is slavery to the self, to its wayward wants and desires. That is why . . . the true teachers of mankind have proclaimed that the highest—and, alas, rarest—form of freedom is the freedom of self-possession, self-discipline: in a word, self-mastery. The free man, whatever his external circumstances, possesses the inner strength to guide his life, and harness his passions, by the reins of reason and faith.[27]

Information, we've seen, is ultimately about finding—or rather *creating*—islands of meaning in the sea of mere potential. It's about the exercise of creative freedom. At every economic stage of development, there are chances to exercise this virtue. For most of human history, however, such chances were few. For people who worked the land as subsistence or tenant farmers, to pick up and move elsewhere was at best a distant dream. My ancestors who first crossed the Atlantic Ocean for the New World hoped for a single new option that they didn't have in the Old World: to own their own farm. My paternal grandfather (born in 1899) lived his entire adult life in twentieth-century America. He had, at best, only a few choices, all tied to farming.

Despite all the challenges ahead—and we'll explore these in detail in the next section—we have far more ways to make a living than we could ever explore in a lifetime. You, right now, can study almost any subject from your home. And there have never been so many diverse, useful things to learn as there are at this moment. There will be more to do, and more to know, tomorrow, and the next day, and the day after that. You must simply be willing to constrain yourself in the right ways—in ways that allow you to create new value with and for others. That's why creative freedom—when it channels courage, antifragility, altruism, and collaboration—is the ultimate virtue for the new American Dream.

And as we'll see, these virtues not only allow us to create value for others. They allow us to pursue, and achieve, happiness—as individuals, as communities, and as a country.

# PART III

## HOW TO PURSUE HAPPINESS

# 9

## BLESSED BE

### Happiness and How to Pursue It

The American Dream has always been about the prospect of a happy life for everyday people. We all want to be happy, yet we know that happiness should not be taken for granted. Thomas Jefferson would not have bothered to write in the Declaration of Independence that man has the right to "the pursuit of happiness" if such a pursuit were guaranteed everywhere. And in fact, at the time, his words were literally revolutionary—and it took more than a century for them to be applied to all Americans. Still, to judge by the millions who have left their native homes to come here over the last two and a half centuries, Jefferson's words must resonate.

What is this pursuit of happiness? And is it a good thing? One British writer, Ruth Whippman, moved to California a few years ago when her husband got a job with a software start-up. After several months she concluded that Americans, unlike Britons, are obsessed with happiness—and *it's making us miserable.*

Yankees, to say nothing of Californians, are always suckers

for the next big happiness gimmick: meditation, crystals, yoga, self-help books, mindfulness exercises, empowerment, keeping a "gratitude journal," attending weekend seminars with names like "Unleash the Power Within." And yet, to judge by studies, Americans don't seem, on balance, much happier now than we were in 1972, when the studies began.

If you spend too much time thinking about your happiness, it can backfire and make you anxious instead. There are even a couple of studies by Cal Berkeley psychologists that suggest as much. "The higher the respondents rated happiness as a distinct personal ambition," Whippman explains, describing the studies, "the less happy they were in their lives generally and the more likely they were to experience symptoms of dissatisfaction and even depression."[1]

In 2016, she wrote a book about this American problem of seeking happiness, called *America the Anxious*.[2] Millions of Americans *are* anxious—about jobs, prosperity, and health. Much of this may be left over from the 2008 financial crisis, rather than a clear assessment of historical norms, but it's real nonetheless. For the first time in history, most Americans expect their children to be worse off than they are.[3]

Whippman also has a point about the pursuit of happiness itself. To obsess on one's happiness doesn't seem like a good plan. But notice that Thomas Jefferson never commended *that*. The Declaration of Independence doesn't even mention a right to happiness. It's a right to the *pursuit* of happiness the American founders hoped to guarantee. It doesn't follow that the best way to do that is to focus on happiness itself.

Indeed, that's never been what the American Dream meant. That Dream has always been wrapped up in the idea that there's something worthwhile in pursuing, in striving for, and in earning something you could be proud of. That's the fruit of hard work and virtue, not weekend seminars on How to Release Your Inner Happy Clown.

So let's step back and tie some threads together. If the American

Dream is about the pursuit of happiness, and if it takes certain virtues to achieve the Dream, what do those virtues have to do with happiness? Is it just that the virtues get us to the proverbial pot of gold? Surely there's more to it than that.

These questions take us into deeper waters. We talk about how best to pursue happiness, and we are constantly evaluating whether we're happy with our own lives. But what *is* happiness in the first place? What does it mean to pursue it? And as we've just seen, happiness may not be best achieved by aiming for it but by aiming for something else, one of whose fruits is happiness.

Economist and happiness expert Arthur Brooks notes that the word "happiness" is used for three distinct ideas: "fleeting feelings of happiness," "happiness on balance," and a "moral quality of life."[4] We've all experienced the passing sensation of joy or pleasure— maybe when we see a sunrise or win an award or fall in love. But transient surges of joy do not happiness make.

Happiness on balance, Brooks explains, is "the emotional balance sheet we keep that allows us to tell honestly whether we are living, all things considered, a happy life." It is a life with "more joy than sorrow in it."[5] This is what surveys and studies on happiness try to capture. It's the self-perception people have of whether they are happy overall. When we say we "just want to be happy," or tell our children we want them to be happy, we probably mean something like this.

"What these surveys capture is something like 'contentedness,'" Brooks told me at a recent dinner meeting. Let's call this "psychological happiness."

Our long-term psychological state is part of the story of happiness, but there's more to it. Here is where the third definition of happiness comes in: "a moral quality of life." This refers to the ancient and classical definition of happiness. It's what the ancient Greek philosopher Aristotle called *eudaemonia,* literally "good spirit." For Aristotle, eudaemonia is "an activity of the soul expressing virtue." The happy life, for him and others, is the virtuous life.

This meaning has mostly dropped out of our modern treatment of happiness. That may be because we imagine that one could live a life of both virtue and misery. We might admire a person like Saint Teresa of Ávila, who was virtuous and holy but suffered pain and illness her entire life. We would not wish such a life for our children.[6]

In any case, virtue plus misery is not what Aristotle had in mind. The Stoics, the Buddha, and Socrates advised a life of detachment as a way to endure what might otherwise cause suffering. But eudaemonia for Aristotle is a package deal. It includes virtue (*arête*), health, prosperity, a good reputation, and the other goods we hope for ourselves and our children. As Aristotle says in his *Nicomachean Ethics*, "He is happy who lives in accordance with complete virtue and is sufficiently equipped with external goods, not for some chance period but throughout a complete life."[7] Virtue is necessary for a happy life, but it's not sufficient.

No need to do a deep dive into ancient Greek thought. The main point is that true happiness is more than a state of mind. It's not just having more pleasant than unpleasant experiences day to day. Many of the characters in Aldous Huxley's *Brave New World* enjoy life. They are free from want, have lots of sex, and take a pill, Soma, that keeps them all nice and chipper. But for all that, *Brave New World* is known as a dystopian novel every bit as much as George Orwell's *1984*. Huxley's book disturbed my older daughter far more than Orwell's did, perhaps because so many of its prophecies have come true.

But what if we could create our own illusions? Would we be happy? The play *The Nether* by Jennifer Haley depicts a future in which the internet has evolved into vast virtual realms. Men and women live and play out their darkest fantasies in an imaginary world of their own making. This includes a region called the Hideaway where pedophiles can enjoy what would get them locked up in the real world. (Sounds more like a prediction than science fiction, right?) Does all that sound like happiness? That queasiness in your stomach is your sense that such a future is not one we should wish for our enemies, let alone our children.

Our gut tells us that true happiness should be rooted in goodness and reality, not evil and illusion. No loving mother would tell her son who likes to torture small animals or spend fifteen hours a day playing *World of Warcraft*: "Oh, well, whatever makes you happy." On the contrary, most parents are like me. "It's better to be a person dissatisfied than a pig satisfied," I tell my daughters when they try to weasel out of some short-term drudgery. "Better to be Socrates dissatisfied than a fool satisfied."

What does this have to do with the American Dream? Everything. The same Thomas Jefferson who inscribed "the pursuit of happiness" in the Declaration said elsewhere that "happiness is the aim of life, but virtue is the foundation of happiness." We could quote any number of the Founding Fathers to make the same point. Here's one other representative sample. "There is no truth more thoroughly established," said George Washington in his First Inaugural Address,

> than that there exists in the economy and course of nature, an indissoluble union between virtue and happiness, between duty and advantage, between the genuine maxims of an honest and magnanimous policy, and the solid rewards of public prosperity and felicity: Since we ought to be no less persuaded that the propitious smiles of Heaven, can never be expected on a nation that disregards the eternal rules of order and right, which Heaven itself has ordained.[8]

In other words, don't expect true happiness and divine blessing if you ignore right and wrong. If you want to be happy, pursue virtue that will allow you to create and share value with and for others.

Again, happiness includes the creature comforts we all associate with it. Abraham Maslow's "hierarchy of needs" captures the idea nicely. We must eat, drink, stay warm, sleep, and feel safe—these form the base of Maslow's pyramid. But we're more than cattle or house pets. We're "rational animals" (to quote Aristotle again): We are rational and moral beings. To really flourish, we need friendships, a sense of accomplishment, and fulfillment—the needs that come at the top of the pyramid. And no one gets from the base to the top without virtue.

## CAN HAPPINESS BE MEASURED?

Of course, neither Aristotle's philosophy nor Maslow's pyramid was based on scientific research. Can we measure happiness? At first blush, it doesn't seem the sort of thing you could weigh or count. In 1972, Jigme Singye Wangchuck, the young "Dragon King" of the tiny agrarian country of Bhutan in the Himalayas, was told that his kingdom needed to implement political and economic reforms to lift its citizens out of poverty. Rather than take the advice of outside meddlers, though, he instituted a "Gross National Happiness" Index (GNH). "GNH," the official website explains, "is a much richer objective than GDP or economic growth. . . . In GNH, the focus is on having sufficient well-being in a total of nine domains: psychological well-being, community, culture, governance, knowledge, health, living conditions (which include income), time use, and harmony with the environment."[9]

King Wangchuck had a point. Isn't it shallow to measure how much money households take in but ignore their spiritual well-being? Isn't it better to be wise than rich? To live at peace with the birds and the trees than to destroy them to build parking lots and smokestacks that can be counted in the GDP?

Well, yes. But a skeptic might argue that it was in the king's interest to take the focus off the dismal failure of his kingdom to improve the material well-being of his subjects and aim it on things much harder to measure. In 1972, Bhutan's GNP per capita was an abysmal $212 (in current dollars).[10] If I were the king of a country whose subjects made less than a dollar a day, I, too, would want to focus on "knowledge" and "community" rather than per capita income.

I would also want to skew the index toward the outcome I favored. A simple, well-defined 1-to-10 scale would be a bit too revealing. Instead, I would use a fuzzy scale with four choices: "deeply happy," "extensively happy," "narrowly happy," and "unhappy." Guess which scale Bhutan uses? Yep, that one. Is it any surprise that most people end up "happy" with this taxonomy? In 2015, 91.2 percent of the population was reported to be deeply, extensively, or narrowly happy.

Alas, the UN liked the Bhutanese approach so much that in 2011 the General Assembly unanimously adopted "happiness" as part of its global agenda. It even aimed to "empower the Kingdom of Bhutan to convene a high-level meeting on happiness" at that year's General Assembly.[11] The UN hailed the tiny kingdom as a country that others could emulate. Would you be surprised to learn that, per the UN, "sustainable development" (read: high taxes, population control, and government control of the economy) is now deemed vital to achieve Bhutanese levels of national elation? Every year since then, the UN has issued an annual World Happiness Report.[12]

Here's the reality. Bhutan remains one of the poorest countries on the planet. In 2014, its GNP per capita was $2,390.[13] It ranks 115th on the 2015 Index of Economic Freedom.[14] In the last twenty years or so, 100,000 people in the country of only three-quarters of a million were stripped of their citizenship and consigned to UN refugee camps. (One wonders whether anyone asked them if they were "deeply happy.") Since 2007, many have been relocated to other countries, although thousands remain.[15] In other words, Bhutan is one of the last places that other countries would want to imitate.

Such mischief feeds my skepticism about surveys that try to measure true happiness. "Not everything that can be counted counts," Einstein observed, "and not everything that counts can be counted." Still, if they're not over-hyped, such surveys can tell us something about psychological happiness. After all, the good ones are based on self-reports. Surely people have some sense of how happy they are.

Culture clearly plays a role. Although it ignores the role of heredity in psychological happiness,[16] the UN report found a strong correlation between political culture and happiness—especially at the extremes. Free and prosperous countries with low levels of corruption show up much higher than unfree, poor, and corrupt ones. Is anyone surprised that Denmark, Switzerland, Canada, the United States, Luxembourg, and Austria—despite their less-sunny, northern latitudes—are near the top, while Rwanda, Afghanistan, Syria, and Burundi are at the bottom? The fact that people risk their lives to get into the countries at the top, and to escape from the ones at the bottom, speaks volumes.

When we turn to surveys on (psychological) happiness *within* the United States, we can have even more confidence. We now have decades of consistent research on the subject from the General Social Survey conducted by the University of Chicago. Based on this data, Arthur Brooks boils down the predictors of happiness to three: "genes, events, and values."[17]

Just as some people start with more than their fair share of kindness, some people have a higher happiness baseline than others. Studies with identical twins conducted by University of Minnesota psychologists between 1936 and 1955 suggest that we inherit as much as 48 percent of our happiness from our parents.[18] You read that right: Almost half of our psychological happiness could be hardwired. Depressing.

Then, too, Brooks's other two predictors of happiness—"events and values"—include some things beyond our control, such as the details of our birth and upbringing. Even among the events over which we have control, some—such as winning a game or buying a new car—are like simple carbs. They give us only short bursts of happiness and then recede into the background.

What remaining factors best predict long-term psychological happiness? Faith, family, friends, and work. Of course, it's tough to untangle cause and effect. Does faith make us happier, or is it that happy people tend to have faith? Hard to say. As a statistical matter, though, if you're married and attend worship at least once a week, you're much more likely to be happy than if you're single and secular.[19] This fits the over seventy-five-year study of male Harvard graduates—the longest ever—which shows that high-quality, long-term social ties are the key predictor of both emotional and physical well-being.[20]

The final ingredient that Brooks mentions—work—stands out from the rest. We're not used to thinking of our labor as a *source* of happiness, beyond the fact that it allows us to make money. Income may not buy happiness, but income and happiness do correlate at lower income levels. At the very bottom of the income ladder, un-employment stinks. "Abstracted from money," notes Brooks, "joblessness seems to increase the rates of divorce and suicide, and the severity of disease."[21] If you look at a map of US unemployment distributions, you'll also be looking at a map of disability claims. Some of that is due to on-the-job injuries. Some is due to fraud. But some could be the outcome of a vicious circle: Long-term unemployment takes a toll on the body, and then a broken body makes it hard, or unpleasant, to find work.[22] Remember that the next time you talk to someone on long-term disability.

Note that this misery is not due to utter destitution: The jobless receive Supplemental Security income and other government assistance. And, yes, some of them prefer this state, choosing the short-term pleasures of sloth to the long-term happiness that a productive job could provide.[23] Still, long-term joblessness in general leads to distress, not joy.

Among the employed, monetary wealth and emotional well-being cluster together up to about $75,000 in annual income.[24] In other words, more money tracks with more happiness. But after a person reaches the upper middle class, growth in income begins to matter less and less.[25] In fact, once people reach that threshold, money is more likely to bring happiness if it's given away. That's right, charitable giving—government extraction doesn't count—brings happiness not just to grateful recipients but to donors.[26]

So why do so many wealthy Americans work so hard? If more money adds less and less happiness after we hit the upper middle class, why don't we all start to take longer vacations when we reach that level? Maybe it takes a long time to figure out that money doesn't buy happiness. But there's a more interesting reason: the value of work itself. Most economists treat work as a cost, a "bad"—as something we do only because we must. They assume that people will trade idleness for work if they can get away with it.

According to the evidence, though, that's way too simple. Happy people don't work mainly for money—even if that's part of the story. They derive satisfaction from meaningful work, from what Brooks calls "earned success." That can be true even for those who work by necessity:

> Franklin D. Roosevelt had it right: "Happiness lies not in the mere possession of money; it lies in the joy of achievement, in the thrill of creative effort."
>
> In other words, the secret to happiness through work is earned success.
>
> This is not conjecture; it is driven by the data. Americans who feel they are successful at work are twice as likely to say they are very happy overall as people who don't feel that way. And these differences persist after controlling for income and other demographics.
>
> You can measure your earned success in any currency you choose. You can count it in dollars, sure—or, in kids taught to read, habitats protected or souls saved. When I taught graduate

students, I noticed that social entrepreneurs who pursued non-profit careers were some of my happiest graduates. They made less money than many of their classmates, but were no less certain that they were earning their success. They defined that success in nonmonetary terms and delighted in it.

If you can discern your own project and discover the true currency you value, you'll be earning your success. You will have found the secret to happiness through your work.[27]

This is great news. It means work, done right and in its proper place, need not sap your happiness but can add to it.

The happy life is the "well-lived life." It's a fulfilled life that includes physical, emotional, and spiritual flourishing. It's a life that enjoys and creates value, a life of meaning.

The Founding Fathers, remember, didn't promise happiness. They promised *the right to pursue it*. Newt Gingrich likes to point out that the Declaration contains an active verb: "Not happiness stamps; not a department of happiness; not therapy for happiness. Pursuit."[28] The government, if it does its job, makes the dream possible. But since happiness is the fruit of a virtuous life, it can't be guaranteed. Virtue can only be freely pursued through struggle and hard work. In pursuing virtue, we work to overcome our weak will (*akrasia* in Aristotle), the penchant to pursue short-term pleasure such as idleness over real, long-term, happiness.

Done right, the pursuit of happiness sets up a virtuous circle of virtue, so to speak. Here's how it works. Some of your happiness is beyond your control. It's rooted in your genes or happenstance. If you're in the United States, however, count yourself lucky. Despite its flaws, our country is still freer and wealthier than most places on earth. On top of that, modern technology offers us countless ways to create and share value. The remainder—the path of virtue—is up to you. You may be tempted to live on the dole or in your parents' basement. You might think the instant pleasure of marching to your own drummer—like Dustin Hoffman's character Benjamin Braddock in *The Graduate*—will add up to happiness. But that way lies despair and a loss of meaning—as Braddock found before the summer was over.

If, in contrast, you work to get outside of yourself—if you seek ways to create value with and for others—you are likely to succeed at some point, especially if you treat your failures as lessons rather than excuses to give up. These actions call for short-term effort and sacrifice. But they will contribute to your true long-term happiness—not only by allowing you to flourish, but to flourish with and for others.

Do you have your basic needs met? If so, good. That's vital for happiness, not to mention mere survival. But it's not the whole recipe. For true happiness, we also need to meet the needs of others. We need to add value. And to do this well our new economy demands that we nurture key virtues. These virtues just happen to be the ones most likely to make us happy. The American Dream, then, is not a fool's errand or a Faustian bargain. As we saw in the stories of people like Brad Morgan and Danielle Tate, we need not sell our souls or our neighbors' silver to get ahead. If we work to create value with and for others, we can not only pursue but compound our happiness—together.

But there are plenty of obstacles that can keep us from engaging in the kind of work that leads to true, sustainable happiness. Let's turn to those next and see how to overcome them.

# 10

## FIGHT THE GOOD FIGHT

### Overcoming Obstacles to the Third American Dream

The main cost of our information economy is the rapid destruction of industries and jobs. The pain it metes out isn't evenly distributed. Often those who suffer the most are the ones who can least afford it. Both as individuals and as a society, we want to do whatever we can to blunt the pain and reduce the cost of change.

Unfortunately, as we've seen, every era of rapid change gives rise to fear. And that fear inspires political "solutions" that we later discover do more harm than good. We should steel ourselves against this pattern, then, lest we fall into the same problems all over again.

The best antidote to the destruction of old industries and jobs is the creation of new ones. Many of those new jobs, however, require virtues, including courage and a willingness to learn from failure, that many will find challenging.

The key barriers to the third American Dream will therefore be whatever hinders new job growth and impedes the virtues that allow us to thrive. These barriers include red tape. They also include efforts to subsidize the American Dream that instead create harmful incentives. If we want the next American Dream to be widely enjoyed, we'll need to overcome these barriers. Let's take each of these in turn.

## REGULATORY SCLEROSIS

For over a century, progressive politicians and much of the media have insisted that businesses, left to their own devices, will lie, steal, cheat, and defraud their customers and the public at large. The only cure for this, they routinely claim, is more regulation. Hence the constant growth of the regulatory state over the last century. Just since 1975 the total pages in the Code of Federal Regulations has swelled from 65,000 to 180,000.[1]

Oddly, progressives tend not to apply their dim view of private actors to government regulators, who, presumably, are above reproach.

The American founders had a more consistent view: They knew that the same flaws that beset merchants and bankers also afflict senators and bank regulators. So the best arrangement is one in which people, whether in the public or private sector, have an incentive to do the right thing. Sometimes that's best done with the market, sometimes with a law or regulation, sometimes with all of the above.

I'm with the founders on this one. But let's grant, for the sake of argument, that every regulation is well motivated and every regulator is noble. That still wouldn't mean that any given regulation is a good idea. During the Great Depression, for instance, the government bought grain from farmers and destroyed it to help raise prices. They were worried that falling grain prices would hurt American farmers. Alas, the policy led to a shortage of food, and a lot of Americans went hungry. This is but one episode in the long history of bad regulatory ideas that shows why good intentions are not enough. We need to consider something else—namely, their effects.

We should measure effects by honestly weighing both costs and benefits. If an antipollution law keeps a paper mill from polluting the water of landowners nearby, with less drag on the paper market than any alternative, then it's a good regulation. The danger is that the cost of many regulations wildly exceeds their benefits. And in almost every case there are alternatives that could better achieve the goal.

We know that regulations affect jobs, for good and for ill. The government has a poor track record of creating jobs in the private sector. What it can and should do is provide the legal setting for individuals and companies to innovate, create, and deliver value to customers, and to take risks with their own money. Our economy needs a regulatory climate that neither feeds foolish risk through bailouts and protectionist schemes nor turns the failures of enterprise into death sentences. Ideally, it should provide the arena for individuals and firms to be antifragile rather than fragile or even merely robust.

As it is, our regulatory state doesn't just protect consumers and align incentives within markets. It tends to protect large firms. These firms help write regulations that make it harder for small upstarts to enter the market. In sectors from banking to auto sales, our economy is more cronyist than capitalist. That's bad, since small businesses create most of the new jobs.

This pattern may be why the number of new start-ups has declined steadily since 1980. Growth in regulations has a way of doing that. The big corporations have enough lawyers and deep pockets to navigate the regulatory thicket, but the little start-ups don't.[2] Financial rules passed under the 2010 Dodd-Frank Wall Street Reform and Consumer Protection Act were supposed to prevent another financial crisis. Instead the law secured the dominance of massive banks, helped destroy small community banks, and made it even harder for small businesses to secure loans. In November

2015, the *Wall Street Journal* reported that "together, 10 of the largest banks issuing small loans to business lent $44.7 billion in 2014, down 38% from a peak of $72.5 billion in 2006."

Per one study, there was a net increase of 421,000 new businesses from 1992 to 1996, and 405,000 from 2002–2006. In contrast, "2009, 2010 and 2011 saw a net loss of new companies year-over-year—the first time in a generation."[3] Only in 2016 was there an uptick. Though the US economy has fared better than many other advanced economies since the 2008 financial crisis, it's still sluggish.

In the past, mid-sized companies sought the cash to expand in an initial public offering (IPO). Now more and more such companies seek to be bought out by a larger firm.[4] This risk aversion is what you would expect when regulations—such as the ill-conceived Sarbanes-Oxley Act—make it harder to launch and then grow new ventures. During President Obama's two terms, business was burdened with over 20,000 new regulations. This added some 572,000 pages to the Federal Register and cost our economy almost a trillion dollars.[5]

Although it's hip to talk up small business, the best economy would not be one with nothing but small start-ups. Most start-ups *fail*. Ventures launched by only one person are especially risky. That means they both create and destroy a lot of jobs. For long-term job growth, some small enterprises must prosper and grow into larger businesses, since that's where most of the more stable jobs end up.

Start-ups are like sea turtle eggs buried on the beach. Most turtle hatchlings die in the surf or get eaten by predators before they make it to the open sea. The only reason there are any sea turtles is because the mamas lay lots of eggs. Fewer eggs, and before long, no sea turtles. It's the same story with business and jobs. We need lots of fresh start-ups so that at least a few of them can grow into large, healthy enterprises. Happily, failed entrepreneurs aren't the baby turtles in this story. They don't get eaten and die. If all goes well, they try again, or go to work for one of the businesses that did succeed.

What's the take-home lesson here? If we want lots of small start-ups, some of which go on to create many new jobs, then we need a soil that isn't so choked with regulatory weeds that only the big established trees can survive.

The take-home is *not* "Get rid of all rules and laws." That may sound good in anarchist bull sessions, but not in the real world. Vibrant economies need sensible laws to protect freedom and the environment.

However, our regulatory system is now far beyond the sensible. Our economy is not only overregulated, many of its regulations are obsolete. New industries—such as peer-to-peer platforms—don't fit the regulatory cookie-cutters built for the last century. Uber and Lyft drivers aren't employees but aren't quite independent contractors, either. Drivers choose their own hours and use their own cars like contractors. But they also get customers through the smartphone platform as employees would. Ham-fisted efforts to dub them employees could destroy rather than discipline the sector. Visit Austin, Texas, sometime, where city fathers regulated Uber and Lyft out of the city. You'll have a hard time getting around. You'll also be more at risk from drunk drivers on the road.

Likewise, folks who rent out their homes on Airbnb aren't opening hotels. Forcing them to comply with hotel rules—which hotels favor—would kill the platform and the value it delivers.

In a regulatory no-man's-land, peer-to-peer platforms tend to seek forgiveness rather than permission. Uber launched without fanfare in Washington, DC, in 2011. It relied on word of mouth from customers, many of whom were fed up with the third-world ambience of Metro. By the time the city and nearby state governments woke up, Uber had already built a large and influential customer base that made it too painful for regulators to shut the platform down. If they did, they would have to start riding Metro again.

Doesn't the lack of regulation give these outfits free rein to defraud and put customers more at risk from dangerous drivers and homeowners? No. It makes sense that taxis in big cities were regulated and branded, since people would not otherwise feel safe getting a ride from a perfect stranger. Only verified, medallion-owning drivers could drive cabs, and the cabs were easy to identify. That meant a passenger could be pretty sure that she was not riding with the local ax murderer.

But the reputation systems in peer-to-peer platforms solve this safety challenge without the monopoly or regulatory hassle. Both drivers and passengers are pre-registered on the platform, which does basic background checks, then records feedback from customers and providers in every transaction. Unsafe Uber drivers get down-voted, as do homeowners who rent out varmint-infested rooms on Airbnb.

The same thing happens on eBay. That's why millions of people freely exchange billions of dollars with complete strangers on the platform. Their rating and credentialing system creates a form of self-policing better and more transparent than anything a government regulator could pull off. As economist Thomas Sowell observes, "Competition does a much more effective job than government at protecting consumers."

On peer-to-peer platforms, writes Arun Sundararajan, "*reputation* serves as the digital institution that protects buyers and prevents the market failure that economists and policy makers worry about."[6] These tools make whole classes of old regulations obsolete. Rather than throw up roadblocks to such platforms, regulators should study how to apply reputation, review, and customer feedback in other industries that don't yet enjoy these features. As one analyst put it, "regulators continue to operate as if Yelp, Google Reviews, and Angie's List do not exist."[7]

The newest parts of our economy—from peer-to-peer platforms to online marketplaces such as eBay to smartphone apps—have enjoyed "permissionless innovation." That's because they are digital creations that no regulator could anticipate ahead of time. Airbnb has no property inventory. Lyft had no fleet of cars when it launched. Smartphone apps don't have to apply for a building license.

Alas, new technologies in the world of atoms do face regulatory roadblocks. "Innovators who make driverless cars, commercial drones and smart medical devices, for example," notes Adam Thierer, "face mountains of pre-existing regulatory red tape imposed by bureaucracies such as the National Highway Traffic Safety Administration, Federal Aviation Administration and Food and Drug Administration, respectively."[8] Politicians, who think in terms of election cycles, may be tempted to block these upstarts rather than design an environment that fits, and that really protects rather than destroys. If our economy is to create new industries and jobs from the ashes of obsolete ones, however, regulators will need to give innovators room to breathe rather than strangle them in the crib.

## WHEN GOVERNMENT DESTROYS VIRTUE

### *Trying to Subsidize the American Dream*

The worst regulations are those that encourage vice rather than virtue. It's not Washington's job to mold virtuous citizens, but it should at least do no harm. The decades of well-meaning "affordable housing policies," many of which invoked the American Dream, are a prime example of harm disguised as help.

Since home ownership correlated with fiscal virtue, policy makers reckoned they could boost such virtue by boosting homeownership. They mistook correlation for causation. There's a difference between merely having property that you've gotten easily versus disciplining yourself so you can acquire and keep it, just as there's a difference between earning a million dollars from hard work and winning a million dollars in the lottery.

In a healthy housing market, folks get a mortgage loan because of what they have *already* done. They've worked hard, kept their jobs, paid their debts, delayed gratification, and saved for a down payment. In this virtuous circle, wise behavior makes it possible to acquire a home, and acquiring a home reinforces wise behavior.

But when government short-circuited that loop of incentives—by making a stable job, savings, down payment, and good credit unnecessary to get a mortgage—it produced a vicious circle of bad financial choices. A meltdown was inevitable.[9]

Housing policy wasn't the only way the federal government tried to force-feed the American Dream. Starting in the 1930s, it launched rearguard actions to keep the older kinds of farming profitable. I noted above that in the depths of the Great Depression, when millions went hungry, policy called for the mass destruction of grain harvests. This strategy went well beyond cereal crops. Fruit and pigs were also destroyed to raise prices in those markets as well. Such efforts did not stop farmers from moving to the cities and suburbs.

Some of these policies linger on. Subsidies mostly go to big agribusinesses rather than struggling family farmers, while tariffs on sugar double its cost for Americans. This is why Coca-Cola and Pepsi use cheaper high-fructose corn syrup, made with subsidized corn.[10]

Americans have just started to notice the same problems in higher education. Since middle-class people tended to go to college, politicians thought that if they subsidized college, they'd get more middle-class people. Maybe. But they also jacked up the price and undermined the value of a college education. And they cause some, who would have been better off in trade school, to get BAs in gender studies instead.[11]

The lesson? Well-meaning government efforts to force the current American Dream, or to preserve the previous one, often fail, and can erode rather than reinforce virtue.

## The War on the Poor

It's the same story with Lyndon Johnson's Great Society initiatives. His War on Poverty was designed to help lift the poor out of poverty. But half a century of data, along with a huge body of anecdotal evidence, suggest that instead it kept many poor stuck in place. The poverty rate was on its way down *before* these programs went online in the mid-1960s. Then the poverty rate leveled off. In other words, the poverty rate stopped declining about the time these anti-poverty programs were launched.

Not only did these programs not eradicate poverty, they helped give rise to generational cycles of poverty and pathology in certain pockets even as society grew far more prosperous.

Few Americans outside this "safety net" realize what a Shelob's Lair it has become. There are now eighty(!) federal programs that provide housing and energy subsidies, cash, food stamps, training, and education. About a third of the population receives services from one of these programs in any given month. Some of this helps those who can't help themselves. For others, though, the programs foster the problems they're meant to solve. On average, if you pay people not to work, not to move out of stagnant, jobless neighborhoods, and to have more children out of wedlock, they pretty much will. As former Clinton advisor and economist Larry Summers put it, welfare provides "an incentive, and the means, not to work."

In late 2016, writer Ronald Bailey returned to his Appalachian place of origin in McDowell County, West Virginia. It was already in decline when he left there forty years earlier. The area had once been the top coal producer in the country. "Out of a population of nearly 100,000 in 1950," he writes, "15,812 worked as miners." But that was near its peak. Mine closings then began to take a toll. "By 1960 that number was just 7,118. Today there are only about 1,000 employees working for coal companies in the county."[12] Now most of the good jobs are in government and social services.

Bailey's essay, entitled "Stuck," is a search for the answer to what he admits is a "rather unsentimental question," namely, "Why don't people just leave?" Short answer: Most already have. The population of the county is less than a fifth of what it was in 1950. Those who remain suffer the common pathologies of those left behind. There is so much suicide and so many drug overdoses that the mortality rate among men between the ages of forty-five and fifty-four is the highest in the country. Half the children are raised by single mothers who subsist on government programs, which induces them to stay put. And everywhere there is a delusional pining for an industry that has been on the decline for decades. "The government," Bailey concludes, "is paying people to be poor."

No one intends this. But the law of unintended consequences eats good intentions for breakfast, lunch, and dinner. If you point this out, you'll be accused of blaming the victim. But here's the truth: This rat's nest of government programs undercuts the virtues needed to pursue the American Dream.

Progressive Robert Putnam[13] and libertarian Charles Murray[14] have scrutinized the social science data. Each found the same problems in poor pockets around the country: Children from wealthier homes, on average, still benefit from discipline, married parents, and religious practice. All these things are plummeting, however, for lower-income Americans.

In another 2015 study, scholars at the American Enterprise Institute and Brookings Institution found that family breakdown among low-income Americans leads to much worse economic and educational outcomes.[15] The wealthy, meanwhile, who might be able to afford rehab after abusing drugs and cushion the harm of a disastrous family life, are more likely to have intact families than the poor, who can least afford it.

Since a healthy family life tends to foster good education, wealthier Americans tend to do better in school. And since education helps economic success . . . well, you get the idea. Everybody fixates on the income gap—yet another fruit of the inequality myth. They need to focus on the virtue gap, or, better, the *virtue deficit.* The problem, after all, isn't that some people acquire the virtues they need to succeed. The problem is that many of those who most need to do so don't.

When it comes to cultural institutions—families, neighborhoods, churches, and schools—there's a nasty example of the Matthew effect: To those who have much, even more is given. And to those who have less, even what they have is taken away. A virtuous circle at the top of the spectrum; a vicious circle at the bottom. It's as if policy makers had sought to destroy the very institutions and virtues that lower-income Americans most need to succeed.

The point is *not* that poor people always lack virtue. Far from it. Throughout history, circumstance dictated who was poor and kept most of them there. And, of course, many of the greatest saints of history were poor. But in the past two hundred years, rule of law, economic freedom, and innovation have given people with certain virtues a way out of poverty. Hundreds of millions of poor people have taken that path. The problems here are policies and perverse incentives that invite people onto a different path, one strewn with short-term incentives that lead to generations of poverty.

### A Universal Basic Income?

Alas, many who study these problems offer the same old, same old as the cure. Robert Putnam wants to raise taxes sky-high on the investor class and spend far more on education, day care, and other government goodies that have little record of helping the poor improve their lot. Charles Murray's proposal might seem heretical for a libertarian: a universal basic income (UBI). Actually, it's not that heterodox. Free-market economist Milton Friedman proposed the idea in the 1970s in the form of a negative income tax. So did the great Austrian economist Friedrich Hayek before him. Murray proposes a $13,000 annual grant for every American over age twenty-one in monthly direct deposits, with $3,000 dedicated to health insurance. That leaves $10,000 in cash per person, per year, free and clear. Portions are slowly taxed away for those who work their way up the income scale.[16]

Wouldn't this swell government debt and spur even more Americans to be slothful? Murray has thought of that. He argues that "a UBI will do the good things I claim only if it replaces all other transfer payments and the bureaucracies that oversee them."[17] And by "all," he means *all*. The UBI would replace "Social Security, Medicare, Medicaid, food stamps, Supplemental Security Income, housing subsidies, welfare for single women and every other kind of welfare and social-services program, as well as agricultural subsidies and corporate welfare." Murray's UBI would thus avoid a fiscal Armageddon. In fact, by stopping the runaway train of entitlements, it would be cheaper than our current system.

Would some folks still live on the dole? Yep, but it could be a lot better than what we have now. Marriage would no longer cut into welfare payments, since the UBIs would go to individuals. More baby-daddies might marry the mothers of their children. More unemployed people would take low-pay jobs that would get them back on the ladder to meaningful work without getting cut off completely.[18]

In short, a simple UBI could be better for recipients, for society, and for the federal budget than what we have now.

Could this happen? Sure. An asteroid could also destroy all life on earth in January 2032. Murray's scenario has about the same odds. In 1996, Congress passed and President Clinton signed the Welfare Reform Act. It added a work requirement to *one* program— Aid to Families with Dependent Children (AFDC). Opponents howled that it would cause an epidemic of homelessness and poverty among single mothers and their children. Instead, those mothers found jobs, dignity, and a way out of poverty. And yet, under President Obama, even that modest reform was undone. Work requirements for food stamps also were waived away in 2009 as part of Obama's "stimulus" program. As a result, the program has exploded, especially among ABAWDs—able-bodied adults without dependents.[19] The tendency for such programs is always to grow, never to shrink. The stars must align just to fix one of them.

Now envision a campaign not just to tweak but to abolish *eighty* programs spread across a dozen or more federal agencies, along with entitlement programs like Social Security and Medicare—which Americans have paid into—and to replace them all with a modest, universal basic income. Ain't gonna happen, short of a Venezuelan-style collapse followed by a benevolent dictator who'd interned at the Heritage Foundation and the American Enterprise Institute.

If against all odds a huge bipartisan coalition someday supports zeroing out all entitlements and means-tested welfare programs in exchange for a UBI, then we can talk.[20] Until then, let's focus on the main reason Murray and many others advocate a UBI: the belief that technology will destroy far more jobs than it will create. This is now global wisdom among academics and policy wonks. Efforts to run the experiment have popped up everywhere. French socialists are plugging a UBI. Switzerland held a public referendum on it in 2016 (which failed). Limited trials are under way in Finland, Canada, and the Netherlands, and Y Combinator has launched a pilot in Oakland, California.[21] This will give us some real data to balance out the fact-free stories told in support of the policy. Still, the best we'll get from these tests is evidence of the short-term effect of a basic income. They won't tell us what would happen, long term, with a *universal* basic income. That data would only come later, after the damage is done.

## Why We Should Avoid the UBI

Moreover, most who propose a UBI don't want to replace the current system but add to it. Martin Ford, for instance, seems to have written *Rise of the Robots* to make the case for just that. If you're already convinced that a UBI is a bad idea and don't care about the details, you can skip to the next section. But since I'm convinced that a UBI would undermine the virtues we need the most, I want to show why we should avoid it like the plague.

Ford offers most of the usual arguments, so let's focus on him.

We will soon reach a "tipping point," Ford predicts, when the jobs destroyed will far exceed the new ones created—leading to "permanent technological unemployment" as high as 50 percent. A UBI is the best option to soften the blow for the unemployed. Even if he's right, though, why implement a UBI before the apocalypse arrives? Wouldn't it be more prudent to wait until it happens, before we swell the federal budget by at least $2 trillion per year with no realistic plan to pay for it?

Ford claims that the looming automation of everything is part of a trend that started as far back as 1970 in the form of stagnant middling wages and rising inequality. That's why we need to start phasing in his plan now. He ponders several possible reasons for these troubles: globalization, financialization, women entering the workforce, deregulation that has shrunk the power of labor unions, and technology. All, he thinks, have had an effect, but automation will soon deal a lethal blow to jobs.

But much of what Ford says about flat wages and income inequality is misleading. He confuses, for instance, the stagnation of actual people's wages with a change in how wages are distributed over time. In truth, most Americans move through different income brackets throughout their lives. About two-thirds of the "hollowing out" of the middle class in the last forty years is because people moved *up* the income scale, not down. That's a good thing! Then, too, many who are now in the low-income segment are recent, low-skill immigrants.[22] Whatever you think of US immigration policy, the fact that poor immigrants do better here than in their place of origin suggests that our economy still has jobs for low-income, low-skill workers.

Ford's claims about inequality are equally suspect. Harvard economist Martin Feldstein notes that many studies based on the US Census undercount government transfers and other forms of income. They also don't account for the value of cheap and free digital goods. And if we compare consumption rather than income—surely the more pertinent factor—we find that the overall well-being of middle-income Americans has gone up in recent decades, not down.[23] The dysfunctional pockets we hear about are just that: pockets.

Ford also confuses the rich getting richer with the poor getting poorer. One doesn't entail the other. That's the zero-sum-game myth again. Inequality is often the result of upper incomes going up, or going up faster than others, not of lower incomes going down.

Information technology *has* led to a spike at the very top of the income scale because of all the features we've discussed in this book. It often grows exponentially, it's digital, and it's often non-rival, hyper-scalable, and highly connective. A handful of coders with a little cash and a good idea can attract millions of customers and grow a billion-dollar business in eighteen months, while a related lumbering industrial-age firm goes bankrupt. In 2012, Facebook bought the image-sharing platform Instagram for about a billion dollars. Kodak, which was slow to leap on the digital photography revolution, filed Chapter 11 bankruptcy.

That's the information economy: highly creative and highly destructive. Some tech entrepreneurs get fabulously wealthy, but their wealth is not a tax on everyone else. It's the fruit of value creation. In the future, we should expect both "bounty" and "spread." That is, growing bounty for society as well as a growing spread in incomes, in which the top 1 percent pulls away from the 99 percent, the top one-tenth of 1 percent pulls away from the top 1 percent, and so on.[24] If the top one-hundredth of 1 percent gets there by creating value rather than extracting it from others, then it's not a problem. At least it's not a problem the government can prevent without making life worse for everyone.

Still, surely some people in the lower and middle incomes make less than they *could* have under other circumstances. What circumstances? Martin Ford ignores, or is unaware of, all sorts of likely culprits for sluggish growth among some lower-income Americans. There's the misguided War on Poverty, which has eroded the creative virtues and seduced many into generational poverty. There are the sexual revolution and no-fault divorce, which have helped spread out-of-wedlock births and divorce like a contagion among lower-income families (1960s).[25] There's the abandonment of a gold-backed currency and embrace of pure fiat money (1970).[26] There's government intervention in college, health care, and housing, which swelled their cost. There's the degrading of education with intellectual fads; the 2008 financial crisis; and massive growth in government regulation across the economy. That's only a partial list. I'd venture that if none of these had taken place, the real incomes of many non-immigrant Americans would be much higher than they are in our timeline.

Finally, Ford's argument is one-sided. He fails to grapple seriously with the arguments of optimists such as Peter Diamandis, who maintains that automation will make it much cheaper to meet our basic needs.[27] That's just what has happened in the past. For instance, if you have a smartphone, then you have access to tools that would have cost more than $900,000 in 1980. Indeed, many technologies have little effect on GDP *precisely* because they make things less expensive.[28] If those examples aren't concrete enough, try this one: The cost of food—in number of hours worked—has gone down thirteenfold in the last century.[29] If these trends continue— bet on it—then one could have a lower-paying job in the future and still have far more purchasing power.

In short, Ford's argument is a house of cards, stacked with economic myths and mistakes. And at its base is our old friend, the lump of labor myth. Thus, inevitably, he concludes that since he can't imagine what jobs the future will bring, then it won't bring any.[30] As we've seen, this gloom follows the advent of every general-purpose technology. Such "pessimism," economist Deidre N. McCloskey notes, "has consistently been a poor guide to the modern economic world."[31] It's an especially poor guide for crafting government programs.

Ford has one final argument for the UBI. Rather than creating an army of freeloaders, he asserts that it would free up recipients to get more training and take more entrepreneurial risks—since their survival wouldn't hang in the balance.[32] But this undercuts his main argument for a basic income. If automation leaves nothing for most people to do, why would anyone take such entrepreneurial risks? To do what?

Also, the United States already spends about *a trillion dollars a year* on public assistance at the state and federal level. Today, no one need starve after a business fails. Have these programs been a boon to micro-entrepreneurship? No. Would an extra $10,000 for everyone change that? Maybe for some: The self-motivated, courageous, and disciplined might use the extra money for school or to start a tiny business. But they probably aren't on government assistance and already have what it takes to succeed.

In contrast, take your average government-dependent OxyContin addict. Would an extra ten grand cause him to sprout entrepreneurial wings or study for a trade? Not likely. It would just make his idleness even more tempting and debilitating. A universal basic income, Rob Tracinski notes, "is a plan to lure a large group of people into withdrawing from the economy and living in a state of economic helplessness and stagnation, separate from a technological elite who enjoy wealth and influence."[33] It's cruelty disguised as compassion.

What if such a policy had been in place in the nineteenth century, when farming ceased to be viable for most Americans? Surely the average farmer in the Midwest had far fewer options than the average American does today—when almost any knowledge can be had free online. Many of these former farmers would happily have drawn a paycheck to do nothing. And how many of their descendants would now be listless wards of the state?

Incentives matter. It's just human nature. Call it the Homer

Simpson Principle: We are tempted to be lazy, to avoid hard work, stress, and risk. We're tempted to ignore the needs of others, to act for short-term pleasure rather than work for long-term gain. If we're offered something for nothing, we'll take it. The paradox is that many will take it, even if the long-term result is despair and a loss of meaning. But this shouldn't be too surprising. We all prefer glazed donuts to kale.

That's the bad news. The good news is really good news. When we *must* work with and for others, when we *must* cultivate the virtues needed to fulfill our short-term needs, and when we are free to create value for ourselves and others, we may find not just the prosperity but the happiness of earned success that we might never have discovered otherwise.

Happiness isn't delivered by the Department of Labor. It's something we pursue. Any government program that thwarts that pursuit is hostile to the American Dream.

## BETTER OPTIONS

Since the American Dream is about earned success, any program for the able-bodied should at least not undercut virtues that lead to earned success. To treat the poor as if they don't respond to incentives is to deny them the basic dignity due every person. That means welfare programs should be converted to workfare. The work requirement added to AFDC in 1996 should be a guide for reform of the rest of the government-managed part of our safety net. We need to adapt the safety net to the many new options of the gig economy. Driving for Uber, mowing lawns through TaskRabbit, cleaning houses through Handy—none are lucrative, but these and dozens of other such jobs provide income, experience, and a way to create value for others. They may not offer a long-term solution, but for now they can offer an on-ramp to a life of fruitful work. These platforms have very low barriers to entry, and many, like Uber and

Lyft, have flexible hours. Our safety net needs to take account of that fact.

This is what Cesar Conda and Derek Khanna propose. "The government should expect that able-bodied safety net beneficiaries be willing to engage in the gig economy before collecting benefits," they urge in a recent *Politico* essay. "But transitioning to such a system requires policymakers to rethink the entire safety net, affecting nearly every federal entitlement program, so that it is oriented around the gig economy."[34]

Congress should also replace welfare provisions that cut off at the slightest whiff of work with a more robust earned-income tax credit, which does not.[35] Subsidizing the work of low-income earners is much wiser than subsidizing their non-work.

## The Dark Downside of High Technology

Government isn't the only hindrance to virtue—not by a long shot. Throughout this book, I've treated job disruption as the main cost of information technology. But we should not overlook its power to degrade us if we let it.[36]

In Plato's dialogue *Phaedrus*, Socrates tells the story of an ancient king who lamented *literacy*. "If men learn this, it will implant forgetfulness in their souls," the king complained, "they will cease to exercise memory because they rely on that which is written, calling things to remembrance no longer from within themselves, but by means of external marks. What you have discovered is a recipe not for memory, but for reminder. And it is no true wisdom that you offer your disciples, but only its semblance." His complaint wasn't crazy. Illiterate oral cultures are much better than literate cultures at memorizing long sagas. When cultures learn to read and write, they seem to lose this skill. That's a cost of literacy. Now raise your hand if you think the cost exceeds the benefits.

Nicholas Carr updates the ancient king's argument in his book

*The Shallows: What the Internet Is Doing to Our Brains.* Carr's conclusion: It's making us stupid.[37] Overnight, almost everyone in the
developed world now devotes our extra bits of time—when we wait
in line at the grocery store or wait for a red light to change or wait
for the Metro to arrive—to screens: big, small, and in between. Not
long ago, I was in a crowded airport tram. I looked up from my
smartphone to find everyone else staring down at theirs. Perhaps
most of them were reading email or the newspaper. Still, it's unset-
tling that such a profound cultural change could happen so quickly.

A study by Microsoft claimed that since 2000 the average attention span had dropped from twelve to eight seconds. We may
be better multitaskers, but we flitter around like moths carrying
our own flames.[38] I've felt the distraction while writing this book.
Some authors retreat to a quiet cabin in the woods when under a
book deadline. I can't do that. I have a family and a job that involves keeping track of breaking news on social media. I've coped
by learning to tune out the world around me, which has its own
costs. Ask my wife.

Some, though, are crippled by the "blooming, buzzing confu-
sion." Columnist Andrew Sullivan confessed in 2016 that he had
become a "manic information addict" who suffered from "distraction sickness." He had been a blogging "web obsessive" for years,
and finally went to a meditation retreat center to detox. The illness,
he realized, wasn't unique to him. It was an epidemic:

> Facebook soon gave everyone the equivalent of their own blog and
> their own audience. More and more people got a smartphone—
> connecting them instantly to a deluge of febrile content, forc-
> ing them to cull and absorb and assimilate the online torrent as
> relentlessly as I had once. Twitter emerged as a form of instant
> blogging of microthoughts. Users were as addicted to the feed-
> back as I had long been—and even more prolific. Then the apps
> descended, like the rain, to inundate what was left of our free
> time.[39]

I have a friend in Seattle who, like Sullivan, became so hooked on social media that he had to cut it off cold turkey and spend six weeks at a clinic for addictive disorders.

These are real drawbacks. But anything can be abused, including computers and smartphones. Gluttony doesn't prove that food is bad, and a Facebook fetish doesn't prove the internet is evil.

Okay, but does the technology, on balance, make us stupid? I doubt it. In *Smarter Than You Think*, Clive Thompson catalogs the many ways computers and the internet can expand our intelligence and abilities—*if we use them properly*.[40] For instance:

- They open up education to everyone.
- They can help us adapt more quickly to work in new environments.
- They can give us new skills: Think of the speed chess players who work with chess programs.
- Network tech acclimates us to work with people that we might never have met in person.
- Many people develop highly refined auditory and visual judgment from exposure to editing software.

To speak for myself, I would not give up the internet and Google search for any realistic amount of money, because they make research so much faster and more fruitful. Still, I rely more on them, and less on my memory, than I would if I had been born in the thirteenth century.

"In every age of human civilization," notes Edward Niedermeyer, "our ability to create transformative new technology has consistently outpaced our ability to understand its full impact. As a result, we tend to project ourselves onto our potent but baffling creations, imagining them to be the heralds of utopian bliss or dehumanizing decline depending on our established values."[41] Whether one inclines toward bliss or decline often seems a function of age. The old curmudgeon grouses about the latest gadget, while the teenager can't imagine how anyone could live without it. The path of wisdom is to see both the costs and the benefits in every technology, and then work to mitigate the costs and milk the benefits.

It need not make us stupid, but if we're not careful, it can make us more vicious. Social media allow ordinary people to debunk fake news. They also allow trolls and hackers to harass people with impunity. Twitter and Facebook connect long-lost friends. They also feed the madness of crowds. The internet and smartphones don't just connect future spouses through eHarmony and Match.com. They also enable free hookups through Tinder and Grindr. Like it or not, every advance in video and VR technology for remote surgery and board meetings will also lead to higher-quality porn and ever more ruinous porn addictions.

And then there are the sex robots.[42] A character in C. S. Lewis's 1945 novel *That Hideous Strength* prophesied the moment that is now upon us. Computing professor Adrian Cheok predicts that copulation with robots is "coming a lot sooner than most people expect."[43] Realbotix, which is under development by the California firm RealDoll, "will include convincing AI, with a robotic head that blinks and opens and closes its mouth."[44] It will also have other skills . . .

The Realbotix customer—to paraphrase Orwell—is a rich man whose failure with women leads him to take up with a sex doll, and his intimacy with a sex doll leads him to fail with women. But what the Realbotix gives him is not intimacy, since only one person is involved. The company has created a $50,000 tool to help lonely men (and a few women) masturbate. Before long, this vicious circle will be available to all—once the sexbot version of Moore's law brings the price down.

If we're not careful, the very tools that allow us to collaborate and connect and create can also enable us to descend ever deeper into a self-absorbed and self-regarding hell, where we live in and for our machines.

It's hard to improve on Neil Postman's diagnosis of the downside to entertainment technology. Here is what he wrote in *Amusing Ourselves to Death* in 1985:

> We were keeping our eye on 1984. When the year came and the prophecy didn't, thoughtful Americans sang softly in praise of themselves . . .
>
> But we had forgotten that alongside Orwell's dark vision, there was another—slightly older, slightly less well known, equally chilling: Aldous Huxley's Brave New World. Contrary to common belief even among the educated, Huxley and Orwell did not prophesy the same thing. Orwell warns that we will be overcome by an externally imposed oppression. But in Huxley's vision, no Big Brother is required to deprive people of their autonomy, maturity and history. As he saw it, people will come to love their oppression, to adore the technologies that undo their capacities to think.

All technology is Janus-faced: a smiling promise on one side, a snarling threat on the other. Any tool that extends our power to connect and create can be used to divide and destroy. Anything that entertains can become a source of addiction, in which "people . . . come to love their oppression."

Once again, the only real antidote to these dangers is virtue. It takes self-control to properly use the internet, email, smartphones, social networks, VR goggles, AIs, and, someday soon, robot personal assistants. To instill virtue, the virtue-forming institutions, not government, must lead. It is in healthy families, churches, synagogues, summer camps, ballet and martial arts studios, sports teams, charities, Scout troops, well-formed schools, and accountability groups that we learn the rudiments of virtue. The bad news is that, in the years ahead, the sheer speed of change, along with ever more elaborate ways to amuse ourselves to death, will put the squeeze on these very institutions, just when we need them the most.

The good news is that not just the moral but the economic value of jobs and institutions that instill virtue could go way up. Robots won't parent, preach, pray, hear confession, write philosophy and poetry, guide Socratic discussions of the great books, heal the downtrodden, or counsel the brokenhearted. Who knows? Maybe someday, when we've delegated most of the drudgery to machines, it will be more lucrative for mothers to nurse their infants and for monks to lead monastic retreats than for anyone to do data analysis.

For that to be more than an idle fantasy, however, there's one final myth—the mother of all myths—that we need to cast off. And in doing so, we can glimpse what it means to be truly human.

## 11

# CONCLUSION

## THIS QUINTESSENCE OF DUST

Intelligent machines will transform industry and the job market in the next few decades. As we've seen, this will be an opportunity rather than a crisis for those who prepare. To do so, we must focus on our absolute advantage over machines so they will supplement rather than supplant our work. A machine isn't free. It doesn't have a will. It can't be virtuous or vicious.

You, in contrast, are a person with a will, emotions, thoughts, ideas, and aspirations. You have some freedom over your actions. You can give in to temptation or resist it. With help and toil, you can become, through your choices, vicious or virtuous. You know all this more directly than you can know any truth of history, science, or politics. Reading popular-science books might help you pretend that you don't know these truths. But deep down you will still know better.

This hasn't stopped some from trying to forget. For a century and a half, materialism—the notion that matter is all that matters, that man is a mere machine—has overrun our culture. This *materialist myth* has so bewitched intellectuals that they routinely make claims they deny by their actions. To fully understand why machines won't replace us and destroy the American Dream, you have to see why materialism is false.

Materialism peaked in the mid-twentieth century with thinkers such as B. F. Skinner, the father of behaviorism and the "Skinner box," and Bertrand Russell, the atheist English philosopher. "Autonomous man . . . has been constructed from our ignorance," Skinner wrote in a book entitled *Beyond Freedom and Dignity*. He believed that "as our understanding increases, the very stuff of which he is composed vanishes," and argued that this was a plus: "To man *qua* man we readily say good riddance. Only by dispossessing him can we turn to the real causes of human behavior. Only then can we turn from the inferred to the observed, from the miraculous to the natural, from the inaccessible to the manipulable."[1]

Russell went just as far. "When a man acts in ways that annoy us," he wrote, "we wish to think him wicked, and we refuse to face the fact that his annoying behavior is the result of antecedent causes which, if you follow them long enough, will take you beyond the moment of his birth and therefore to events for which he cannot be held responsible by any stretch of the imagination."[2]

The views of Skinner and Russell haven't aged well. But their materialism lingers in the air like the smell of burnt toast. "Our belief in morality," E. O. Wilson and Michael Ruse assure us, "is merely an adaptation put in place to further our reproductive ends." As they go on to explain, "Ethics as we understand it is an illusion fobbed off on us by our genes to get us to cooperate. It is without external grounding. . . . Ethics is illusory inasmuch as it persuades us that it has an objective reference."[3]

In a recent book, *The Atheist's Guide to Reality*, Alex Rosenberg goes so far as to argue that beliefs and thoughts aren't about anything at all. "The notion that thoughts are about stuff is illusory," he contends. "Think of each input/output neural circuit as a single still photo. Now, put together a huge number of input/output cir-cuits in the right way. None of them is about anything; each is just an input/output circuit firing or not."[4]

And from this, it's not much of a leap to the conclusion that consciousness is an illusion, "a kind of con game the brain plays with itself." That's how George Johnson summarizes the views of Princeton neuroscientist Michael Graziano:

> The brain is a computer that evolved to simulate the outside world. Among its internal models is a simulation of itself—a crude approximation of its own neurological processes.
>
> The result is an illusion. Instead of neurons and synapses, we sense a ghostly presence—a self—inside the head. But it's all just data processing.
>
> "The machine mistakenly thinks it has magic inside it," Dr. Graziano said. And it calls the magic consciousness.[5]

To sum up the view, "you" as a distinct person don't exist, you aren't free or responsible, morality has no objective referent, your thoughts aren't about anything, and consciousness is an illusion. Got it?

These aren't fringe ideas. They are what follows from material-ism, as articulated not by its crazy critics but by its A-list advocates. That makes them no less crazy.

Most of the claims above are what philosophers call self-refuting. If there are no persons, whom was Skinner trying to persuade? To whom does the "our" refer in "our understanding"? If freedom is an illusion, why did Russell bother to write a book? Wouldn't people believe whatever they must believe? If thoughts aren't about any-thing, what are those scribbles on paper with Rosenberg's name on the cover? What of his thought that thoughts aren't about anything? Is *that thought* about anything? And if Graziano's consciousness is an illusion, do we really need to take his argument seriously?[6] No, we don't. But we do need to take seriously the damage such a mass delusion has done and could do to the pursuit of true happiness in our day.

## WHY ROBOTS WON'T REPLACE US

Albert Einstein once said that a theory should be as simple as possible, but no simpler.[7] In other words, the best theory will be the simplest one that explains what needs explaining, rather than explaining it away. Here's a principle derived from Einstein's: Any theory that asks you to believe you don't exist is a terrible theory. But that's just what the materialist myth requires of us.[8] It's so loony it takes the autistic consistency of a Skinner or Russell or Rosenberg to bring it into stark relief.

Most thinkers prefer misleading metaphors drawn from technology to hide the absurdities. Futurist Ray Kurzweil, for instance, sees us not as lumps of mindless atoms but as fleshy computers. Our bodies serve as the hardware and our minds, the software. (Computer pioneer Marvin Minsky once said that "the brain is just a computer made of meat.") That one premise pays astonishing dividends. It allows Kurzweil to predict a coming "Singularity" as soon as 2029 and no later than 2043. That's when technology, following the law of accelerating returns, will transcend our understanding. Machine intelligence, he claims, will outstrip the human intelligence, not just of one person but of the whole human race. However, rather than be left behind, we will merge with our machines, upload ourselves to much sturdier hardware, and cast off this mortal coil. No need to fear the coming robot overlords. They'll be us, or at least our much more accomplished grandchildren![9]

When Kurzweil speaks of us uploading ourselves, what he imagines is that we are software housed in mushy, fragile hardware. So there's no reason, in principle, that we could not be transferred to a more robust hard drive.[10] This sounds better than the bullet-biting materialism of a B. F. Skinner or Bertrand Russell. Don't imagine, though, that Kurzweil sees our software self as an immaterial soul, seat of consciousness, or Aristotelian form. In his detailed account of "how to create a mind"—the title of his 2013 book—he identifies the mind, not with consciousness or a person, but with a physical pattern in the brain. That's why he can make the massive leap from 3-D brain scans to minds. Get a high enough resolution scan of your brain, and the upload should work.[11] Kurzweil, for all his cutting-edge heterodoxy, is still stuck in the musty maze of materialism.

One consequence of Kurzweil's futurist talk: It has provoked a reaction from a new batch of Luddites, not all of whom live on organic kale farms in the Pacific Northwest. I was present for one of the most famous such reactions in 1998, when Kurzweil presented his ideas to tech executives at George Gilder's Telecosm conference in Lake Tahoe. Bill Joy of Sun Microsystems was there and talked with Kurzweil at the bar after the lecture. Joy was so shocked by the tech guru's forecasts that he wrote a famous essay in *Wired* magazine calling for governments to restrict "GNR" technologies—genetics, nanotechnology, and robotics.[12]

Joy is not alone. We now hear daily warnings about AI from luminaries such as Bill Gates, Stephen Hawking, and Elon Musk. "The development of full artificial intelligence," Hawking told the BBC in 2014, "could spell the end of the human race." Musk speaks of releasing an AI "demon" and sees it as "our greatest existential threat."

I share a bit of this worry. When Musk, Hawking, Apple co-founder Steve Wozniak, and others released a letter in 2015 warning of the dangers of AI, they had in mind autonomous weapons.[13] Robots roaming the earth armed with tactical nukes are worth a worry or two.

But much of the panic comes from a dubious view of both man and machine. It's a view Kurzweil shares with many of his critics. It shows up in Hawking's BBC interview, where he fretted that "humans, limited by slow biological evolution, couldn't compete and would be superseded by A.I."[14]

No. This belief that our machines will soon become conscious is a misguided one. The greatest delusion of our age is the paradoxical penchant to deny our own agency while attributing agency to the machines we create. A recent story claimed that the AI Watson had produced a movie trailer. Dig into the details, however, and it becomes clear that a human producer merely *used* Watson to create the trailer.[15]

The image of a conscious robot is popular, in part, because computers are black boxes for most of us. Anyone with the right training, though, knows exactly what happens inside computers. It has nothing to do with the *computer's* consciousness, self-awareness, purposeful choices, or agency. It involves the complex manipulation of symbols, of 0s and 1s, of transistor states, following algorithms designed to perform tasks.

Consider the (weak) AI we most often experience: the vast search magic of Google. Google search takes account of feedback from billions of user choices. This is machine learning, a sort of algorithm-building algorithm. I ask Google: Is John Searle retired? It offers me a list of choices based on previous searches. When I pick one of the options—Searle's faculty page at UC Berkeley—I help "teach" the Google filter how best to answer the question. But it's not literally intelligent. It *mimics* intelligence with the help of countless real agents—the programmers and Google users. The system isn't conscious, and there's no evidence it's inching its way toward self-awareness. Ditto with the recommendation engines at Amazon, Netflix, eBay, and Airbnb.

Kurzweil and his devotees try to get around this objection to conscious computers by invoking the Turing Test. At some point, they claim, we'll have a device that will be able to answer questions so well that we won't be able to tell if it's man or machine. In other words, our AIs will tell us they're conscious, and we'll simply have to believe them.

This is a weak argument. The fact that we feel uncertain if something is conscious does not mean that it is conscious, or that we ought to pretend it is. We attribute consciousness to one another, in part, because we have direct access to our own consciousness and realize that other humans are the same type of being we are. We can't say the same thing about computers.

"We'll spend the next three decades—indeed, perhaps the next century—in a permanent identity crisis, continually asking ourselves what humans are good for," predicts Kevin Kelly.[16] But that need not be, if we keep in mind the difference between us and our machines. Instead, as we get better at devising machines that mimic intelligence, we could develop a clearer sense of how they differ from us, and how we differ from them. By studying our greatest inventions and abandoning an absurd myth, we could learn more about ourselves.

Rather than wake up one morning and realize that Siri 12.0 is conscious and speaks like Scarlett Johansson, we should expect something like the ship's computer on the starship *Enterprise* in every nook and cranny of our lives: fast, cheap, ubiquitous, competent, interactive, voice-commandable, and no more a free, conscious agent than were those old PCs with the Intel 486 microprocessors.

## WHY COMPUTERS WON'T BECOME PERSONS: SEARLE'S CHINESE ROOM AND OUR MENTAL STATES

The most formidable objection to strong AI is the Chinese Room argument proposed by philosopher John Searle. Searle asks you to picture yourself locked in a room. You're given a batch of Chinese symbols through a slot in the wall, then a second batch, along with a detailed set of rules in English that tells you how to correlate the first batch with the second. Based on the rules, you are to hand back symbols from the second batch. (If you know Chinese, pick a language you don't know for this thought experiment.)

Now imagine you start getting Chinese symbols through the slot in the wall. You follow the rules as instructed, and then send back symbols from the second batch through the slot. You follow the rules so well that the Chinese man on the other side of the wall assumes he is chatting with a Chinese speaker.

Since you don't know Chinese, however, the Chinese script is merely a set of visual symbols that you manipulate based on formal rules. They don't *mean* anything to you. You don't fathom what's being said, or even *that* anything is being said. "I do not understand a word of the Chinese stories," explained Searle in the paper where he first introduced this thought experiment, with himself in the Chinese Room. "I have inputs and outputs that are indistinguishable from those of the native Chinese speaker, and I can have any formal program you like, but I still understand nothing."[17] This is how computers work: at the level of syntax—formal rules and symbols that we provide. They don't work at the level of semantics—that is, of meaning.

Our thoughts and consciousness—our "mental contents"—can't be reduced to formal rules or mere physical properties.[18] That's why a computer can simulate intelligence but does not have consciousness, intentions, or real intelligence. (See notes for more details.)[19]

If you tell a strong AI enthusiast that computers, unlike us, aren't conscious, he will go in one of two directions. Either he will wave his hands and talk about future technology that nobody knows anything about. Or he will insist that human beings don't have thoughts either. After all, if we don't have thoughts, then he doesn't need to claim that computers could have them as well. Rather than claiming that a machine will become man, he demotes man to a machine.

Now, if anyone tells you that you aren't conscious or that your thoughts aren't about anything, the best response is a hearty laugh—since he must assume what he denies.

## FREE TO CREATE

Once we put the baseless idea of conscious computers out to pasture, several truths come into focus. Yes, our machines will do many tasks better and cheaper than we can do them. Rather than replace us, though, they can magnify our capacity to collaborate and create, in an "exponential feedback between technology and intelligence," as one *Wall Street Journal* article put it.[20] IT is "humanity's accelerant."[21] To miss this is to miss the key fact of our economy. Grasp it, and you have reason for hope.

Alas, the current fashion is to deny our creativity, to reduce innovators to tinkerers. Our ideas are mere "works of bricolage . . . cobbled together with spare parts that happened to be sitting in the garage," as Steven Johnson puts it.[22]

I wish this were just a tic among tech writers. But it's long been the trend in economics as well. Economists want repeatable data to test their theories. That's why they tend to focus on material factors, such as "land, labor, and capital"—which they can measure. The result is that the surprising creative spark of free men and women slips through their nets.

Even when economists talk about entrepreneurs—the big change agents in our economy—they tend to underplay creativity's place in the story of success. Israel Kirzner, the economist most focused on the subject, describes entrepreneurs as "arbitrageurs" who exploit some "information asymmetry" in a market. In plain English: A clever entrepreneur finds that she can profit by buying milk for fifty cents a gallon from farmers in Iowa and selling it for three dollars a gallon in Manhattan. While this might help the Iowa dairy farmer and the New Yorker, it's not an inspiring story of creativity. And it's hardly the whole story.

We find the same reticence in Joseph Schumpeter, who developed the theory of "creative destruction." "The problem that is usually being visualized," he wrote, "is how capitalism administers existing structures, whereas the relevant problem is how it creates and destroys them." Schumpeter makes a helpful point here. Innovations often do far more than tinker around the margins of an industry. But notice the subject in his sentence: "it." Maybe that usage is just a shorthand. But this happens all too often when economists speak of innovation. The flesh-and-blood entrepreneur is eclipsed, replaced with the Machine of Capitalism, that faceless Darwinian creator and destroyer of industries.

Some recent thinkers go even further. For Steven Johnson and Kevin Kelly, creative agents seem to disappear altogether, in favor of an impersonal entity that has acquired the traits of agency. "Good ideas may not want to be free, but they do want to connect, fuse, recombine," writes Johnson in his captivating 2010 book *Where Good Ideas Come From*.[23] "They want to reinvent themselves by crossing conceptual borders. They want to complete each other as much as they want to compete."[24]

Note that Johnson refers not to *people with ideas* who compete and cooperate in a market, but to ideas themselves. Where do good ideas come from? Johnson asks. From prior ideas that fell in love and decided to recombine into new ideas. And where do those ideas come from? Apparently, it's ideas all the way down. Real human beings, who love, hate, create, remember, combine, modify, and share ideas, have disappeared down a dark hole. The ideas themselves have been granted the power to act. Rather than agents of creation, Johnson downgrades men and women to functions of the environment.

Johnson confers agency on ideas. Kevin Kelly of *Wired* magazine confers it on technology in recent books with telling titles such as *The Inevitable* and *What Technology Wants*. Kelly, like Johnson, sees technological evolution as a stage in the larger Darwinian story. Man is a mere inflection point between biology and technology. Kelly and Johnson banish not just *the* Creator but human creators themselves.

The need to put intelligent agency somewhere in the story is irresistible, though, even for materialists. Banish God and man, and before long, you're writing about ideas that want to have sex with other ideas, and software that wants to be free. "This inability of modern techno-philosophers to grasp the difference between machines and human beings is a great *trahison des clercs* of our time," George Gilder observes. "They would have us believe that inventors and entrepreneurs are passive figures in an evolutionary process that these self-serving intellectuals alone transcend. They must transcend it, after all, if they can see through it and unveil the great illusion of human creativity."[25]

MIT professors Erik Brynjolfsson and Andrew McAfee hew more closely to common sense, and hence closer to the truth. In *The Second Machine Age*, they argue that innovation is about real people working together, recombining not just material goods or atoms but *ideas* in new and creative ways. This allows them to challenge skeptics such as economist Robert Gordon, who claims that the kind of economic growth we enjoyed in the twentieth century is over.[26] "Not a chance," they insist. "It's just being held back by our inability to process all the new ideas fast enough."[27]

"Because combinatorial possibilities explode so quickly," they explain, "there is soon a virtually infinite number of potentially valuable recombinations of existing knowledge pieces." The word "valuable" is key. Valuable recombinations will be the ones that have value to other people, that have meaning. Some of these involve recombinations of physical objects. Maybe a man thinks to replace the roller in a self-feeding roller gin with wires. That's what Eli Whitney did with the cotton gin. Later, a guy realizes he can put a steam engine on a horse carriage. That's a car. Pull a roll of film between a lightbulb and camera lens with spools and sprockets? A movie projector. Use cathode tubes to receive radio signals? TV. Use a bad adhesive on the back of paper for temporary notes? 3M's Post-it note.[28]

In other cases, most of the matter drops away. A software firm creates a program that allows normal folks to forgo an accountant? TurboTax. A tech company figures out that it can use GPS data from its users to track real-time traffic information? Inrix and Waze. Two other ventures create apps that use traffic maps and smartphones to connect drivers with passengers? Uber and Lyft. These innovations depend on physical technology, of course, but they reside mostly in the realm of information.

We are still left with a chicken-and-egg riddle. Where do original ideas come from? Are we to believe that we forever combine and recombine ideas, but never originate them? That makes no sense. Human beings don't just copy, tweak, and remix ideas but also enjoy leaps of insight and inspiration. "Of course, it's easier to copy a model than to make something new," observes PayPal cofounder and venture capitalist Peter Thiel. "Doing what we already know how to do takes the world from 1 to $n$, adding more of something familiar. The act of creation is singular, as is the moment of creation, and the result is something fresh and strange."[29]

Our hyper-connected information economy allows not just great entrepreneurs but ordinary people to recombine ideas of value to others—to take the world from 1 to $n$. And our humanity—as conscious, free, and creative—means that, every so often, as Thiel puts it, one of us takes a blank patch of the world from zero to one.

## What Is Man?

So, what exactly is the central character in this drama? It's not a *what*. It's a *who*. Or, rather, billions of whos.

To bring the drama into focus, we must summon an alternative to nineteenth-century materialism. The alternative is close at hand, just out of sight since the first page of this book. It's a view that we take for granted unless we've been bullied and bamboozled out of it. And even then, we still act as if it's true: Human beings are neither ethereal souls nor mere beasts. We are, as Aristotle put it, rational animals, a unity of dust and breath, of the material and the immaterial. We are bound to the material world, but not enslaved to it. We can tell right from wrong, and in our better moments we struggle to do the former rather than the latter.

This view is anchored in the thought of Plato, Aristotle, and the ancient Israelites, and has been fleshed out by great thinkers for the last two millennia. At some level, it's just common sense. If you don't like the pedigree, though, then treat it as a heuristic mental picture. Compare its explanatory power with the materialist myth that urges us to explain away what we all know to be true. With this picture, all that we've discussed in these pages comes into focus. *We* can create, conceive, share, and recombine ideas in the face of staggering societal change. We use them to transform, to *inform*, both the social and physical world. And since we have now entered the age when machines and networks bear more and more of the marks of our own intelligence—of our ideas—we will surely have more to do, more value to create for ourselves and others than we did in earlier, more isolated stages of history.

## The Death of Materialism

"The end of all our exploring," T. S. Eliot wrote, "will be to arrive where we started and know the place for the first time." Let's now step back and reinterpret our economic story in light of our exploration.

The immaterial sources of information are ideas in our minds that we conceive, share, and remix. (Recall that we get our word "idea" from the Greek *eidos*, a near synonym for the Latin word *informare*.) For these ideas to have social or economic meaning, they must make their way into the world of matter. This has been going on a long, long time. When our caveman Grok first chipped two flint rocks together to start a cooking fire, or rolled round logs to move a block of stone, or scratched a furrow in the ground to plant seeds, he *in-formed* the world. That is, he infused the physical world with information.

Let's zero in on the fire-starting. Think of the information here in terms of Grok in his leopard-skin tunic intelligently choosing from a vast range of choices: rock rather than mud, flint rather than sandstone, two stones rather than one, or three, or five, or fifty, striking them together rather than rubbing them, striking them over dry bits of grass rather than over a thousand and one other choices, and on it goes. The information is the shift from the vast range of passive possibilities to the applied know-how that yields a warm, controlled fire in a pit in a cave, roasting some ibex.[30] In fact, the word "intelligence" derives from two Latin words, *inter* (between) and *lego* (to choose). To act intelligently is to choose rightly among alternatives for a purposeful end. It is, in effect, how we create information. It's also how we create wealth.

Since information is non-rival, Grok doesn't forget how to start a fire when he shares what he knows with others. On the contrary, he has added value for his tribe. The channel for this information, however, is limited to speech. Only if one member of the tribe tells another will the information, the knowledge, on fire-starting get passed on. With one bout of cholera, it could be lost.

Fast-forward a few thousand years, to the early Iron Age. Now whole civilizations not only know how to control fire but how to use it to separate copper and iron and gold from ore, to melt it and mold it. They herd cattle, sheep, and goats. They cultivate fruit trees and plant, tend, water, harvest, and grind wheat. This knowledge makes great cities possible. And the know-how is no longer left to oral tradition: It can be recorded and preserved in written records, though such records are fragile, rare, and hard to produce. Elite rulers hoard this knowledge. They lord it over vast hordes of slaves, who are forced to build great monuments of stone.

A couple thousand years pass. Some have found new ways to channel nature for human purposes. Water mills and windmills can grind grain. The harrow has been invented. Oxen and horses can now pull metal plows, dig deep, and turn the dirt back over seeds in one clean movement. Farming is much more fruitful. Texts can now be printed. Far more people have access to books and can devote their time to texts rather than the plow. Literacy begins to spread beyond elites.

Then, in a flash, in one corner of the world, people crack the code of chemistry, invent and improve the steam engine, build railroads, refine oil, devise the telegraph and telephone and internal combustion engine. Electricity and lights and indoor plumbing and clean water and household appliances abound. With mass production, everyday people have access to food, shelter, and technology that the kings and queens of yore could scarcely have imagined. Millions of men, women, and children have spare time.

You might suppose, as Kevin Kelly and Ray Kurzweil do, that all this was inevitable, that once things got started, they evolved on their own. But this is an illusion. These events are the fruit of an elaborate informational system. None of them would have taken root in a world of small isolated tribes of illiterate and innumerate hunter-gatherers. Indeed, in the twentieth century, there were still such groups stuck in the Stone Age.

Rather than wires, fiber-optic cables, or radio waves, the stable channels that carried this creative profusion were human ideas, beliefs, rules, and institutions that allowed information to be preserved, shared, and improved upon. "Adam Smith defined those

essential features of the channel as free trade, reasonable regulations, sound currencies, modest taxation, and reliable protection of
property rights," notes George Gilder. "No one has improved much
on this list."[31]

We might add specialization and division of labor, which vastly
amplify the signal. "What is prudence in the conduct of every private family, can scarce be folly in that of a great kingdom," observed Adam Smith himself. "If a foreign country can supply us
with a commodity cheaper than we ourselves can make it, better
buy it of them with some part of the produce of our own industry,
employed in a way in which we have some advantage." Very little
IT could exist but for a vast and global supply chain.[32] Thousands
of patents and millions of people in over a dozen countries were
needed to produce and deliver that smartphone in your pocket. No
man or woman oversees this system. No one *could* oversee it. Without a stable market and price system following fixed rules, it would
not exist.

It's neither an easy channel to maintain nor wholly free of noise.
Fickle kings and presidents, wobbly currency, broken banks, petty
corruption, marauding pirates, the denial of human dignity,[33] trade
barriers, high tariffs, public and private vice, economic myths, byzantine regulations, and burdensome taxation are all *noise on the
channel* for trade, supply chains, innovation, investment, business,
and enterprise. Get enough noise and some start to mistake the
noise for the signal. Then they turn against the system, making
more noise, less signal, and ever less freedom to communicate and
create.

As long as man has roamed the earth, there have been a channel, a signal, and noise. Yet, until 1837, when the telegraph was
invented, the signal could travel no faster than the pace of a horse
along a well-trodden path.[34] And the Pony Express and then the
telegraph had very little bandwidth.

About half the world is now connected to one another at roughly
the speed of light. And we've just gotten started. "Thousands of

years from now," Kevin Kelly predicts, "our ancient time here at the beginning of the third millennium will be seen as an amazing moment. This is the time when inhabitants of this planet first linked themselves together into one very large thing."[35]

Man has infused our world with information from the start. If we step back, though, we see a trend. When Grok set that controlled fire, he unleashed a bit of the power of the physical world. He did just a little more than nature could do on its own. This early act was a creative spark, a mix of matter and information, with the preexisting structure of matter doing a lot of the work. The same is true in primitive hunting and agriculture. But over time we have added more and more information to the mix.

In the industrial era, we built machines that could vastly exceed the work of the strongest beasts. We now construct integrated circuits and fiber-optic cables from humble sand, and inform these technologies with "software"—one part matter and a million parts information.

Since meaningful information comes only from intelligent agents, our new economy is fit for us. It's an economy in which our unique gifts begin to predominate. In such a mindscape, or "noosphere,"[36] weird things start to happen. On that hockey stick graph that represents economic growth over human history, the Industrial Revolution marks the inflection point where the horizontal line turns sharply upward. Our economy now resides to the right of the elbow, on a nearly vertical slope. That's because this economy, far more than the economies of farm and factory, channels our gifts as free, social, creative beings—if only we will nurture the right virtues.

Materialism blots out this picture. It makes virtue itself a figment. If we lack real freedom to make the kindly or brave or magnanimous choice over the cruel or cowardly or stingy one, then we cannot choose virtue, since we cannot truly choose at all.

But of course we can.

We must now reeducate ourselves after a long diversion in the metaphysical dark. C. S. Lewis, in the dark night that was World War II, pierced the heart of the problem:

> Such is the tragicomedy of our situation—we continue to clamor for those very qualities we are rendering impossible. You can hardly open a periodical without coming across the statement that what our civilization needs is more "drive," or dynamism, or self-sacrifice, or "creativity." In a sort of ghastly simplicity, we remove the organ and demand the function. We make men without chests and expect from them virtue and enterprise. We laugh at honor and are shocked to find traitors in our midst. We castrate and bid the geldings be fruitful.[37]

Once we have recovered our grasp of who we are, then we will see why we should neither worship our technological future nor dread it. It may distract us. It may ease our burdens. But it need not, and cannot, replace us. With clear vision, we can then seek the American Dream with confidence. It will be different in the twenty-first century than it was in the nineteenth or twentieth, but it will open far more pathways to explore.

"What a piece of work is a man!" Hamlet reflected. "How noble in reason! how infinite in faculties! in form, and moving, how express and admirable! in action how like an angel! in apprehension how like a god! The beauty of the world! the paragon of animals! And yet, to me, what is this quintessence of dust?"

Part of the answer to Hamlet's question is up to you. You can foster the virtues you need. But you must have the courage to suffer, to risk, to learn from failure and adversity. You must pursue work with others that meets the needs of others. You must create value amidst constant change, and embrace an unknown future rather than certain success. Pursue happiness in this way, and you will find a way, perhaps a unique way, to live the American Dream.

What are you waiting for?

# ACKNOWLEDGMENTS

This book pulls together threads and ideas that reach back at least ten years. As a result, it depends on the help and ideas of far more people than I can mention. The endnotes give ample evidence of the writers and thinkers who have shaped my own views.

For helping me get this project off the ground, I'm grateful to my agent, Giles Anderson. For valuable editorial advice over many months, I would like to thank my editor at Crown, Derek Reed. I must also thank Jonathan Witt and John Zmirak, who offered editorial advice on the manuscript at the final stages. Thanks to Casey Luskin and Frederic Sautet for their willingness to read earlier versions of the manuscript and provide helpful feedback.

Thanks also to Kelli Segars, Danielle Tate, and Marcus Daly for taking the time to share their stories with me, and to Arthur Brooks for his helpful thoughts on happiness studies.

And, finally, thanks to my wife, Ginny, and my daughters, Gillian and Ellie, who have had to tolerate lots of dinner conversations about Moore's law, autonomous cars, and cultivating virtue.

# NOTES

## INTRODUCTION

1. Tricia Romano, "Fitness Blender Couple-Next-Door Have 2.5 million YouTube fans," *Seattle Times* (Oct. 30, 2015), at: http://www.seattletimes.com/life/wellness/fitness-blender-couple-next-door-have-25-million-youtube-fans/.

2. See Nicholas Eberstadt, *Men Without Work* (Conshohocken, PA: Templeton Press, 2016).

3. Peter Coy, "Why Are So Many Men Not Working? They're in Pain," *Bloomberg Businessweek* (Oct. 7, 2016), at: http://www.bloomberg.com/news/articles/2016-10-07/why-are-so-many-men-not-working-they-re-in-pain.

4. See, for instance, "The American Middle Class Is Losing Ground," Pew Research Center (Dec. 9, 2015), at: http://www.pewsocialtrends.org/2015/12/09/the-american-middle-class-is-losing-ground/. There are all sorts of complicated details in this Pew study, and it doesn't, contrary to impressions, mean that the average American has gotten poorer

since 1970. Quite the contrary: It simply means that the distribution of household income in a snapshot in time is different now than it was four decades ago, with more in the upper brackets and a few more in the lower brackets. But that could simply be because people tend to move from lower- to upper-income brackets more quickly than they used to. In any case, studies like this are always taken to mean that Americans are getting poorer, even if the study itself shows just the opposite. For more discussion, see James Pethokoukis, "7 Reasons Why the US Is Not the 'Cesspool of the Developed World,' as Gawker Claims," AEIdeas (Dec. 11, 2015), at: http://www.aei.org/publication/7-reasons-why-the-us-is-not-the-cesspool-of-the-developed-world-as-gawker-claims/.

5. In the recent poll of ten nations by the Legatum Institute, "What the World Thinks of Capitalism" (Nov. 3, 2015), at: https://social.shorthand.com/montie/3C6iES9yjf/what-the-world-thinks-of-capitalism.

6. David Leonhardt, "The American Dream, Quantified at Last," *New York Times* (Dec. 8, 2016), at: http://www.nytimes.com/2016/12/08/opinion/the-american-dream-quantified-at-last.html.

7. Generation Opportunity, "2016 State of the Millennial Report" (Jan. 12, 2016), at: https://generationopportunity.org/wp-content/uploads/2016/01/State_of_the_Millennial_2016.pdf.

8. Tyler Cowen, *The Great Stagnation: How America Ate All the Low-Hanging Fruit of Modern History, Got Sick, and Will (Eventually) Feel Better* (New York: Dutton, 2011).

9. Mark Aguiar and Erik Hurst, "Measuring Trends in Leisure: The Allocation of Time over Five Decades," *Quarterly Journal of Economics* 122, no. 3 (Aug. 2007), at: http://www.nber.org/papers/w12082.pdf.

10. Eliza Barclay, "Your Grandparents Spent More of Their Money on Food Than You Do," NPR (March 2, 2015), at: http://www.npr.org/sections/thesalt/2015/03/02/389578089/your-grandparents-spent-more-of-their-money-on-food-than-you-do.

11. In real, nominal, and per capita dollars. See discussion and data in Scott Grannis, "The U.S. Is Richer Than Ever," Calafia Beach Pundit (March 11, 2016), at: http://scottgrannis.blogspot.com/2016/03/the-us-is-richer-than-ever.html.

12. Chelsea German and Marian Tupy, "Putting Income Inequality in Perspective," HumanProgress (Nov. 10, 2015), at: http://humanprogress.org/blog/putting-income-inequality-perspective.

13. Grannis, "The U.S. Is Richer Than Ever."

14. "Little Change in Public's Response to 'Capitalism,' 'Socialism,'" Pew Research Center (Dec. 28, 2011), at: http://www.people-press.org/2011/12/28/little-change-in-publics-response-to-capitalism-socialism/.

15. See Jay W. Richards, *Money, Greed, and God: Why Capitalism Is the Solution and Not the Problem* (San Francisco: HarperOne, 2009).

16. I refer here and throughout the book to disruption. But in most cases I am not referring to the specialized idea, developed by Clayton Christensen, which he calls "disruptive innovation." For an explanation of this concept, see Clayton M. Christensen, Michael E. Raynor, and Rory MacDonald, "What Is Disruptive Innovation?," *Harvard Business Review* (Dec. 2015), at: https://hbr.org/2015/12/what-is-disruptive-innovation.

17. Allison Schrager, "Why People Feel Poorer, Even If They're Not," *Quartz* (Oct. 25, 2016), at: http://qz.com/800219/why-americans-feel-poorer-even-if-they-are-earn-the-same-amount-in-one-chart/.

18. All tech companies know this. See Clayton Christensen's modern classic *The Innovator's Dilemma: When New Technologies Cause Great Firms to Fail* (Cambridge: Harvard Business Review Press, 2013).

19. James C. Bennett and Michael J. Lotus speak of "America" but not the American Dream in *America 3.0: Rebooting American Prosperity in the 21st Century—Why America's Greatest Days Are Yet to Come* (New York: Encounter Books, 2013). See also Walter Russell Mead, "Getting to the Next American Dream," *American Interest* (Nov. 27, 2015), at: http://www.the-american-interest.com/2015/11/27/getting-to-the-next-american-dream/.

20. I'm referring here not only to the much-vaunted "creative class" but to larger numbers of people. Richard Florida, *The Rise of the Creative Class—Revisited* (New York: Basic Books, revised and expanded, 2014).

## CHAPTER 1

1. David Attenborough featured just such a hunt in the BBC special *Life of Mammals* (2009).

2. See, for example, the charts at Max Roser, "GDP Growth over the Very Long Run," OurWorldInData.org, at: http://ourworldindata.org/data/growth-and-distribution-of-prosperity/gdp-growth-over-the-very-long-run/.

3. From chapter 12 of Hobbes's *Leviathan*.

4. Louis C. Hunter and Eleutherian Mills-Hagley Foundation, *A History of Industrial Power in the United States, 1780–1930: Stream Power* (Charlottesville, VA: University of Virginia Press, 1979), pp. 601–30. Cited in Erik Brynjolfsson and Andrew McAfee, *The Second Machine Age: Work, Progress and Prosperity in a Time of Brilliant Technologies* (New York: W. W. Norton, 2014), p. 6.

5. Ibid., p. 7.

6. Steven Johnson describes the surprising stories of these innovations in *How We Got to Now: Six Innovations That Made the Modern World* (New York: Riverhead Books, 2014). The six innovations are glass, cold, sound, clean, time, and light.

7. J. Bradford DeLong, "Rethinking Productivity Growth," Project Syndicate (March 3, 2017), at: https://www.project-syndicate.org/commentary/rethinking-productivity-growth-by-j—bradford-delong-2017-03.

8. "Towards the End of Poverty," *Economist* (June 1, 2013), at: http://www.economist.com/news/leaders/21578665-nearly-1-billion-people-have-been-taken-out-extreme-poverty-20-years-world-should-aim.

9. Chelsea German, "Poverty's Decline and Its Causes," HumanProgress (Feb. 8, 2016), at: http://humanprogress.org/blog/povertys-decline-and-its-causes.

10. Bjorn Lomborg, "Gambling the World Economy on Climate," *Wall Street Journal* (November 16, 2015), at: http://www.wsj.com/articles/gambling-the-world-economy-on-climate-1447719037.

11. Ibid.

12. See "Food Consumption, per Person, per Day," HumanProgress, at: http://humanprogress.org/story/2535.

13. Don't overlook the religious backdrop. Contrary to the Dark Ages myth, the Middle Ages were the seedbed of every good idea and institution that flowered in the early modern period. These innovations either were born in the creative ferment of this time and place, or were transported from abroad and then cultivated.

     Those raised on myths about the warfare between science and religion are shocked to learn what careful historians know: It was the Judeo-Christian idea of a unified, rational, and intelligible universe that laid the foundation for natural science and the advanced technology that followed. For details, see Rodney Stark, *For the Glory of God: How*

*Monotheism Led to Reformations, Science, Witch-Hunts, and the End of Slavery* (Princeton: Princeton University Press, 2003).

14. Walter Russell Mead and others have called this American Dream 1.0. Walter Russell Mead, "The Death of the American Dream 2.0," *American Interest* (June 2, 2011), at: http://www.the-american-interest.com/2011/06/03/the-death-of-the-american-dream-ii/.

15. Walter Russell Mead, "Beyond Blue Part One," *Crisis of the American Dream* (Jan. 29, 2012), at: http://blogs.the-american-interest.com/2012/01/29/beyond-blue-part-one-the-crisis-of-the-american-dream/.

16. See *Human Progress* graph compiling data from the census and US Department of Agriculture at: https://twitter.com/humanprogress/status/670685648236503041.

17. Arun Sundararajan, *The Sharing Economy: The End of Employment and the Rise of Crowd-Based Capitalism* (Cambridge, MA: MIT Press, 2016), introduction.

18. US Census Bureau, "Historical Census of Housing Tables," at: https://www.census.gov/hhes/www/housing/census/historic/owner.html.

19. Lendol Calder, *Financing the American Dream: A Cultural History of Consumer Credit* (Princeton, NJ: Princeton University Press, 1999), p. 96.

20. Ibid., p. 101.

21. Ibid., p. 160.

22. Ibid., p. 162.

23. Thorstein Veblen, *The Theory of the Leisure Class* (New York: Macmillan, 1899).

24. Christopher Lane, "Hoarding, Collecting, Accumulating: DSM-5 and American Life," *Psychology Today* (July 25, 2013), at: https://www.psychologytoday.com/blog/side-effects/201307/hoarding-collecting-accumulating-dsm-5-and-american-life.

25. Jillian Berman, "More Than Half of Millennials Have Less Than $1,000," MarketWatch (Dec. 19, 2015), at: http://www.marketwatch.com/story/more-than-half-of-millennials-have-less-than-1000-2015-12-14.

26. Associated Press, "Federal Reserve Report Shows Homeowner Equity Dipping Below 50 Percent, Lowest on Record," *Deseret News* (March 6, 2008), at: http://www.deseretnews.com/article/695259338/Federal-Reserve-report-shows-homeowner-equity-dipping-below-50-percent-lowest-on-record.html.

27. For proof, just look north to our Canadian neighbors. Their banking rules prevented a high-risk subprime loan market from developing, and as a result they were only mildly affected by the financial crisis.

## CHAPTER 2

1. Derek Thompson, "A World Without Work," *Atlantic* (July-Aug. 2015), at: http://www.theatlantic.com/magazine/archive/2015/07/world-without-work/395294/.

2. Martin Ford, *Rise of the Robots: Technology and the Threat of a Jobless Future* (New York: Basic Books, 2015).

3. Grigory Milov, "Smart Computers, Skilled Robots, Redundant People," *McKinsey & Company/McKinsey Russia* (May 28, 2013), at: http://www.mckinsey.com/global-locations/europe-and-middleeast/russia/en/latest-thinking/smart-computers. This is a summary of the McKinsey report, James Manyika, Michael Chui, Jacques Bughin, Richard Dobbs, Peter Bisson, and Alex Marrs, "Disruptive Technologies: Advance That Will Transform Life, Business, and the Global Economy," *McKinsey & Company* (May 2013), at: http://www.mckinsey.com/business-functions/business-technology/our-insights/disruptive-technologies. Another estimate is that seven million jobs globally could disappear by 2020, and two million jobs added, for a net loss of five million. Jill Ward, "Rise of the Robots Will Eliminate More Than 5 Million Jobs," *Bloomberg* (Jan. 18, 2016), at: http://www.bloomberg.com/news/articles/2016-01-18/rise-of-the-robots-will-eliminate-more-than-5-million-jobs.

4. Chien-Liang Fok, Fei Sun, Matt Mangum, Al Mok, Binghan He, and Luis Sentis, "Web-based Teleoperation of a Humanoid Robot," currently unpublished, at: https://arxiv.org/ftp/arxiv/papers/1607/1607.05402.pdf.

5. Alan Yuhas, "Would You Bet Against Sex Robots? AI 'Could Leave Half of World Unemployed,'" *Guardian* (Feb. 13, 2016), at: http://www.theguardian.com/technology/2016/feb/13/artificial-intelligence-ai-unemployment-jobs-moshe-vardi.

6. George Lorenzo, "How to Avoid Being Replaced by a Robot," *Fast Company* (April 12, 2016), at: http://www.fastcompany.com/3058800/the-future-of-work/how-to-avoid-being-replaced-by-a-robot.

7. Nathaniel Popper, "The Robots Are Coming for Wall Street," *New York Times Magazine* (Feb. 25, 2016), at: http://www.nytimes.com/2016/02/28/magazine/the-robots-are-coming-for-wall-street.html.

8. Carl Benedikt Frey and Michael A. Osborne, "The Future of Employment: How Susceptible Are Jobs to Computerisation?" (Sept. 17, 2013), at: http://www.oxfordmartin.ox.ac.uk/downloads/academic/The_Future_ of_Employment.pdf.

9. Maximiliano Dvorkin, "Jobs Involving Routine Tasks Aren't Growing," Federal Reserve Bank of St. Louis (Jan. 4, 2016), at: https://www .stlouisfed.org/on-the-economy/2016/january/jobs-involving-routine-tasks-arent-growing.

10. Todd Bishop, "15,000 Robots and Counting: Inside Amazon's New Fulfillment Centers," *GeekWire* (Nov. 30, 2014), at: http://www.geek wire.com/2014/video-amazons-robot-future-arrived-new-distribution-centers/.

11. John Markoff, *Machines of Loving Grace: The Quest for Common Ground Between Humans and Robots* (New York: Ecco, 2015).

12. Quoted in Todd Bishop, "Rise of the Robots at Amazon? John Markoff's New Book Foresees Fully Automated Fulfillment Centers," *GeekWire* (Aug. 26, 2015), at: http://www.geekwire.com/2015/rise-of-the-robots-at-amazon-john-markoffs-new-book-foresees-fully-automated-fulfillment-centers/.

13. Ibid.

14. To see how the last step of the process may be automated, see Nick Lucchesi, "Robotic Imitation of Human Behavior Just Took a Big Step Forward," *Inverse* (May 16, 2017), at: https://www.inverse.com/ article/31665-robots-imitation-skills.

15. Angel Gonzalez, "Amazon's Robot Army Grows by 50 Percent," *Seattle Times* (Dec. 28, 2016), at: http://www.seattletimes.com/business/amazon/ amazons-robot-army-grows/; Matt McFarland, "Amazon Only Needs a Minute of Human Labor to Ship Your Next Package," *CNN* (Oct. 16, 2016), at: http://money.cnn.com/2016/10/06/technology/amazon-warehouse-robots/.

16. James Vincent, "Jeff Bezos Looks a Little Too Happy Piloting a Giant Mechanical Robot," *Verge* (March 20, 2017), at: http://www.theverge .com/2017/3/20/14979620/jeff-bezos-robot-method-2-mars2017-conference.

17. Announced by Ford CEO Mark Fields on Aug. 16, 2016, "Ford Targets Fully Autonomous Vehicle for Ride Sharing in 2012; Invests in New Tech Companies, Doubles Silicon Valley Team" (August 16, 2016), at: https://media.ford.com/content/fordmedia/fna/us/en/news/2016/08/16/ ford-targets-fully-autonomous-vehicle-for-ride-sharing-in-2021.html.

18. Max Chafkin, "Uber's First Self-Driving Fleet Arrives in Pittsburgh This Month," *Bloomberg* (Aug. 18, 2016), at: http://www.bloomberg.com/news/features/2016-08-18/uber-s-first-self-driving-fleet-arrives-in-pittsburgh-this-month-is06r7on.

19. Carolyn Said, "Uber Sees Future of Flying Cars Zooming over Traffic," *SFGate* (Oct. 27, 2016), at: http://www.sfgate.com/business/article/Uber-sees-future-of-flying-cars-zooming-over-10417167.php.

20. David Roberts, "1.8 million American Truck Drivers Could Lose Their Jobs to Robots. What Then?" *Vox* (Aug. 3, 2016), at: http://www.vox.com/2016/8/3/12342764/autonomous-trucks-employment.

21. Quoctrung Bui, "Map: The Most Common Job in Every State," NPR: Planet Money (Feb. 5, 2015), at: http://www.npr.org/sections/money/2015/02/05/382664837/map-the-most-common-job-in-every-state.

22. Twelve years earlier in Hamburg, Germany, Kasparov had played thirty-two of the best chess computers at the same time over a five-hour period, and beaten them all. Garry Kasparov, "The Chess Master and the Computer," *New York Review of Books* (Feb. 11, 2010), at: http://www.nybooks.com/articles/2010/02/11/the-chess-master-and-the-computer/.

23. Cristine Russell, "The Alarming Rate of Errors in the ICU," *The Atlantic* (Aug. 28, 2012), https://www.theatlantic.com/health/archive/2012/08/the-alarming-rate-of-errors-in-the-icu/261650/.

24. Bertalan Mesko, "Can an Algorithm Diagnose Better Than a Doctor?," *Medical Futurist* (May 19, 2016), at: http://medicalfuturist.com/2016/05/19/can-an-algorithm-diagnose-better-than-a-doctor/.

25. Ibid.

26. One student considered Jill the best of the nine available TAs. Only at the end of the semester did students learn the truth. Computer science professor Ashok Goel had the idea, to solve the problem of TAs "getting bogged down answering routine questions," as many as ten thousand per semester. Melissa Korn, "Imagine Discovering That Your Teaching Assistant Is Really a Robot," *Wall Street Journal* (May 6, 2016), at: http://www.wsj.com/articles/if-your-teacher-sounds-like-a-robot-you-might-be-on-to-something-1462546621.

27. In 2012, I interviewed an executive of a financial services company. I asked him how many of his resources were dedicated to government regulations. He brought me to a large, warehouse-sized room filled with cubicles. "You see that section over there?" he said as he waved his hand

over about a fourth of the room. "Every one of those employees deals with compliance."

28. Quoted in Julia Kirby and Thomas H. Davenport, "The Knowledge Jobs Most Likely to Be Automated," *Harvard Business Review* (June 23, 2016), at: https://hbr.org/2016/06/the-knowledge-jobs-most-likely-to-be-automated.

29. Ibid.

30. Fred Imbert, "Google Robot Is 'the End of Manual Labor': VC," CNBC (Feb. 25, 2016), at: http://www.cnbc.com/2016/02/24/google-robot-is-the-end-of-manual-labor-vc.html.

31. Quoted in Derek Thompson, "A World Without Work," *Atlantic* (July-Aug. 2015), at: http://www.theatlantic.com/magazine/archive/2015/07/world-without-work/395294/. See the entire document online at: http://www.educationanddemocracy.org/FSCfiles/C_CC2a_TripleRevolution.htm.

32. Jeremy Rifkin, *The End of Work: The Decline of the Global Labor Force and the Dawn of the Post-Market Era* (New York: Tarcher, 1996).

33. Calum Chace, *The Economic Singularity: Artificial Intelligence and the Death of Capitalism* (Three Cs, 2016).

34. This story may be apocryphal. Friedman did visit China with George Gilder in the late 1980s, but I haven't been able to verify the quote.

35. James Bessen, "The Automation Paradox," *Atlantic* (Jan. 19, 2016), at: http://www.theatlantic.com/business/archive/2016/01/automation-paradox/424437/.

36. Robert Bryce, *Smaller Faster Lighter Denser Cheaper: How Innovation Keeps Proving the Catastrophists Wrong* (New York: PublicAffairs, 2014).

37. In 1929, there were about 49 million people in the civilian labor force in the United States. By the end of 2010, that had tripled to 153,690,000. In Council of Economic Advisers, "Table B-35. Civilian population and labor force, 1929–2010," *Economic Report to the President* (2011), at: https://www.gpo.gov/fdsys/pkg/ERP-2011/pdf/ERP-2011-table35.pdf.

38. Martin Ford, *Rise of the Robots: Technology and the Threat of a Jobless Future* (New York: Basic Books, 2015), p. xii.

39. Julia Kirby and Thomas H. Davenport, "The Knowledge Jobs Most Likely to Be Automated," cited in note 28 above. This essay is a summary of their excellent book *Only Humans Need Apply: Winners and Losers in the Age of Smart Machines* (New York: HarperBusiness, 2016).

40. Carl Shapiro and Hal R. Varian, *Information Rules: A Strategic Guide to the Network Economy* (Cambridge, MA: Harvard Business Review Press, 1998), p. 173.


CHAPTER 3

1. Romans 7:14–15, Revised Standard Version.

2. Malcolm Gladwell, *Outliers: The Story of Success* (New York: Little, Brown, 2008).

3. Anders Ericsson and Robert Pool, *Peak: Secrets from the New Science of Expertise* (New York: Eamon Dola/Houghton Mifflin Harcourt, 2016).

4. William M. Struthers, "The Effect of Pornography on the Male Brain," *Christian Research Journal* 34, no. 5 (2011), at: http://www.equip.org/article/the-effects-of-porn-on-the-male-brain-3/.

5. Matt Fradd reports on two drug tests and two scientific studies that arrive at this conclusion in "When Did Masturbating to Images of Women Pretending to Like Us Become 'Adult Entertainment'?," *The Huffington Post* (Sept. 19, 2016) at: http://www.huffingtonpost.com/entry/57e01f91e4b0d5920b5b323f.

6. Hannah Devlin, "From Porkies to Whoppers: Over Time Lies May Desensitise Brain to Dishonesty," *Guardian* (Oct. 24, 2016), at: https://www.theguardian.com/science/2016/oct/24/from-porkies-to-whoppers-over-time-lies-may-desensitise-brain-to-dishonesty.

7. For a readable treatment of the role of heredity in athletic prowess, see David Epstein, *The Sports Gene: Inside the Science of Extraordinary Athletic Performance* (New York: Current, 2013). Epstein's book was written to challenge Malcolm Gladwell's argument in *Outliers*. The examples he gives involve sporting events in which height, size, and muscularity are decisive, such as sprinting.

8. As the authors put it in Anders Ericsson, Michael J. Prietula, and Edward T. Cokely, "The Making of an Expert," *Harvard Business Review* (July–Aug. 2007), at: https://hbr.org/2007/07/the-making-of-an-expert.

9. Quoted in David Goldman, "The Witches of the Ivy League," *Asia Times* (Nov. 23, 2015), at: http://atimes.com/2015/11/the-witches-of-the-ivy-league/.

10. Carol S. Dweck, *Mindset: The New Psychology of Success* (New York: Random House, 2006).

## CHAPTER 4

1. See his website at: http://www.dairydoo.com/.

2. David W. Madden, "Great Irish Famine," at: http://immigrationtounit-edstates.org/528-great-irish-famine.html.

3. Timothy Noah, "Stay Put, Young Man," *Washington Monthly* (Nov.-Dec. 2013), at: http://www.washingtonmonthly.com/magazine/november_december_2013/features/stay_put_young_man047332.php.

4. Derek Thompson, "How America Lost Its Mojo," *Atlantic* (May 27, 2016), at: http://www.theatlantic.com/business/archive/2016/05/how-america-lost-its-mojo/484655/.

5. From US Census data at: http://www.census.gov/library/visualizations/2016/comm/30-year-olds.html.

6. "New Poll Explores Plight of the Unemployed," Express Employment Professionals (June 8, 2016), at: https://www.expresspros.com/Newsroom/America-Employed/New-Poll-Explores-Plight-of-Unemployed.aspx.

7. Jeff Guo, "Mexican Immigrants Will Move for Low-Skilled Jobs. No One Else Will," *Washington Post* (Aug. 6, 2014), at: https://www.washingtonpost.com/news/storyline/wp/2014/08/06/mexican-immigrants-will-move-for-low-skill-jobs-no-one-else-will/.

8. Kevin Williamson, "The White Ghetto," *National Review* (Dec. 2013), published online on Jan. 9, 2014, at: http://www.nationalreview.com/article/367903/white-ghetto-kevin-d-williamson.

9. Thompson is reporting on the findings from a recent study by economist Eric Hurst. Derek Thompson, "The Free Time Paradox in America," *Atlantic* (Sept. 13, 2016), at: http://www.theatlantic.com/business/archive/2016/09/the-free-time-paradox-in-america/499826/.

10. In an essay entitled "Economic Possibilities for Our Grandchildren," in *Essays in Persuasion* (New York: Harcourt Brace, 1932), pp. 358–73.

11. David Kestenbaum, "Keynes Predicted We Would Be Working 15-Hour Weeks. Why Was He So Wrong?," NPR (Aug. 13, 2015), at: http://www.npr.org/2015/08/13/432122637/keynes-predicted-we-would-be-working-15-hour-weeks-why-was-he-so-wrong.

12. Yoni Heisler, "Apple's Biggest Product Disasters of All Time," BGR (Feb. 18, 2016), at: https://bgr.com/2016/02/18/apple-product-failures-all-time-lisa-pippin-newton/.

13. See Randall E. Stross, *The Wizard of Menlo Park: How Thomas Alva Edison Invented the Modern Word* (New York: Crown, 2007), and Ernest

Freeberg, *The Age of Edison: Electric Light and the Invention of Modern America* (New York: Penguin, 2013).

14. Scott Adams hammers home this point in *How to Fail at Almost Everything and Still Win Big: Kind of the Story of My Life* (New York: Portfolio, 2014).

15. Sallie Krawcheck, "Reasons to Think Twice Before Starting Your Own Company," *Fast Company* (Nov. 16, 2015), at: http://www.fastcompany.com/3053254/lessons-learned/9-reasons-to-think-twice-before-starting-your-own-company.


## CHAPTER 5

1. Heather Clancy, "Hearsay Social CEO Clara Shih: 5 Ways for Female Tech Entrepreneurs to Get Ahead," *Fortune* (Oct. 19, 2015), at: http://fortune.com/2015/10/19/clara-shih-5-ways-female-tech-entrepreneurs-get-ahead/.

2. Nassim Nicholas Taleb, *Antifragile: Things That Gain from Disorder* (New York: Random House, 2012).

3. Organisms shaped by Darwinian evolution might seem to be a good example of antifragility. But being antifragile is more than simply being adaptable, especially in the Darwinian sense.

   Take antibiotic resistance in bacteria. This is the best example we have of natural selection and random genetic mutation in the real world (as opposed to beloved just-so stories). Neither an individual bacterium nor the entire species gets stronger from exposure to antibiotics. What happens is that a few bacteria have a mutation that give them resistance within a quirky ecosystem—a body being flooded with an antibiotic. The antibiotic kills most of the bacteria, leaving the mutant to reproduce and fill out the ecosystem. This allows bacterial *populations* to adapt to certain changes. But the mutants haven't gained a cost-free strength.

   In no known case does such a mutation *strengthen* the surviving bacterium or the population that descends from it. The mutation results in a loss of function, which just happens to confer a survival advantage in an isolated environment—a body jacked up on amoxicillin. When the mutant bacteria return to the wild, they don't fare well.

4. See Dominic Bouck, "The Revenge of the Coddled: An Interview with Jonathan Haidt," *First Things* (Nov. 18, 2015), at: http://www.firstthings

.com/blogs/firstthoughts/2015/11/the-revenge-of-the-coddled-an-interview-with-jonathan-haidt. This interview is based on the important essay by Greg Lukianoff and Jonathan Haidt, "The Coddling of the American Mind," *Atlantic* (Sept. 2015), at: http://www.theatlantic.com/magazine/archive/2015/09/the-coddling-of-the-american-mind/399356/.

5. April Kelly-Woessner, "How Marcuse Made Today's Students Less Tolerant Than Their Parents," *Heterodox Academy* (Sept. 23, 2015), at: http://heterodoxacademy.org/2015/09/23/how-marcuse-made-todays-students-less-tolerant-than-their-parents/. See also Arthur Brooks, "The Real Victims of Victimhood," *New York Times* (Dec. 26, 2015), at: http://www.nytimes.com/2015/12/27/opinion/sunday/the-real-victims-of-victimhood.html.

6. Scott Adams, *How to Fail at Almost Everything and Still Win Big* (New York: Portfolio, 2013), p. 17.

7. Ibid., p. 25.

8. Ibid., p. 8.

9. Angela Duckworth, *Grit: The Power of Passion and Perseverance* (New York: Scribner, 2016).

10. Richard Foster and Sarah Kaplan, *Creative Destruction: Why Companies That Are Built to Last Underperform the Market—and How to Successfully Transform Them* (New York: Crown Business, 2001).

11. Gordon E. Moore, "Cramming More Components onto Integrated Circuits," *Electronics* 38, no. 8 (April 19, 1965), pp. 114–17. Available online at: https://www.cs.utexas.edu/~fussell/courses/cs352h/papers/moore.pdf.

12. The earliest extant version of this story is in the poem *Shahnameh,* written by the Persian Perdowsi around AD 1000, and involves wheat and a chessboard.

13. Ray Kurzweil tells this story in *The Age of Spiritual Machines: When Computers Exceed Human Intelligence* (New York: Penguin, 2000), p. 37.

14. Ray Kurzweil, *The Singularity Is Near: When Humans Transcend Biology* (New York: Viking, 2005), pp. 35–110.

15. This technology will soon reach its physical limit, which has encouraged armies of prophets to predict the end of Moore's law. But these predictions focus on the current technology, on the physical layer. Referring to the inherent limits of silicon-based integrated circuits, the *Economist* in 2015 claimed, "In our physical world exponential growth eventually comes to an end." That claim assumes that the underlying technology

can't change—hardly a safe assumption, since it changed five times in the last century. If the trend is to continue, that will need to happen again, but we have no reason to assume it can't. The *Economist* article admitted as much. "Predictions of the death of Moore's law," its author conceded, "are nearly as old as the forecast itself." L. S., "The End of Moore's law," *Economist* (April 19, 2015), at: http://www.economist.com/blogs/economist-explains/2015/04/economist-explains-17.

16. See the statistics at "U.S. Cost of Technology," *HumanProgress*, at: http://humanprogress.org/static/1440.

17. Ibid., pp. 48–50.

18. Holman W. Jenkins, Jr., "Will Google's Ray Kurzweil Live Forever?," *Wall Street Journal* (April 12, 2013), at: http://www.wsj.com/articles/SB10001424127887324504704578412581386515510.

19. There has also been growth of a sort in frothy financial instruments and currency trading. Some of this, I would argue, is wealth producing, some not. In any case, it has only been possible because of the rise of networks and computing.

20. United Nations Development Programmes, "Mean Years of Schooling (of Adults) (Years)," *Human Development Reports* (2013), at: http://hdr.undp.org/en/content/mean-years-schooling-adults-years.

21. Lisa Ruddick, "When Nothing Is Cool," *Point* (2015), at: http://thepointmag.com/2015/criticism/when-nothing-is-cool.

22. "The Age of Uncertainty," *National Review* (Feb. 15, 2015), at: http://www.nationalreview.com/article/398625/age-uncertainty-kevin-d-williamson.

23. Jonathan Haidt, "The Yale Problem Begins in High School," Heterodox Academy (Nov. 24, 2015), at: http://heterodoxacademy.org/2015/11/24/the-yale-problem-begins-in-high-school/.

24. John Zmirak, "7 Ridiculous Courses at Top Colleges," *Intercollegiate Review* (Spring 2015), at: https://home.isi.org/journal-issue/spring-2015.

25. Heather McDonald, "Who Killed the Liberal Arts?," *Prager University* (Oct. 26, 2015), at: https://www.youtube.com/watch?v=6Sxttk5REkM.

26. Quoted in Bret Stephens, "Radical Parents, Despotic Children," *Wall Street Journal* (Nov. 23, 2015), at: http://www.wsj.com/article_email/radical-parents-despotic-children-1448325901-lMyQjAxMTE1ODIxNDYyMTQ0Wj.

27. "College ROI Report," *PayScale* (2016), at: http://www.payscale.com/college-roi.

28. For a clear road map for how to get a college education without lots of debt, see Alex Chediak, *Beating the College Debt Trap: Getting a Degree Without Going Broke* (Grand Rapids, MI: Zondervan, 2015).

29. Glenn Harlan Reynolds, *The Education Apocalypse: How It Happened and How to Survive It* (New York: Encounter Books, 2015); Clayton Christensen, Curtis W. Johnson, and Michael B. Horn, *Disrupting Class, Expanded Edition: How Disruptive Innovation Will Change the Way the World Learns,* 2nd ed. (New York: McGraw-Hill Education, 2010).

30. Steven Pearlstein, "Four Tough Things Universities Should Do to Rein in Costs," *Washington Post* (Nov. 25, 2015), at: https://www.washington post.com/opinions/four-tough-things-universities-should-do-to-rein-in-costs/2015/11/25/64fed3de-92c0-11e5-a2d6-f57908580b1f_story. html.

31. Don't mistake me for a utilitarian who reduces education to dollars and cents. I wish *everyone* could get a real liberal arts education, with ample time to digest the great books of civilization surrounded by wise tutors who guide them through Socratic dialogues, with no thought of a job (although I suspect its value for future jobs would be much greater than what passes for liberal arts in most colleges). I hope more people can have such experiences in a more prosperous future.

32. On the importance of networking in Ivy League schools, see Glenn Reynolds, "To Reduce Inequality, Abolish Ivy League," *USA Today* (Nov. 2, 2015), at: http://www.usatoday.com/story/opinion/2015/11/01/ glenn-reynolds-reduce-inequality-abolish-ivy-league-elitist-discrimination-column/74998648/.

33. See Minerva Schools at KGI, at: https://www.minerva.kgi.edu.

34. Ironically, Khan himself couldn't teach in a public school, because he lacks a teaching certificate. He wasted his time getting a couple of graduate degrees from MIT instead. This is the kind of silly credentialing designed to keep college education departments and teachers' unions in business, not educate kids for the twenty-first century.

35. For instance, massively open online courses (MOOCs) are meeting the dilemma of how to credential students who take the courses. Skeptics, of course, assume that troubles in the transition mean a transition isn't really happening. They'll be proved wrong. See, for instance, the gloating by Daniel Drezner, in "Twilight of the MOOCs," *Foreign Policy* (July 22, 2013), at: http://foreignpolicy.com/2013/07/22/twilight-of-the-moocs/. What Drezner misses is that while Bill Gates and other

high-profile thought leaders were putting money into MOOCs, other online and distance learning programs by other colleges he's never heard of were turning a profit and graduating students.

36. This is a reference to the biblical text of Matthew 25:29: "For whoever has will be given more, and then will have an abundance. Whoever does not have, even what they have will be taken from them."

## CHAPTER 6

1. With Nathaniel Branden (New York: Signet, 1964).

2. Ayn Rand, *Capitalism: The Unknown Ideal* (New York: Signet, 1967), p. 195.

3. Ayn Rand, *Atlas Shrugged* (New York: Random House, 1957), Appendix.

4. Ayn Rand, "Brief Summary," *Objectivist* (Sept. 1971).

5. As she puts it in *The Virtue of Selfishness*: "Altruism declares that any action taken for the benefit of others is good, and any action taken for one's own benefit is evil. Thus the beneficiary of an action is the only criterion of moral value—and so long as that beneficiary is anybody other than oneself, anything goes."

6. Adam Smith, *An Inquiry into the Nature and Causes of the Wealth of Nations*, ed. Edwin Cannan (New York: Modern Library, 1994).

7. Ibid., p. 148.

8. Ibid., p. 15.

9. Ibid., p. 485.

10. See the article on this point by Robert A. Black, "What Did Adam Smith Say About Self-Love?," *Journal of Markets & Morality* 9, no. 1 (Spring 2006): 7–34. For an entertaining study of Smith's moral views, see Russ Roberts, *How Adam Smith Can Change Your Life: An Unexpected Guide to Human Nature and Happiness* (New York: Portfolio, 2014).

11. See also Jerry Z. Muller, *Adam Smith in His Time and Ours* (New York: Free Press, 1993), p. 71.

12. Matthew 7:12.

13. Smith understood this, but is often misinterpreted by later economists working in a more thoroughgoing, utilitarian, and individualistic mind-

set. As James Halterman puts it: "Clearly Smith's notion of self-interest is not expressed as the isolated preference of an independent economic agent, but, rather, as the conditioned response of an interdependent participant in a social process." In "Is Adam Smith's Moral Philosophy an Adequate Foundation for the Market Economy?," *Journal of Markets & Morality* 6, no. 2 (Fall 2003): 459.

14. Robin Klay and John Lunn develop this idea in their excellent article, "The Relationship of God's Providence to Market Economies and Economic Theory," *Journal of Markets & Morality* 6, no. 2 (Fall 2003): 547–59.

15. Adam Smith, *The Theory of Moral Sentiments*, part IV, chapter 1.

16. George Gilder, *Wealth and Poverty* (New York: Basic Books, 1981), p. 37. See also the new and updated edition (Washington, DC: Regnery, 2012).

17. Robert A. Sirico, *The Entrepreneurial Vocation* (Grand Rapids, MI: Acton Institute, 2001).

18. Andrew Flowers, "The Best Jobs Now Require You to Be a People Person," FiveThirtyEight (Aug. 25, 2015), at: http://fivethirtyeight.com/features/the-best-jobs-now-require-you-to-be-a-people-person.

19. Erik Brynjolfsson and Andrew McAfee, *The Second Machine Age: Work, Progress and Prosperity in a Time of Brilliant Technologies* (New York: W. W. Norton, 2014), p. 61. They are drawing on the earlier work of Carl Shapiro and Hal R. Varian, *Information Rules: A Strategic Guide to the Network Economy* (Cambridge, MA: Harvard Business Review Press, 1998).

20. Brynjolfsson and McAfee, *The Second Machine Age*, p. 62.

21. Thomas Jefferson, "Letter to Isaac McPherson" (Aug. 13, 1813), at: http://press-pubs.uchicago.edu/founders/documents/a1_8_8s12.html. Quoted in George Gilder, *Knowledge and Power* (Washington, DC: Regnery, 2013), p. 93.

22. I'm saying near-zero to avoid the fallacy that Jeremy Rifkin commits in spades in his recent tome *The Zero Marginal Cost Society* (New York: St. Martin's Press, 2014). Rifkin predicts a future in which all goods and services will be pretty much free, and thinks that such dynamics will overturn the basic logic of the capitalist economy. He speaks of "the paradigm shift from market capitalism to collaborative commons." He has been misinterpreting and overinterpreting trends for decades, especially as they relate to energy and capitalism. The zero or near-zero mar-

ginal costs of digital goods and services do have significant economic consequences, but it doesn't mean what Rifkin thinks it means. I see no reason other than communitarian wishful thinking to conclude that it will overturn the basic logic of "capitalism," which Rifkin never manages to define accurately.

23. Shapiro and Varian, *Information Rules*, p. 21.

24. Brynjolfsson and McAfee, *The Second Machine Age*, p. 63.

25. Economist Paul M. Romer anticipated this in his famous paper, "Endogenous Technological Change," *Journal of Political Economy* 98, no. 5, pt. 2 (1990), at: http://pages.stern.nyu.edu/~promer/Endogenous.pdf.

26. Since these magnitudes are generated as multiples of 2, a megabyte is 1,048,576 bytes or 1,024 kilobytes, but we'll stick with the round numbers.

27. Note that we're talking about digital information here, not information in the broader sense. In particular, don't think of this as a measure of, say, knowledge of new facts. For instance, a thousand digital copies of "Roar" by Katy Perry gets counted in this measure.

28. Rupert Jones, "Out of Tune: How Music Festival Ticket Prices Keep Moving On Up," *Guardian* (May 2, 2015), at: https://www.theguardian.com/money/2015/may/02/music-festival-ticket-prices-rising-latitude-inflation.

29. From Marc and Angel Chernoff, "40 Quotes to Help You Follow Your Passion," at: http://www.marcandangel.com/2012/09/14/40-quotes-to-help-you-follow-your-passion/.

30. It also has the downside of feeding the narcissism of our age. A recent scientific study found that narcissistic personality disorder has increased by more than half among college students since the 1980s, reaching 30 percent. Arthur Brooks, "Narcissism Is Increasing. So You're Not So Special," *New York Times* (Feb. 13, 2016), at: http://www.nytimes.com/2016/02/14/opinion/narcissism-is-increasing-so-youre-not-so-special.html.

## CHAPTER 7

1. James Surowiecki, *The Wisdom of Crowds* (New York: Doubleday, 2004). See also Keith Sawyer, *Group Genius: The Creative Power of Collaboration* (New York: Basic Books, 2006).

2. This is a modernized version of his language. He actually wrote: "If I have seen further it is by standing on ye sholders of Giants." See the facsimile, "Item: Letter from Sir Isaac Newton to Robert Hooke," Historical Society of Pennsylvania, at: http://digitallibrary.hsp.org/index.php/ Detail/Object/Show/object_id/9285.

3. Ken Kaplan, "5G vs. 4G: Will 5G Technology Bring New Dimensions to Wireless?," iQ (2016), at: http://iq.intel.com/5g-vs-4g-will-5g-technology-bring-new-dimensions-to-wireless/.

4. David Curry, "A Seventh of the World's Population Visits Facebook Every Day," *Digital Trends* (Nov. 5, 2015), at: http://www.digitaltrends .com/social-media/how-many-people-use-facebook/.

5. James Surowiecki, "Uber Alles," *New Yorker* (Sept. 16, 2013), at: http:// www.newyorker.com/magazine/2013/09/16/uber-alles-2.

6. The term is from Donald Tapscott and Alex Tapscott, *Blockchain Revolution: How the Technology Behind Bitcoin Is Changing Money, Business, and the World* (New York: Portfolio, 2016).

7. Arun Sundararajan, *The Sharing Economy: The End of Employment and the Rise of Crowd-Based Capitalism* (Cambridge, MA: MIT Press, 2016), chap. 2.

8. James Surowiecki discusses the research establishing this in *The Wisdom of Crowds*.

9. See the discussion of network effects in Geoffrey G. Parker, Marshall W. Van Alstyne, and Sangeet Paul Choudary, *Platform Revolution: How Networked Markets Are Transforming the Economy—and How to Make Them Work for You* (New York: W. W. Norton, 2016), chapter 3.

10. These two-sided-network firms usually have a chicken-egg dilemma at the beginning. Uber, for instance, needs drivers to get customers. Who wants to go through the hassle of signing up to be a driver, though, if no one has downloaded the Uber app in your area? They get over the hump with incentives, such as offering free rides and discounts to early subscribers.

11. Chris Isidore, "New York City's Yellow Cab Crisis," CNN (July 22, 2015), at: http://money.cnn.com/2015/07/21/news/companies/nyc-yellow-taxi-uber/.

12. These peer-to-peer platforms butt heads not just with established businesses but with government regulators who try to jam square pegs into round holes. Is an Uber driver an employee, an independent contractor, a freelancer, or something else? Must people who rent out their house

through Airbnb comply with regulations designed for hotel chains? These are thorny issues that must be resolved, and there will be casualties. The FAA shuttered one promising platform, Flytenow, which connected private plane pilots with potential passengers going to the same place. Follow the saga at: http://blog.flytenow.com. Expect a lot of these conflicts in years ahead as regulators and legacy companies fight and then adjust to disruptions they failed to plan for and can't stop forever.

13. A good primer is Donald Tapscott and Alex Tapscott, *Blockchain Revolution*.

14. As Clay Shirky puts it in *Cognitive Surplus: How Technology Makes Consumers into Collaborators* (New York: Penguin, 2011).

15. *The Rise of the Creative Class—Revisited* (New York: Basic Books, revised and expanded, 2014).

16. The term was coined by futurists Alvin and Heidi Toffler in *Revolutionary Wealth* (New York: Knopf, 2006), chapter 26.

17. Some of the most popular YouTube videos are genuinely disturbing, such as the "murder prank" video escapades of Sam Pepper. See Caitlin Dewey, "Whatever Happened to the 15 People the Internet Hated Most in 2015?," *Washington Post* (Dec. 22, 2015), at: https://www.washington post.com/news/the-intersect/wp/2015/12/22/whatever-happened-to-the-15-people-the-internet-hated-most-in-2015/.

18. Chris Anderson, *The Long Tail: Why the Future of Business Is Selling Less of More* (New York: Hachette Books, 2008).

19. Pundits and academics often bemoan the fact that kids waste their time sending Snapchats and playing video games. My response: Sure, but what were *they* doing as teenagers? If they're over forty and at all like me, they probably spent thousands of hours watching reruns of *Gilligan's Island* and *M*A*S*H*. My fourteen-year-old daughter, Ellie, in contrast, spends her free time on an iPad or iMac building an elaborate Minecraft estate with her friend Abigail. They connect on Ellie's iPod via FaceTime, since Abigail is in Seattle and we're in DC. No one taught her how to do this. *I'm* not even sure how to do it.

When Ellie can't do that, she watches instructional cooking and drawing videos on YouTube and then she cooks and draws what she's just seen. She also watches episodes of *Dirty Jobs*, which I would assign if she didn't watch them voluntarily. This is what she freely chooses to do with her "cognitive surplus," *after* she's finished her school day, guitar and basketball practice, and homework. I'm pretty sure that's an improvement over a *Gilligan's Island* marathon. There was a time when I could list the entire sequence of *Gilligan's Island* episodes from memory. Not time well spent.

There's no doubt that the advent of the television harmed the culture of reading. It's embarrassing to compare the readers that children used in the decades before the TV to the decades after. Reading scores on standardized tests started dropping while TVs proliferated (although I doubt that this is the sole cause of the decline). In less than fifty years, our culture shifted from getting its most widespread information from written text, to audio broadcast, to video broadcast. That last shift happened in just a few years, when the American population shifted from gathering around radios to gathering around what my mom called "the blue-eyed monster." There were benefits to this shift, but the costs are obvious.

With the proliferation of screens in the computer era, bookish curmudgeons expected reading and writing to disappear entirely. But that hasn't happened. With the advent of word processing, email, and texting, more people write and read more text every day than at any time in history. It might not be good writing or good reading, but it qualifies.

TV was never going to be text friendly for the simple reason that the early screens were simply too blurry. I now have a smartphone and laptop with resolution better than any ink and paper. You probably do as well.

20. Don Tapscott and Anthony P. Williams tell the story at the beginning of *Wikinomics: How Mass Collaboration Changes Everything* (New York: Portfolio Hardbacks, 2006).

21. Coase argued famously that firms exist to reduce transaction costs. They coordinate the work of employees, standardize production processes, protect trade secrets, vet and place employees, make sure the right people get paid the right amount at the right time, and so forth. If every interaction depended on one-off contracts, not much would get done. So as long as it's more efficient and less costly to perform a task inside the firm, a firm will tend to internalize the task. R. H. Coase, "The Nature of the Firm," *Economica* 4 no. 16 (Nov. 1937): 386–405.

22. As Donald Tapscott and Anthony D. Williams put it in "Ideagora, a Marketplace for Minds," *Bloomberg* (Feb. 15, 2017), at: https://www .bloomberg.com/news/articles/2007-02-15/ideagora-a-marketplace-for-mindsbusinessweek-business-news-stock-market-and-financial-advice.

23. Ibid.

24. Jessica Lahey and Tim Lahey, "How Loneliness Wears on the Body," *Atlantic* (Dec. 3, 2015), at: http://www.theatlantic.com/health/archive/2015/12/loneliness-social-isolation-and-health/418395/.

25. As in Jeremy Rifkin, *The Zero Marginal Cost Society: The Internet of Things, the Collaborative Commons, and the Eclipse of Capitalism* (New York: St. Martin's Press, 2014).

26. The idea of a hybrid economy is prominent in economist Lawrence Lessig's book *Remix: Making Art and Commerce Thrive in the Hybrid Economy* (New York: Penguin Press, 2008). He also refers to a "third way."

27. In Clay Shirky, *Here Comes Everybody: The Power of Organizing Without Organizations* (New York: Penguin Press, 2008).

## CHAPTER 8

1. See "The FTC Funeral Rule" at: https://www.consumer.ftc.gov/articles/0300-ftc-funeral-rule.

2. This designation of "most liberal place" set off complaints from others hoping for that honor. For some objections, see Charles Mudede, "Why Vashon Island Is Not the Most Liberal Place in the US," *Stranger* (Dec. 18, 2015), at: http://www.thestranger.com/blogs/slog/2015/12/18/23274224/why-vashon-island-is-not-the-most-liberal-place-in-the-us.

3. Quotes in Amy Larocca, "Etsy Wants to Crochet Its Cake, and Eat It Too," *New York Magazine* (April 4, 2016), at: http://nymag.com/thecut/2016/04/etsy-capitalism-c-v-r.html.

4. Ibid.

5. Really, this exists. At the time of writing, you can nab one of these silver-plated nose rings for a paltry $25.90 plus shipping: https://www.etsy.com/listing/268539640/octopus-tentacle-septum-ring-nose-ring.

6. Sohrab Vossoughi, *Harvard Business Review* blog (November 23, 2012), at: http://blogs.hbr.org/2013/11/welcome-to-the-designed-by-me-era/.

7. CNC millers and routers use machine tools to shape materials such as wood or metal. "CNC" stands for "computer numerical control." That means these tools can follow instructions from a digital file. All the design takes place on the screen. It is then brought to life at the click of a mouse.

   Laser cutters carve out 2-D shapes, many of which can be put together to create 3-D figures, such as 3-D puzzles and those wooden dinosaur skeleton kits that populate the rooms of elementary schools. Like CNC millers, these laser cutters convert digital designs into real objects.

8. Chris Anderson, *Makers: The New Industrial Revolution* (New York: Crown Business, 2012), p. 56.

9. Ibid., p. 196.

10. Marc Andreessen, "Software Is Eating the World," *Wall Street Journal* (Aug. 20, 2011), at: http://www.wsj.com/articles/SB1000142405311190 34809045765122509156294 60.

11. All the elements of the information economy—exponential growth, digitization, hyper-connectivity, and the massive growth of information—come together in DIY manufacturing. You can get CAD programs online, from free and open source to high-powered and costly—for example, Google SketchUp and Autodesk 123D on the free side, Solidworks Premium and AutoCAD for purchase.

Everything you need to know about digital design you can learn with little expense at your computer from online tutorials. With an inexpensive 3-D scanner (or even a good camera and the right software) you can scan a 3-D object, digitize it, modify the file, and then fabricate the replicas. You can download, modify, and share scads of designs at Thingiverse (thingiverse.com) to create 2-D objects with a laser cutter and 3-D objects with your 3-D printer at resolutions as fine as 0.1mm (so far).

With an inexpensive residential 3-D printer, at the moment, you'll be limited to smallish objects made of plastic—iPhone holders, modified Lego kits, game pieces, action figures, scale models of cars and buildings, Christmas ornaments, dolls and dollhouse furniture, key chains, plastic whistles, wire-frame skull pencil holders, plastic appliance parts, and so on.

You can take lessons and access better equipment at one of the Tech-Shops or other makerspaces around the country. Just as many of us take larger printing jobs to FedEx Office, these makerspaces allow folks to do more than they could in their offices or basements.

What if you want to design jewelry that mimics traditional Chinese art but can't bear the cost of a high-end 3-D printer that fabricates metal objects? No biggie. You can perfect the prototype at home in plastic and then connect with fabricators at Shapeways (shapeways.com), who will produce the jewelry for you. From the user's point of view the process is no more complex than getting images printed on T-shirts at Threadless or on coffee mugs at CafePress. But how do you market your products? Don't worry. You can also sell and market them on the same platform.

Since this is small-batch manufacturing for niche goods, it lacks the economies of scale of mass production. But it benefits from the variety and rarity enjoyed by handcrafted goods, and so will be priced above commodity goods but below handmade. This is "the maker's premium," notes Chris Anderson, "the ultimate antidote to commodification."

Want a much larger batch? You can connect with first-rate manufacturers at Ponoko and MFG.com. At Alibaba, the massive Chinese platform founded by Jack Ma, you can even negotiate directly with big manufacturers in China, with your messages translated from English to Chinese and back again. No middleman needed.

12. George Gilder, *Knowledge and Power* (Washington, DC: Regnery, 2013), p. 101.

13. Our entire information economy rests atop the insights of great twentieth-century intellectuals such as Kurt Gödel (1906–1978), friend of Einstein and author of the famous incompleteness theorems that helped dethrone determinism; John von Neumann (1903–1957), the great Hungarian-American mathematician and polymath; and Alan Turing (1912–1954), who led the British intelligence team during World War II that cracked the German Enigma code using an advanced computer built solely for the purpose. Turing is also famous for his concept of an abstract computer architecture and for the eponymous "Turing Test." A computer, he proposed, could pass his test if it could pass itself off to a human observer as another human being rather than a computer. We're still working on that one.

14. George Gilder summarizes Shannon's initial academic work:

> His award-winning master's thesis at MIT jump-started the computer age by demonstrating that the existing "relay" switching circuits from telephone exchanges could express the nineteenth-century algebra of logic George Boole invented, which became the prevailing logic of computing. A key insight came from the analogy with the game of twenty questions: paring down a complex problem to a chain of binary, yes-no choices, which Shannon may have been the first to dub "bits."

Shannon, like Alan Turing, had worked in cryptography during World War II at Bletchley Park—a Victorian mansion turned secret code-cracking facility northwest of London—and benefited from conversations with Turing. After the war, Shannon repaired to AT&T's Bell Labs, and in 1948 published a monograph in the *Bell System Technical Journal* entitled "The Mathematical Theory of Information." That same year, also at Bell Labs, the transistor was invented. Imagine: The physical and conceptual foundations of our modern information and telecommunications economy, of what Gilder has dubbed the "telecosm," both emerged at the same time from the same research hub of one American company.

Unfortunately, Shannon's explanation was confusing, because he took the advice of John von Neumann. As the story goes, around 1940, the two had a conversation at MIT (or maybe at the Institute for Advanced Study in Princeton) about Shannon's ideas. Von Neumann suggested he use a term from thermodynamics as the measure of information: entropy. The greater the information content of a message, the higher its "entropy."

"According to Shannon," Gilder reports, "Neumann liked the term because no one knew what it meant" (*Knowledge and Power*, p. 19). That's a problem when your goal is to explain it. Entropy in physical systems refers to disorder, or to usable energy. Imagine a room in which all the heat—that is, the energetic molecules—is collected in one corner. This is its lowest entropy state. As the heat dissipates throughout the room, entropy increases until the room reaches the same average temperature.

The Second Law of Thermodynamics states that any closed physical system will move over time from a state of low entropy/high order to a state of high entropy/low order. In other words, a closed physical system will move from order to disorder, from order to chaos.

According to modern cosmology, the universe itself must have started in a state of unimaginably low entropy—that is, order—for us to be able to observe its current state. Physicist Roger Penrose calculated that the chances of this low-entropy state occurring by chance was 1 part in $10^{10^{23}}$!

It's no surprise that many of us think this mind-boggling fine-tuning is evidence of a cosmic fine-tuner. Still, governed as it is by the iron fate of the Second Law, the universe will eventually dissipate into a state of uniform temperature and static equilibrium, in which nothing interesting or surprising will happen. (Don't worry: This state of cosmic boredom would take about $10^{150}$ years to arrive. And it all depends on the assumption that the universe is a closed system.)

Physical and informational entropy do have something in common.

Maximum entropy in a physical system means disorder or equilibrium. At the point of maximum physical entropy, there is no more useful energy. Maximum entropy in an information system, however, is reached "when all the bits in a message are equally improbable and thus cannot be further compressed without loss of information" (*Knowledge and Power*, p. 1).

If you're confused, welcome to the club. The more chaos or disorder there is in a communication, the more information it contains? That's certainly counterintuitive. I confess that I've always found the concept of entropy, even in physics, confusing. It can refer to a movement from maximum usable energy to no usable energy. It can also refer to a descent from order to disorder. Those seem like different ideas. Do we really need to use the same confusing concept when measuring information as well? I would say no—please, no—but no one asked me, so we're stuck with it. For this reason, however, I have avoided Shannon's use of "entropy" in my explanation of information.

15. Gilder, *Knowledge and Power*, p. 19.

16. This minimal approach has its benefits. As Gilder puts it:

> It was Shannon's caution, his disciplined reluctance to contaminate his pure theory with wider concepts of semantic meaning and creative content, that made his formulations so generally applicable. . . . Shannon offered a theory of messengers and messages, without a theory of the ultimate source of the message in a particular human mind with specific purposes, meanings, projects, goals, and philosophies. Because Shannon was remorselessly rigorous and restrained, his theory could be brought to bear on almost anything transmitted over time and space in the presence of noise or interference. Ibid., p. 22.

17. The danger, however, is that people would take Shannon's reduced definition of "information," so generally applicable but so devoid of content, as if it captured information itself. "Shannon said the notion of information has nothing to do with meaning," explains James Gleick to Kevin Kelly in an interview in *Wired* about Gleick's book *The Information: A History, a Theory, a Flood* (New York: Pantheon books, 2011). "A string of bits has a quantity, whether it represents something that's true, something that's utterly false, or something that's just meaningless nonsense. If you were a scientist or an engineer, that idea was very liberating; it enabled you to treat information as a manipulable thing." Kevin Kelly, "Why the Basis of

the Universe Isn't Matter or Energy—It's Data," *Wired* (Feb. 28, 2011), at: http://www.wired.com/2011/02/mf_gleick_qa/.

Fair enough, but Shannon *did not show* that "information has nothing to do with meaning." How could he? He simply showed that one could calculate the carrying capacity of a channel in terms of improbability or surprise, without considering meaning, and define information as such. It doesn't follow that information is *nothing but* surprise, still less that it has nothing to do with meaning.

18. Another, similar way to think of information is in terms of complexity or improbability. The more information a sequence or event has, the more complex or improbable it is. (Complexity and improbability are the same thing in these contexts.) The number 1476398470821576029547 has a good bit of information because there's no simple rule that predicts what number comes next. (I typed the sequence by closing my eyes and hitting the number keys mindlessly.) It probably can't be compressed. The shortest way to send that number over a telegraph wire would be just to punch out the symbols for the entire number.

A highly repetitive message, in contrast, doesn't have much complexity or improbability. 121212121212121212121212121212121212 is a much longer number than 1476398470821576029547, but it can be compressed with a simple rule: "1, 2, repeat 18 times." So it has less information in Shannon's sense, or, if you prefer, less entropy than does 1476398470821576029547.

19. We can also think of the laws of physics as simple or orderly, since they allow us to predict certain regularities, such as the orbit of the planets around the sun, the movement of a projectile above a field, or how long it will take for a falling metal ball to get from the top of the Leaning Tower of Pisa to the ground. If information is surprise, then, given our knowledge of certain physical principles—in the last case, how quickly a falling object will accelerate toward the earth—we won't be surprised at what happens when we run this experiment. The constants of physics are the stable background to all the surprising events that happen in the world. This includes the electromagnetic spectrum. It is the same from one end of the universe to the other and is governed by the speed of light, which is also a physical constant.

20. "Information is the thing that we care most about," notes James Gleick in an interview about his book *The Information*. In Kevin Kelly, "Why the Basis of the Universe Isn't Matter or Energy—It's Data," *Wired* (Feb. 28, 2011), at: https://www.wired.com/2011/02/mf_gleick_qa/.

21. This point is often muddled. Even James Gleick in his illuminating book *The Information* (see note 18) has an entire chapter entitled "Information Is Physical." To say that information is physical, as Gleick and others do, is clearly a mistake. Why does he say so? It's surely because he senses the modern tribe's prejudice against the idea that something nonphysical could be so important. Robust information has the unsavory whiff of magic and spirituality, even—horror of horrors—real purpose and creativity. Haven't all right-thinking people been taught since the middle of the nineteenth century that matter is all that matters? How could something so important, so real, be immaterial?

 Gleick clearly tries to resolve the problem and senses the trouble, which makes him an inconsistent materialist. It should be no surprise that, for his trouble, John Horgan, one of *Scientific American*'s resident materialists, complained about Gleick's book, or at least Gleick's invocation of Wheeler's it-from-bit aphorism (which, we must admit, is hardly illuminating). The "hard-hearted part of me," Horgan writes, "sees ideas like the 'it from bit' as the kind of fuzzy-headed, narcissistic mysticism that science is supposed to help us overcome." John Horgan, "Why Information Can't Be the Basis of Reality," *Scientific American* (March 7, 2011), at: http://blogs.scientificamerican.com/cross-check/why-information-cant-be-the-basis-of-reality/. Horgan had reviewed Gleick's book positively in the *Wall Street Journal* but couldn't let this niggling issue rest.

22. Norbert Wiener, *Cybernetics: Or Control and Communication in the Animal and the Machine*, 2nd ed. (Cambridge, MA: MIT Press, 1965), p. 132.

23. Henry Quastler, *The Emergence of Biological Organization* (New Haven, CT: Yale University Press, 1964), p. 16.

24. For many, the implication is disturbing. They speak of the universe as a computer program or a computer simulation but avoid the obvious follow-up question: Who's running the program?

 These are subjects for other books. On the fine-tuning of the initial conditions, laws, and constants of physics and of the local requirements for life, see Guillermo Gonzalez and Jay W. Richards, *The Privileged Planet: How Our Place in the Cosmos Is Designed for Discovery* (Washington, DC: Regnery, 2004). Stephen Meyer argues that the information in the biological world points to intelligence in *Signature in the Cell: DNA and the Evidence for Intelligent Design* (San Francisco: HarperOne, 2009) and in *Darwin's Doubt: The Explosive Origin of Animal Life and the Case for Intelligent Design* (San Francisco: HarperOne, 2013).

25. Michelangelo actually carved two *David* statues, both of which are in Florence, Italy.

26. From a comment posted on George's Facebook page.

27. Theodore Dalrymple, "Your Limits Are Your Freedom," *Intercollegiate Review* (Spring 2016), at: https://home.isi.org/your-limits-are-your-freedom.

## CHAPTER 9

1. Ruth Whippman, "America Is Obsessed with Happiness—and It's Making Us Miserable," *Vox* (Dec. 22, 2016), at: https://www.vox.com/first-person/2016/10/4/13093380/happiness-america-ruth-whippman.

2. Ruth Whippman, *America the Anxious: How Our Pursuit of Happiness Is Creating a Nation of Nervous Wrecks* (New York: St. Martin's Press, 2016).

3. In a recent poll of ten nations by the Legatum Institute, "What the World Thinks of Capitalism" (Nov. 3, 2015), at: https://social.shorthand.com/montie/3C6iES9yjf/what-the-world-thinks-of-capitalism.

4. Arthur C. Brooks, *Gross National Happiness: Why Happiness Matters for America—and How We Can Get More of It* (New York: Basic Books, 2008), p. 4.

5. Ibid., p. 5.

6. Saints often experience a supernatural form of happiness even in suffering that transcends ordinary experience, but here we're just talking about the happiness of ordinary, natural life.

7. *Nicomachean Ethics*, 1101a10.

8. George Washington, First Inaugural Address, April 30, 1789, in John C. Fitzpatrick, *The Writings of Washington from the Original Manuscript Sources, 1745–1799*, vol. 30, p. 294.

9. See the official website at: http://www.grossnationalhappiness.com/.

10. See table at: http://macroeconomics.kushnirs.org/index.php.

11. Timothy W. Ryback, "The U.N. Happiness Project," *New York Times* (March 28, 2012), at: http://www.nytimes.com/2012/03/29/opinion/the-un-happiness-project.html.

12. Some of the variables used by the UN have less to do with reported happiness than with the political preferences of UN honchos. For instance,

"GDP per capita," "health life expectancy," and "freedom to make life choices" are among the variables used to explain the scores, but so is something called "social support." Moreover, the fact that the report doesn't even try to take account of the massive hereditary component of psychological happiness is enough justification to sit loosely on it, especially when it is used for political purposes.

13. From the World Bank data for Bhutan, at: http://data.worldbank.org/country/bhutan. The World Bank uses "GNI" (for "gross national income") rather than "GNP."

14. 2015 Index of Economic Freedom, "Bhutan," at: http://www.heritage.org/index/country/bhutan.

15. Deepesh Das Shrestha, "Resettlement of Bhutanese Refugees Surpasses 100,000 Mark," *UNHCR* (Nov. 19, 2015), at: http://www.unhcr.org/en-us/news/latest/2015/11/564dded46/resettlement-bhutanese-refugees-surpasses-100000-mark.html.

16. Heredity seems especially relevant with comparisons among countries with diverse ethnic makeups. A 2014 study looked at the "average genetic makeup of people" in 141 countries, "and compared how similar their genes were to people living in Denmark—a measure called genetic distance." The scientists controlled for factors such as GDP, since rich countries also tend to be happy countries. The result?

They found that the greater a nation's genetic distance from Denmark, the lower the reported well-being of that nation. Countries near Denmark, like the Netherlands and Sweden, ranked among the happiest. Given their close proximity, these countries are some of the most genetically similar to Denmark. Countries that ranked particularly low on the happiness scale, like Ghana and Madagascar, have the least genetic similarity to Denmark.

Kelly Dickerson, "Is There a Happiness Gene?," *LiveScience* (July 18, 2014), at: http://www.livescience.com/46877-denmark-happiness-genetics.html. The paper is Eugenio Proto and Andrew J. Oswald, "National Happiness and Genetic Distance: A Cautious Exploration," *IZA (Institute for the Study of Labor) Discussion Paper No. 8300* (July 2014), at: http://ftp.iza.org/dp8300.pdf.

17. Arthur Brooks, "A Formula for Happiness," *New York Times* (Dec. 14, 2013), at: http://www.nytimes.com/2013/12/15/opinion/sunday/a-formula-for-happiness.html.

18. Brooks, *Gross National Happiness*, pp. 10–11. He is reporting on David Lykken and Auke Tellegen, "Happiness Is a Stochastic Phenomenon," *Psychological Science* 7, no. 3 (1996).

19. In brief and on average, women are happier than men, conservatives are happier than liberals, the married are happier than singles, and the actively religious much happier than the non-religious. "It turns out that conservative women are particularly blissful: about 40 percent say they are very happy. That makes them slightly happier than conservative men and significantly happier than liberal women. The unhappiest are liberal men, only about one-fifth of whom consider themselves very happy." Married, conservative religious women hit the jackpot— again, on average. Arthur Brooks, *The Conservative Heart* (New York: Broadside Books, 2015), p. 27. If they exercise regularly, that's even better. Emily E. Berstin and Richard J. McNally, "Acute Aerobic Exercise Helps Overcome Emotion Regulation Deficits," *Cognition and Emotion* (April 4, 2016), at: http://www.tandfonline.com/doi/full/10.1080/0269 9931.2016.1168284. Happiness and health correlates most highly with *social connections*. Severe loneliness kills people. See the TED lecture by Robert Waldinger (Jan. 25, 2016), at: https://www.youtube.com/watch?v=8KkKuTCFvzI.

20. The current director of the study is Harvard psychiatrist Robert Waldinger. Colby Itkowitch, "Harvard Researchers Discovered the One Thing Everyone Needs for Happier, Healthier Lives," *Washington Post* (March 2, 2016), at: https://www.washingtonpost.com/news/inspired-life/wp/2016/03/02/harvard-researchers-discovered-the-one-thing-everyone-needs-for-happier-healthier-lives/.

21. Brooks, "A Formula for Happiness."

22. Brendan Greeley, "Mapping the Growth of Disability Claims in America," *Bloomberg Businessweek* (Dec. 16, 2016), at: https://www.bloomberg.com/news/features/2016-12-16/mapping-the-growth-of-disability-claims-in-america.

23. This, of course, doesn't go for every unemployed person, and we shouldn't rush to judgment about the long-term unemployed person we happen across. Life happens. Sometimes a person gets dealt a string of strangely bad hands through no fault of his own.

But the opposite impulse is no solution, either. If you rush to assume that every person suffering from long-term unemployment is a helpless victim, you have consigned him or her to the status of a child. That isn't a classy move. The right response is simply to face up to the messy complexity of long-term unemployment and resist pat simplifications. We can do all this and still look for clues in our effort to understand the art of happiness.

24. Daniel Kahneman and Angus Deaton, "High Income Improves Evaluation of Life but Not Emotional Well-being," *PNAS* (*Proceedings of the National Academy of Sciences of the United States of America*) 107, no. 38 (Aug. 4, 2010), at: http://www.pnas.org/content/107/38/16489.

25. Brooks, *Gross National Happiness*, p. 114.

26. Ibid., pp. 175–92. If you've followed the details, you might already have guessed that religious conservatives give more money to charity than liberals do. Arthur Brooks, *Who Really Cares: The Surprising Truth About Compassionate Conservative Conservativism* (New York: Basic Books, 2006).

27. Brooks, "A Formula for Happiness." This commentary is a summary of the findings in his book *Gross National Happiness*.

28. In Pete DuPont, "Pursue Happiness, Vote GOP," *Wall Street Journal* (Nov. 29, 2004); quoted in Brooks, *Gross National Happiness*, p. 32.


CHAPTER 10

1. See "Total Pages, Code of Federal Regulations (1975–2015)," Regulatory Studies Center, at: https://regulatorystudies.columbian.gwu.edu/sites/regulatorystudies.columbian.gwu.edu/files/downloads/Pages_CFR_0.JPG.

2. Laura Jones, "Cutting Red Tape in Canada: A Regulatory Reform Model for the United States?," Mercatus Center (Nov. 11, 2015), at: http://mercatus.org/publication/cutting-red-tape-canada-regulatory-reform-model-united-states.

3. Michael S. Malone, "A Lost Generation of American Entrepreneurs," *Forbes* (June 1, 2016), at: http://www.forbes.com/sites/mikemalone/2016/06/01/a-lost-generation-of-american-entrepreneurs/#3671e30e537e.

4. Telis Demos and Corrie Driebusch, "Forget Going Public, U.S. Companies Want to Get Bought," *Wall Street Journal* (Nov. 29, 2015), at: http://www.wsj.com/articles/forget-going-public-u-s-companies-want-to-get-bought-1448793190. Banks, unions, trade associations, and large manufacturers have had government affairs offices for decades. The innovative tech sector—Apple, Microsoft, Amazon, eBay, Qualcomm—initially kept its distance from Washington, DC. But for self-protection, they have had to expand to K Street as well. Now, even young start-ups feel the need to lobby the government. Cecelia Kang, "Start-up Leaders

Embrace Lobbying as Part of the Job," *New York Times* (Nov. 22, 2015), at: http://www.nytimes.com/2015/11/23/technology/start-up-leaders-embrace-lobbying-as-part-of-the-job.html.

5. Michael Bastasch, "Obama's Legacy: 8 Years, 3,000 Regulations and 8 Trillion in Debt," *The Stream* (Jan. 20, 2017), at: https://stream.org/obamas-legacy-8-years-3000-regulations-8-trillion-debt/; James Gattuso, "20,642 New Regulations Added in the Obama Presidency," *Daily Signal* (May 23, 2016), at: http://dailysignal.com/2016/05/23/20642-new-regulations-added-in-the-obama-presidency/.

6. Arun Sundararajan, "Why the Government Doesn't Need to Regulate the Sharing Economy," *Wired* (Oct. 22, 2012), at: http://www.wired.com/2012/10/from-airbnb-to-coursera-why-the-government-shouldnt-regulate-the-sharing-economy/.

7. See Jared Meyer, "Social Media Is Making Some Regulators Obsolete," *Economics* 21 (Dec. 8, 2015), at: http://economics21.org/commentary/social-media-making-some-regulators-obsolete.

8. Adam Thierer, "Don't Let Government Stifle the Next Tech Revolution," *Fiscal Times* (May 3, 2016), at: http://www.thefiscaltimes.com/Columns/2016/05/03/Don-t-Let-Government-Stifle-Next-Tech-Revolution. This is based on his book *Permissionless Innovation,* 2nd edition (Arlington, VA: Mercatus Center at George Mason University, 2016).

9. Jay Richards, "How a Virtuous Housing Circle Turned Vicious," *Harvard Business Review* (Aug. 8, 2013), at: https://hbr.org/2013/08/how-a-virtuous-housing-circle. For all the sordid details, see Jay W. Richards, *Infiltrated.*

10. Daniel Mitchell, "The Insane World of Agriculture Subsidies," *International Liberty* (Dec. 14, 2016), at: https://danieljmitchell.wordpress.com/2016/12/14/the-insane-world-of-agriculture-subsidies/.

11. Glenn Reynolds, "Go to College or Go to Jail?," *USA Today* (Dec. 19, 2015), at: http://www.usatoday.com/story/opinion/2015/12/19/bernie-sanders-john-kerry-college-jail-column/77570786/. On the role of increased financial aid and increased costs, see Grey Gordon and Aaron Hudlund, "Accounting for the Rise in College Tuition," NBER Working Paper No. 21967 (Feb. 2016), at: http://www.nber.org/papers/w21967.

12. Ronald Bailey, "Stuck," *Reason* (Jan. 2017), at: http://reason.com/archives/2016/12/10/stuck.

13. In *Our Kids: The Dream in Crisis* (New York: Simon & Schuster, 2015).

14. In *Coming Apart: The State of White America, 1960–2010* (New York: Crown Forum, 2013).

15. Anna Sutherland and W. Bradford Wilcox, "Strengthening the Three Pillars of the American Dream: Education, Work and Marriage," Institute for Family Studies (Dec. 3, 2015), at: http://family-studies.org/strengthening-the-three-pillars-of-the-american-dream/.

16. Murray first proposed this idea in a 2006 book, since reprinted, *In Our Hands: A Plan to Replace the Welfare State* (Washington, DC: AEI Press, 2016).

17. Charles Murray, "A Guaranteed Income for Every American," *Wall Street Journal* (June 3, 2016), at: http://www.wsj.com/articles/a-guaranteed-income-for-every-american-1464969586.

18. Murray also argues that social expectations could shift: "It will be possible," he writes, "to say to the irresponsible what can't be said now: We won't let you starve before you get your next deposit, but it's time for you to get your act together. Don't try to tell us you're helpless, because we know you aren't.'" This seems unlikely, though. All manner of welfare and charity programs keep poor Americans from starving now, but it's still thought cruel to tell able-bodied men to get off their butts.

19. Robert Rector, Rachel Sheffield, and Kevin D. Dayaratna, "Maine Food Stamp Work Requirement Cuts Non-Parent Caseload by 80 Percent," Heritage Foundation Backgrounder 3091 (Feb. 8, 2016), at: http://www.heritage.org/research/reports/2016/02/maine-food-stamp-work-requirement-cuts-non-parent-caseload-by-80-percent.

20. Even then, there would be reasons for skepticism and hesitation. First, a universal basic income might normalize freeloading and the pathologies that go with it far beyond what we have now. Second, even if the government zeroed out all of those other entitlements and means-tested programs, there's nothing to prevent them from leaking back in during the years that followed, at which point we would have both a universal basic income and a thicket of anti-poverty programs, entitlements, and regulations.

21. Peter S. Goodman, "Free Cash in Finland. Must Be Jobless," *New York Times* (Dec. 17, 2016), at: http://www.nytimes.com/2016/12/17/business/economy/universal-basic-income-finland.html.

22. Mark J. Perry, "Yes, America's Middle Class Has Been Disappearing . . . into Higher Income Groups," AEIdeas (Dec. 17, 2015), at: https://www.aei.org/publication/yes-americas-middle-class-has-been-disappearing-

into-higher-income-groups/. See also Mark J. Perry, "Charts of the Day: Another Look at How America's Middle Class Is Disappearing into Higher Income Households," AEIdeas (Dec. 30, 2015), at: http://www .aei.org/publication/charts-of-the-day-another-look-at-how-americas-middle-class-is-disappearing-into-higher-income-households/.

23. See discussion of relevant studies in Edward Conard, *The Upside of Equality* (New York: Portfolio, 2016), chapter 6.

24. "Bounty and spread" is the phrase used by Brynjolfsson and McAfee, *The Second Machine Age*, pp. 164–73. In-country inequality is rising throughout the developed world, suggesting that the cause is large and global rather than the result of economic policies within countries. Katy Barnato, " 'Enormous Increase' in Global Inequality: OECD," CNBC (Oct. 1, 2014), at: http://www.cnbc.com/2014/10/01/enormous-increase-in-global-inequality-oecd.html.

25. Ashley McGuire, "The Feminist, Pro-Father, and Pro-Child Case Against No-Fault Divorce," *Public Discourse* (May 7, 2013), at: http:// www.thepublicdiscourse.com/2013/05/10031/. Cause and effect are hard to prove in studies, but there's some evidence that divorce is contagious. In other words, if a person has a close friend who is divorced, that person is much more likely to get a divorce. Rose McDermott, James H. Fowler, and Nicholas A. Christakis, "Breaking Up Is Hard to Do, Unless Everyone Else Is Doing It Too: Social Network Effects on Divorce in a Longitudinal Sample," *Social Forces* 92, no. 2 (October 8, 2013): 491–519.

26. George Gilder discusses this factor in *The Scandal of Money: Why Wall Street Recovers but the Economy Never Does* (Washington, DC: Regnery, 2016).

27. Ford does spend a couple of paragraphs on this, because he had been criticized for ignoring it in a previous book. But his treatment is quite cursory. For a summary of the optimistic argument, see Peter Diamandis, "Why the Cost of Living Is Poised to Plummet in the Next 20 Years," *Singularity Hub* (July 18, 2016), at: https://singularityhub .com/2016/07/18/why-the-cost-of-living-is-poised-to-plummet-in-the-next-20-years. For somewhat techno-utopian antidotes to Ford's doom-and-gloom, see Peter H. Diamandis and Steven Kotler, *Abundance: The Future Is Better Than You Think* (New York: Free Press, 2012), and Peter H. Diamandis and Steven Kotler, *Bold: How to Go Big, Create Wealth and Impact the World* (New York: Simon & Schuster, 2015).

28. Joel Mokyr, "The Next Age of Invention," *City Journal* (Winter 2014), at: http://www.city-journal.org/html/next-age-invention-13618.html.

29. Diamandis, "Why the Cost of Living Is Poised to Plummet in the Next 20 Years."

30. In "A Guaranteed Income for Every American," Charles Murray at least admits that his worries of a jobless future might be due to a lack of vision:

> It takes a better imagination than mine to come up with new blue-collar occupations that will replace more than a fraction of the jobs (now numbering 4 million) that taxi drivers and truck drivers will lose when driverless vehicles take over. Advances in 3-D printing and "contour craft" technology will put at risk the jobs of many of the 14 million people now employed in production and construction.

31. Deidre McCloskey, "Measured, Unmeasured, Mismeasured, and Unjustified Pessimism: A Review Essay of Thomas Piketty's *Capital in the Twenty-First Century*," *Erasmus Journal for Philosophy and Economics* 7, no. 2 (Autumn 2014): 81, at: http://ejpe.org/pdf/7-2-art-4.pdf.

32. Facebook's Mark Zuckerberg has endorsed a UBI for this reason as well.

33. Rob Tracinski, "The Basic Income Is the Worst Response to Automation," *RealClearFuture* (Aug. 15, 2016), at: http://www.realclearfuture.com/articles/2016/08/15/basic_income_worst_response_to_automation_111934.html.

34. Cesar Conda and Derek Khanna, "Uber for Welfare," *Politico* (Jan. 27, 2016), at: http://www.politico.com/agenda/story/2016/1/uber-welfare-sharing-gig-economy-000031. This piece is based on their white paper "Using the Gig Economy to Reform Entitlements," *The Aspen Institute Future of Work Initiative* (Aug. 31, 2016), at: https://www.aspeninstitute.org/publications/condakhanna/.

35. Abolishing or at least freezing the minimum wage would also help, since it prices the least skilled and least experienced workers out of certain markets. (If you doubt that, explain how the poor are helped by making it harder for employers to hire them.) An EITC is not, however, the panacea that many reform-minded conservatives imagine. It is the source of a great deal of tax fraud and gives IRS workers fits. An expanded EITC would need to be accompanied by more good compliance officers at the IRS.

36. Unfortunately, some digital dissenters overstate the case. With no sense of irony, they use their laptops, the Internet, smartphones, Facebook, and Twitter to warn of the alienating effects of technology. Joel Achenbach, "Techno-Skeptics' Objection Growing Louder," *Washington Post*

(Dec. 26, 2016), at: https://www.washingtonpost.com/classic-apps/
techno-skeptics-objection-growing-louder/2015/12/26/e83cf658-617a-
11e5-8e9e-dce8a2a2a679_story.html.

37. Nicholas Carr, *The Shallows: What the Internet Is Doing to Our Brains*
(New York: W. W. Norton, 2011). Much of the strength of these arguments comes from false comparisons. Perhaps uploading pictures to
Facebook isn't as intellectually stimulating as, say, reading Plato's *Republic*, but that's not the relevant comparison. How does it compare
to, say, watching *Scandal* on ABC or *Survivor* on CBS? That's the more
relevant question.

38. Kevin McFadden, "You Now Have a Shorter Attention Span Than a
Goldfish," *Time* (May 14, 2015), at: http://time.com/3858309/attention-
spans-goldfish/. The story about the short attention span of a goldfish
seems to be an urban legend.

39. Andrew Sullivan, "I Used to Be a Human Being," *New York Magazine* (Sept. 18, 2016), at: http://nymag.com/selectall/2016/09/andrew-
sullivan-technology-almost-killed-me.html.

40. Clive Thompson, *Smarter Than You Think: How Technology Is Changing
Our Minds for the Better* (New York: Penguin, 2014).

41. Edward Niedermeyer, "Robot Cars Aren't Dangerous—People Are,"
*Federalist* (May 11, 2016), at: http://thefederalist.com/2016/05/11/
robot-cars-arent-dangerous-people-are/.

42. Already in 2007 David Levy had given the subject a book-length treatment in *Love and Sex with Robots: The Evolution of Human-Robot Relationships* (New York: HarperCollins, 2007).

43. Glenn McDonald, "Sex Robots Are Coming 'Sooner Than Anyone
Expects,'" *Seeker* (Dec. 22, 2016), at: http://www.seeker.com/sex-robots-
are-coming-sooner-than-anyone-expects-2161089911.html.

44. James Ovenden, "AI and the Future of Sex," Innovation Enterprise
(April 26, 2016), at: https://channels.theinnovationenterprise.com/
articles/ai-and-the-future-of-sex. It seems worth mentioning that
RealDolls' owner, David Mills, is best known for his book *Atheist
Universe: The Thinking Person's Answer to Christian Fundamentalism*
(Berkeley, CA: Ulysses, 2006), which arch-atheist Richard Dawkins
calls an "admirable work." Eva Wiseman, "Sex, Love and Robots: Is
This the End of Intimacy?," *Guardian* (Dec. 13, 2015), at: http://www
.theguardian.com/technology/2015/dec/13/sex-love-and-robots-the-end-
of-intimacy.

## CHAPTER 11

1. B. F. Skinner, *Beyond Freedom and Dignity* (New York: Hackett, 1971).

2. In *Why I'm Not a Christian* (New York: Touchstone, 1967).

3. Michael Ruse and E. O. Wilson, "The Evolution of Ethics," in *Religion and the Natural Sciences: The Range of Engagement*, ed. James E. Huchingson (Orlando: Harcourt Brace, 1993), p. 310.

4. Alex Rosenberg, *The Atheist's Guide to Reality: Enjoying Life Without Illusions* (New York: W. W. Norton, 2012).

5. George Johnson, "Consciousness: The Mind Messing with the Mind," *New York Times* (July 4, 2016), at: https://www.nytimes.com/2016/07/05/science/what-is-consciousness.html.

6. E. O. Wilson and Michael's Ruse claim can be coherently stated, but of course they frequently contradict it by treating moral claims as objectively true. Ruse does just that in Michael Ruse, "Why God Is a Moral Issue," *New York Times* (March 23, 2015), at: https://opinionator.blogs.nytimes.com/2015/03/23/why-god-is-a-moral-issue/.

7. He said "things" rather than "theories," but he was referring to the theories we use to explain things.

8. At least materialism as it's commonly understood by the thinkers discussed here. There is another option called "panpsychism," which claims that matter simply is conscious, at least under certain configurations. In this case, consciousness is not so much the mystery, since it is simply taken as a given. Matter is the mystery, since it doesn't seem to have the properties of mind or consciousness when we inspect it. I'm not considering this view because panpsychism, to be intelligible, would still need to distinguish between, say, a pattern in the brain and the first-person experience of a thought or sensation. See Galen Strawson, "Consciousness Isn't a Mystery. It's Matter," *New York Times* (May 16, 2016), at: https://www.nytimes.com/2016/05/16/opinion/consciousness-isnt-a-mystery-its-matter.html.

9. "Singularitarians" and "transhumanists" now write and attend conferences on these ideas. Some, such as John Zenakis, place the launch date a bit sooner than 2043, the date Kurzweil seemed to prefer for a while. "It's the doubling of computing power every 18 months," he explains, "that makes it all but certain that the Singularity will occur by 2030, whether we like it or not." John J. Xenakis, "World View: Artificial Intelligence Breakthroughs in 2015, the Singularity by 2030," *Breit-*

*bart* (Dec. 29, 2015), at: http://www.breitbart.com/national-security/ 2015/12/29/world-view-artificial-intelligence-breakthroughs-in-2015-the-singularity-by-2030/.

10. A popular theory of the brain among cognitive scientists and philosophers of mind—even those skeptical of Kurzweil's conjectures—is called "computationalism." In a fascinating essay, psychologist Robert Epstein shows how unlike a computer our brain is. See "The Empty Brain," Aeon (May 18, 2016), at: https://aeon.co/essays/your-brain-does-not-process-information-and-it-is-not-a-computer. For a book-length analysis of consciousness by a prominent critic of computationalism, see David Gelernter, *The Tides of Mind: Uncovering the Spectrum of Consciousness* (New York: Liveright, 2016).

11. Ray Kurzweil, *How to Create a Mind: The Secret of Human Thought Revealed* (New York: Penguin, 2013). For a contrary argument, see Jeffrey Schwartz and Sharon Begley, *The Mind and the Brain: Neuroplasticity and the Power of Mental Force* (New York: HarperCollins, 2002).

12. Bill Joy, "Why the Future Doesn't Need Us," *Wired* (April 1, 2000), at: http://www.wired.com/2000/04/joy-2/.

13. Michael Sainato, "Stephen Hawking, Elon Musk, and Bill Gates Warn About Artificial Intelligence," *Observer* (Aug. 8, 2015), at: http:// observer.com/2015/08/stephen-hawking-elon-musk-and-bill-gates-warn-about-artificial-intelligence/.

14. Quoted in ibid.

15. See Steven D. Greydanus, "People Keep Lying About Computer 'Creativity,'" *National Catholic Register* (Sept. 2, 2016), at: http://www.ncregister .com/blog/steven-greydanus/people-keep-lying-about-computer-creativity.

16. Kelly, *The Inevitable*, p. 49.

17. John Searle, "Minds, Brains, and Programs," *Behavioral and Brain Sciences* 3 (1980): 417–24. He offers a modified version of the argument, applied to the chess-playing computer Deep Blue, in John Searle, "I Married a Computer," in Jay Richards, ed., *Are We Spiritual Machines? Ray Kurzweil vs. the Critics of Strong A.I.* (Seattle: Discovery Institute Press, 2002), pp. 61–64.

18. Searle's original thought experiment focused on the simple deterministic computer programs common in 1980. He has updated it to take into account the statistical algorithms common in machine learning. See John Searle, "The Failures of Computationalism," in *Think* 2 (1993): 68–73, available online at: http://users.ecs.soton.ac.uk/harnad/Papers/Harnad/

harnad93.symb.anal.net.searle.html. Ironically, Searle is himself a materialist and speaks of consciousness as being "produced by the brain in the same way that bile is produced by the liver." He argues, nevertheless, that mental properties can't be reduced to the physical properties of brain states. Such is the power of materialism over the academic mind that even philosophers who deny its implications can't deny the whole enchilada.

19. Another argument has to do with the intentional states of our minds. I ask you to think about eating a chocolate ice cream sundae while a doctor does an MRI and takes a snapshot of your brain state. We all assume the following are true:
    (1) You're a person. You have "first-person perspective."
    (2) You have thoughts.
    (3) I asked you to think about eating a chocolate ice cream sundae.
    (4) You freely chose to do so, based on my request.
    (5) Those thoughts caused something to happen in your brain and perhaps elsewhere in your body.
    Notice that the thought—your first person, subjective experience of thinking about the chocolate sundae—would not be the same as the pattern in your brain, or the same as an MRI picture of the pattern. One glaring difference between them: Your brain pattern isn't *about* anything. Your thought is. It's about a chocolate sundae. We have thoughts and ideas—what philosophers call "intentional" states—that are about things other than themselves. We don't know how this works or how it relates to the brain or chemistry or the laws of physics or the price of tea in China. But whenever we speak to another person, we assume it must be true. And in our own case, we *know* it's true. Even to deny it is to affirm it.

    Points (1) through (5) above are common sense. And they all utterly defy materialist explanation. The materialist will want to say one of three things: (a) Your "thoughts" are identical with a physical brain state. (b) Your "thoughts" are *determined* by some physical brain state. Or (c) you don't really have thoughts. And if (a), (b), or (c) is true, then most or all of (1) through (5) are false.

20. Quoted in Christopher Chabris and David Goodman, "Chess-Championship Results Show Powerful Role of Computers," *Wall Street Journal* (Nov. 22, 2013), at: http://online.wsj.com/news/articles/SB1000 1424052702304337404579209980222399924.

21. Kelly, *The Inevitable*, p. 6.

22. Steven Johnson, "The Genius of the Tinkerer," *Wall Street Journal* (Sept. 25, 2010), at: http://www.wsj.com/articles/SB10001424052748 703989304575503730101860838. He develops this thesis in detail in *Where Good Ideas Come From: The Natural History of Innovation* (New York: Riverhead, 2010).

23. Johnson, *Where Good Ideas Come From*.

24. For Johnson, ideas function like genes in Richard Dawkins's account of evolution. For Dawkins, there are no organisms per se, only carriers of genes. (Dawkins completes the reduction by treating ideas as mere "memes.") Johnson is following the ideas of George Dyson, *Darwin Among the Machines: The Evolution of Global Intelligence* (New York: Basic Books, 2nd ed., 2012).

25. Gilder, *Knowledge and Power* (Washington, DC: Regnery, 2013), p. 247.

26. In a widely discussed 2012 paper, economist Robert Gordon claimed that the innovation of the Industrial Revolution is now mostly over and that any new innovations will encounter six "headwinds." Robert J. Gordon, "Is U.S. Economic Growth Over? Faltering Innovation Confronts the Six Headwinds," NBER Working Paper No. 18315 (Aug. 2012), at: http://www.nber.org/papers/w18315. He distinguishes three industrial revolutions. The first, from 1750 to 1830, was fired by the steam engine and railroads. The second, from 1870 to 1900, gave us "electricity, internal combustion engine, running water, indoor toilets, communications, entertainment, chemicals, petroleum," and the third, from 1960 to the present, gave us computers, the internet, and cell phones. All these led to major economic growth in the United States. But Gordon argues that we should not expect such growth in the future, especially for the 90 percent, due to declining population, bad education, "inequality, globalization, energy/environment, and the overhang of consumer and government debt." He continues this claim in his 2016 book, *The Rise and Fall of American Growth: The US Standard of Living Since the Civil War* (Princeton, NJ: Princeton University Press, 2016). Unfortunately, he mostly fails to appreciate both the effects of information technology and its promise for the future. The only growth he can imagine is the easily measurable growth that occurred in the Industrial Revolution.

27. *The Second Machine Age: Work, Progress and Prosperity in a Time of Brilliant Technologies* (New York: W. W. Norton, 2014), p. 82. They draw on the argument of economist Martin L. Weitzman, "Recombinant Growth," *Quarterly Journal of Economics* 113, no. 2 (May 1998), at:

https://dash.harvard.edu/bitstream/handle/1/3708468/Weitzman_RecombinantGrowth.pdf.

28. Mark A. Lemley, "The Myth of the Sole Inventor," Stanford Public Law Working Paper No. 1856610 (July 21, 2011), at: http://dx.doi.org/10.2139/ssrn.1856610; and Derek Thompson, "Forget Edison: This Is How History's Greatest Inventions Really Happened," *Atlantic* (June 15, 2012), at: https://www.theatlantic.com/business/archive/2012/06/forget-edison-this-is-how-historys-greatest-inventions-really-happened/258525/.

29. Peter Thiel and Blake Masters, *Zero to One: Notes on Startups, or How to Build the Future* (New York: Crown Business, 2014), p. 1.

30. Ötzi the Iceman, discovered in the Alps in 1991, died around 3000 BC. Scientists found ibex meat in his stomach.

31. Gilder, *Knowledge and Power*, p. 25.

32. Check out "I, Smartphone" at: https://www.youtube.com/watch?v=V1Ze_wpS_o0.

33. For a compelling study of the importance of the classical liberal, and Judeo-Christian, view of human equality for prosperity, see Deidre McCloskey, *Bourgeois Equality: How Ideas, Not Capital or Institutions, Enriched the World* (Chicago: University of Chicago Press, 2016).

34. There were also drum signals in sub-Saharan Africa, but this was isolated from the processes that gave rise to telecommunications technology.

35. Kelly, *The Inevitable*, p. 291.

36. The term is from the flaky twentieth-century Jesuit Teilhard de Chardin. I use it here with my own meaning, not his.

37. In *The Abolition of Man* (San Francisco: HarperOne, 2015). The book is based on a series of lectures about education, first published in 1943.

# INDEX